CRITICAL PERSPECTIVES ON AGEING SOCIETIES

Edited by Miriam Bernard and Thomas Scharf

First published in Great Britain in 2007 by

The Policy Press
Fourth Floor, Beacon House
Queen's Road
Bristol BS8 1QU
UK

Tel +44 (0)117 331 4054
Fax +44 (0)117 331 4093
e-mail tpp-info@bristol.ac.uk
www.policypress.org.uk

© Miriam Bernard and Thomas Scharf 2007

British Library Cataloguing in Publication Data

A catalogue record for this book is available from the British Library

ISBN 978 1 86134 890 6 (paperback)
ISBN 978 1 86134 891 3 (hardcover)

The right of Miriam Bernard and Thomas Scharf to be identified as editors of this work has been asserted by them in accordance with the 1988 Copyright, Designs and Patents Act.

The statements and opinions contained within this publication are solely those of the editors and contributors and not of The University of Bristol or The Policy Press. The University of Bristol and The Policy Press disclaim responsibility for any injury to persons or property resulting from any material published in this publication.

The Policy Press works to counter discrimination on grounds of gender, race, disability, age and sexuality.

Cover design by In-Text Design.
Front cover: photograph kindly supplied by Digital Vision.
Printed and bound in Great Britain by Hobbs the Printers, Southampton.

This book is dedicated to the memory of Frank Glendenning –
a critical friend and supportive mentor

Contents

List of tables, boxes and figures   vi
Foreword by Chris Phillipson   vii
Acknowledgements   ix
Notes on contributors   x

Part One: Historical, theoretical and policy contexts

one   Critical perspectives on ageing societies   3
Miriam Bernard and Thomas Scharf

two   Critical gerontology: reflections for the 21st century   13
Martha B. Holstein and Meredith Minkler

three   Using human rights to defeat ageism: dealing with policy-induced   27
'structured dependency'
Peter Townsend

four   The re-medicalisation of later life   45
Robin Means

Part Two: Forms of knowing – participatory approaches

five   Narratives as agents of social change: a new direction for   59
narrative gerontologists
Ruth E. Ray

six   Redressing the balance? The participation of older people in research   73
Mo Ray

seven   Revisiting *The Last Refuge*: present-day methodological challenges   89
Julia Johnson, Sheena Rolph and Randall Smith

eight   The road to an age-inclusive society   105
Bill Bytheway, Richard Ward, Caroline Holland and Sheila Peace

Part Three: Future considerations

nine   Justice between generations: the recent history of an idea   125
Harry R. Moody

ten   Progress in gerontology: where are we going now?   139
Tony Warnes and Judith Phillips

References   155
Index   177

List of tables, boxes and figures

Tables

3.1   Levels of material and social deprivation among older people,   39
      Great Britain (2000) (%)

3.2   Types of violations of human rights (ECHR) and possible indicators   40

3.3   Types of violations of human rights (ESC) and possible indicators   41

3.4   International Covenant on Economic, Social and Cultural Rights and   41
      1995 World Summit Action Programme

10.1   Year of first publication of journals with gerontolog* and ag(e)ing   146
      in the titles held by the British Library, 2005

Boxes

3.1   Article 4: Right of elderly persons to social protection   35

4.1   Outcomes for social care   50

4.2   Enabling health, independence and well-being   56

Figures

10.1   The wheel of gerontological interests and the road of change   142

10.2   The foundation of English-language gerontology journals   147

Foreword

Critical gerontology has its roots in the political and economic crisis affecting western societies during the 1970s and 1980s. The nature of this crisis – with major expenditure cuts to welfare programmes – brought profound consequences for the lives of older people. Reductions in the scope and quality of services were one obvious dimension, raising major question marks over the future of the welfare state. Equally damaging, however, was an ideologically driven critique of demographic change, with the labelling of older people as a 'burden' and 'cost' to society. Both these elements were influential forces behind early formulations of critical gerontology, most notably in the political economy perspective developed by researchers such as Carroll Estes, John Myles, Peter Townsend and Alan Walker. Equally significant, however, was a view that welfare and pension arrangements, as they had evolved over the post-war period, were in some senses de-humanising and demeaning to the experience of growing old. This view was clearly enunciated by Carroll Estes (1979) in her pioneering study on the 'ageing enterprise' and was supported by the rise (in the US) of organisations such as the Gray Panthers (led by Maggie Kuhn), together with radical groups of older people in a number of European countries (notably Germany and the UK).

Critical gerontology, from its political economic, feminist and humanist foundations, brought to the study of later life appreciation of the relationship between ageing and economic life, the differential experience of ageing according to social class, gender and ethnicity, and the role of social policy in contributing to the dependent status of older people. Alongside this, however, as many of the contributions in this book make clear, came a commitment to scholarship that 'gave voice' to the experiences of older people; an approach as well that placed them as integral to the research process. It is probably fair to say that this perspective was not the dominant approach in the early phases of critical gerontology, when neo-Marxist and structuralist accounts were at their most influential – in the US and UK at least. Moving into the 1990s, however, the importance of older people as agents within gerontology became a point of reference for a variety of studies. There were probably three main influences at work here: first, from feminism, with its attention to the subjective experience of ageing as a neglected dimension of study; second, the influence of biographical/life history perspectives that rooted an understanding of ageing in experiences over the totality of the life course; third, the rise of humanistic perspectives (drawn from the US), which focused on the crisis of meaning affecting the lives of older people in western societies.

The great achievement of this book is in providing a major assessment of work in critical gerontology, in particular that which emphasises the central position of older people in the ageing and research enterprise. The volume brings together some of the outstanding researchers working in social gerontology over the past decade, the chapters uniquely taking the lens of 'passionate scholarship' with which to view the complex issues affecting older people in the 21st century. This is a highly appropriate time for publication of a volume of this kind. Critical gerontology has been advancing its case, in different guises, for some three decades. But the need for further reflection and development of the core themes of this approach are now acute. Population changes (bringing greater diversity among the older population) alongside economic developments (notably the rise of globalisation) are creating new challenges for the study of ageing. New perspectives and methodologies will need to be developed if effective responses are to be made to the major issues that are presenting themselves both to older people and the discipline of social gerontology. These chapters, with their focus on the complex practical and ethical dilemmas in studying with older people, offer major insights for critical gerontology. The volume draws on the strengths of critical perspectives while bringing new themes and questions for further research. The editors and contributors offer an exciting set of visions and perspectives for the renewal and development of critical gerontology in the years ahead.

Chris Phillipson
Professor of Applied Social Studies and Social Gerontology
Keele University
November 2006

Acknowledgements

Like many books of this nature, this volume has taken a considerable time to put together and draws on contributions from many people who worked with us both prior to, and during, the production process. To our contributors, we thank you for your patience throughout the editorial process and for your generous acceptance of our suggested changes. Any remaining mistakes are ours alone. We would also like to thank current and former colleagues who worked tirelessly 'behind the scenes': Pat Chambers, Jim Hakim, Judith Phillips, Chris Phillipson, Mo Ray, Di Roberts, Brenda Roe, Julius Sim and Chaz Simpson. We owe a particular debt of thanks to Sue Humphries whose quiet efficiency and unfailing good humour, as administrator for the Centre for Social Gerontology at Keele University, has made all our lives so much easier.

Our appreciation also goes to those at The Policy Press: to Alison Shaw, Director; to Judith Phillips (and the late Jo Campling), Series Editor; and to Emily Watt, Editorial Assistant.

Finally, this book is dedicated to the memory of Dr Frank Glendenning, founder member, in 1987, of the Centre for Social Gerontology at Keele University. Frank was a critical friend and supportive mentor to many of us – he is much missed.

Miriam Bernard
Thomas Scharf

Notes on contributors

Miriam Bernard is Professor of Social Gerontology and Director of the Research Institute for Life Course Studies at Keele University. Her research interests focus primarily on the development of new and healthy lifestyles in later life, and she has a long-standing interest in women's lives as they age.

Bill Bytheway is a Senior Research Fellow in the Centre for Ageing and Biographical Studies (CABS) at The Open University. His research addresses issues around ageing over the life course, experience and everyday life, ageism and images and models of ageing.

Caroline Holland is a Research Associate in the Centre for Ageing and Biographical Studies (CABS) at The Open University. Her particular interests are in social, physical and technological aspects of homes and neighbourhoods, in housing policy and provision, and in the use of qualitative/ethnographic methods.

Martha B. Holstein is Adjunct Professor in the Department of Philosophy, Northwestern University, Evanston, Illinois and Co-director of the Center for Long-Term Care Reform in the Health and Medicine Policy Research Group, Chicago, Illinois. For much of her work life, she has worked to link ageing theory and practice. Recently this effort has focused on ethics, especially in the area of ageing.

Julia Johnson is Senior Lecturer in the Centre for Ageing and Biographical Studies (CABS) at The Open University. With a background in social anthropology, her research interests relating to older people include studies of residential care, medication, self-neglect, the social construction of care and the history of post-war social care policies.

Robin Means is Professor of Health and Social Care in the Faculty of Health and Life Sciences at the University of the West of England, Bristol. His research interests relate to issues around public policy and older people, social care, housing and community care, and interagency and interprofessional working.

Meredith Minkler is Professor of Health and Social Behavior in the School of Public Health at the University of California, where she was also Founding Director of the University of California Center on Ageing. Her current research involves studies of health disparities in older North Americans, critical gerontology and community-based participatory research with diverse groups.

Harry R. Moody is Director of Academic Affairs for AARP (previously known as the American Association of Retired Persons) in Washington, DC. He also serves as Senior Associate with the International Longevity Center–USA and is a senior fellow of Civic Ventures. With wide-ranging interests in the study of ageing, he currently edits three e-newsletters: *The Soul of Bioethics*, *Human Values in Aging* and *Teaching Gerontology*.

Sheila Peace is Professor of Social Gerontology and Associate Dean (Research) in the Faculty of Health and Social Care at The Open University. She is also a member of the University's Centre for Ageing and Biographical Studies (CABS). She has long-standing interests in the field of environment and ageing, long-term care for older people, the context of care across the life span and the regulation of social care services for older people.

Judith Phillips is Professor of Social Work and Gerontology in the Department of Applied Social Sciences at Swansea University and Director of the Wales Older People and Ageing Research and Development Network. Her research interests are in social work and social care, ageing and the environment, family and kinship networks, care work and older offenders.

Mo Ray is Lecturer in Social Work at Keele University, and a member of the University's Centre for Social Gerontology. She has recently completed a research fellowship supported by the Economic and Social Research Council (ESRC). Her research addresses issues relevant to critical social work practice, with a particular focus on older people's participation and involvement in research and practice.

Ruth E. Ray is Professor of English at Wayne State University in Detroit, Michigan. Her research has focused on the sociocultural factors that influence the writing of marginalised groups, including of older people. She is particularly interested in how culture, world view, and gender roles affect the ways people write and the effect their writing has on others.

Sheena Rolph is Senior Research Fellow in the Faculty of Health and Social Care at The Open University. She has research interests in the history of community care for people with learning disabilities, using oral history and archival research methods, and in enabling people with learning disabilities to participate in the exploration of their history.

Thomas Scharf is Professor of Social Gerontology and Director of the Centre for Social Gerontology at Keele University. In recent years, his research has addressed issues around poverty and social exclusion of older people, and cross-national comparisons of ageing. A particular focus has been on the experience of ageing in both urban and rural environments.

Randall Smith is a post-retirement Senior Research Fellow in the Centre for Urban Studies, School for Policy Studies, University of Bristol. His research interests include the domestic (UK) impact of European Union policies, practices and procedures, community care policies and practices and policy for older people.

Peter Townsend is Professor of International Social Policy, London School of Economics and Political Science, and Professor Emeritus and Senior Research Fellow in Social Policy at the University of Bristol. He has been at the forefront of poverty studies since the 1950s. As well as challenging the philosophical and theoretical constructs of poverty, he has been instrumental in the development of new methods of measuring and defining poverty and inequality in the UK and around the world.

Richard Ward is a Research Fellow in the Centre for Ageing and Biographical Studies (CABS) at The Open University, where he is currently working on the Research on Age Discrimination (RoAD) Project. His research interests include the social relations of dementia care settings, communication and dementia care and sexuality and ageing.

Tony Warnes is Professor of Social Gerontology in the Sheffield Institute for Studies on Ageing (SISA) at the University of Sheffield. He has pursued research in the social demography of later life and older people's residential choices since the 1970s. His interests in gerontology are multidisciplinary and range from the humanities to the potential of genomic medicine. Recent projects have included analysis of the trends in the international dispersal of pensioners from affluent countries.

Part One
Historical, theoretical and policy contexts

ONE

Critical perspectives on ageing societies

Miriam Bernard and Thomas Scharf

Behold your future.... You will not apply for membership, but the tribe of the elderly will claim you. Your present will not keep pace with the world's. This slippage will stretch your skin, sag your skeleton, erode your hair and memory, make your skin turn opaque so your twitching organs and blue-cheese veins will be semi-visible. You will venture out only in daylight, avoiding weekends and school holidays. Language, too, will leave you behind, betraying your tribal affiliations whenever you speak. On escalators, on trunk roads, in supermarket aisles, the living will overtake you, incessantly. Elegant women will not see you. Store detectives will not see you. Salespeople will not see you, unless they sell stair-lifts or fraudulent insurance policies. Only babies, cats and drug addicts will acknowledge your existence. So do not fritter away your days. Sooner than you fear, you will stand before a mirror in a care home, look at your body, and think, ET, locked in a ruddy cupboard for a fortnight. (David Mitchell, 2004, pp 182-3)

Introduction

Fictional though the above account is, it contains within it some of the deep-seated attitudes and ambivalences many of us have towards ageing and old age despite the fact that recent decades have witnessed the growth of an ever-widening interest in the ageing of societies. In the context of this book, it is the linking of this interest with an explicit critical gerontological focus that provides a unique set of understandings about ageing and later life in the 21st century. Our contributors draw on original and current research and thinking, offering new insights into the past, present and future and complementing more recent texts edited by colleagues on both sides of the Atlantic (see for example, Estes and Associates, 2001; Arber et al, 2003; Estes et al, 2003; Sheets et al, 2005; Phillipson et al, 2006). Close and scholarly analysis of policies affecting the lives of older people, together with an exploration of why research is done in particular ways, offer challenges to us all as gerontologists and as ageing individuals. Locating these discussions in a series on 'ageing and the life course' is also important for it sends a message that ageing is indeed a life course issue and not just something that concerns those whom the rest of society might disparagingly regard as belonging to 'the tribe of the elderly'.

In addition to the life course orientation, other themes thread their way throughout this book. Below, we discuss three particular themes and sets of commitments that stand out in all these explorations. First, all the contributors are committed to illuminating and extending the critical gerontological approach conceptually, methodologically and practically. Second, we are all committed to the importance of research and to the full and proper involvement and participation of older people. Third, all those writing here demonstrate an engagement with what Minkler and Holstein term in the next chapter as "passionate scholarship" which, at heart, aims to bring about change. Before discussing these themes in more detail, we turn first to a brief contextual consideration of what we mean when we talk about 'ageing societies'.

Ageing societies

In order to articulate how society impacts on individual experiences of ageing, we need to understand something of the societies within which ageing occurs and to look at these both together (Sheets et al, 2005). While the demographic features underlying the ageing of advanced industrial societies are very well known by those working in the field, for those who may be less familiar with this literature it is important to highlight the key population trends occurring within the nations that form the backdrop to the contributions to this book. In 2005, approximately 672 million people around the world were aged 60 and over, representing just over 10 per cent of the world's population of 6.5 billion (UN, 2005). In more economically developed nations, the proportion of the population aged 60 and over is now about 20 per cent, compared with only eight per cent in more economically developing nations (UN, 2005). However, while such figures are important as orientation points, they need to be treated with due caution. In particular, it needs to be borne in mind that averages across groups of nations often hide great diversity. For example, while the proportion of the UK population aged 60 and over is currently around 21 per cent, the equivalent figure for Italy is 26 per cent and for the US 17 per cent (UN, 2005). Moreover, although the developed nations have the highest proportions of older people, it is in the less economically developed world that the older population is growing most rapidly (Kinsella and Velkoff, 2001; UN, 2005).

Our societies are ageing as a consequence of three interrelated trends: declining fertility, declining mortality rates and changing patterns of migration. Declining fertility rates in advanced industrial nations have been key to population ageing. Countries that have experienced the greatest decline in fertility are also the ones that are ageing fastest. But here too there are national variations. In the UK, the average number of births per woman was 1.66 in the period 2000-05. This contrasts with figures of 2.04 for the US and 1.28 for Italy (UN, 2005). According to the United Nations (UN) (2005), the current below-replacement level fertility in most economically developed nations is expected to continue until the middle of the 21st century. Changing mortality rates also play a major role in population ageing. A decline in mortality rates across all age groups, but especially among the young, serves to increase average life expectancies. Here, too, there are national variations, even between advanced industrial societies. While life expectancy at birth is currently 80 years in Italy, it is 78 years in the UK and 77 years in the US (UN, 2005). Such average figures also mask significant gender differences. Although the gender gap in life expectancy has been declining in recent years in countries such as the UK (Shaw, 2006), women continue to live longer than men across the economically developed world. A female child born in the UK can expect to live to 81 years and a male child to 77 years (Shaw, 2006). In the US the equivalent figures for women and men are similar, at 80 years and 75 years respectively (Miniño et al, 2006).

Alongside changes in fertility and mortality, migration trends also play a role in population ageing. However, in the world's economically developed countries migration has tended to have the greatest effect in relation to within-nation differences in population structure. In such countries, the move towards modernisation was accompanied by a fairly slow growth of urbanisation as the countries moved from a rural agricultural economy to an urban industrial economy. In economically developed nations, around three quarters of all people aged 65 and over lived in urban areas in 1990 – a figure set to reach 80 per cent by 2015 (Kinsella and Velkoff, 2001, p 49). However, in spite of the increasingly urban nature of the world's older population, rural areas tend to have higher proportions of older people as a result of migration processes. Out-migration from rural areas by young people in order to find work is often compounded by a degree of return migration from urban to rural areas in later age (Kinsella and Velkoff, 2001). In some nations, there is long-standing evidence of processes of retirement migration to rural communities (Cribier, 1982; Grundy, 1987; Warnes, 1993; Longino, 1995). As a result, there can be considerable within-nation variations in the distribution of older populations. For example, in some local authority areas in the UK over 30 per cent of the population was above state pension age at the 2001 Census. This contrasted with other areas, primarily parts of London, where fewer than 12 per cent of the population fell into this age range (Office for National Statistics, 2004, p 3).

While the trends driving the ageing of our societies are similar around the world – and are anticipated to endure at least until the middle of the current century – these play out in somewhat different ways when it comes to considerations of social divisions among the older population (such as gender, 'race' or ethnicity, socio-economic status, disability and sexual orientation), and the responses of different governments in relation to education, policy and practice, and research about ageing and later life. It is now more widely accepted that older people are as heterogeneous demographically, socially and economically as younger people, but again there are some notable differences and challenges to some of the received wisdom about variations within and between more economically developed nations, which it will be important to address for the future. A good example of such variation concerns the proportions of older people who live alone. In the US, around 37 per cent of women and 15 per cent of men aged 65 and over lived alone towards the end of the 20th century. In Sweden the respective proportions were significantly higher, at 50 per cent and 25 per cent (Kinsella and Velkoff, 2001, p 65). Among older people, living alone is most often the result of outliving a spouse (and even children or siblings), especially where women are concerned, and the likelihood of living alone increases substantially with age. However, despite the increased chances of living alone in later life, it is still worth making the point that even in our ageing societies, most older people actually live with someone else. Extending knowledge and understanding of such differing dimensions of our ageing societies is a key task for critical gerontologists. We turn now therefore, to a consideration of the three cross-cutting themes that permeate the rest of these contributions, before providing an overview of each chapter.

Critical gerontology

First, all the contributors to this book are committed to illuminating and extending what has become known as the critical gerontological approach – conceptually, methodologically and practically. Others write more lucidly, both here and elsewhere, about the developments underpinning this perspective, so we simply provide a very brief thumbnail sketch of the critical issues and concerns highlighted in the chapters that follow. As Minkler and Holstein note in the next chapter, it is now 20 years since our colleagues Chris Phillipson and Alan Walker (1987, p 12) contended that critical gerontology was about "a more value-committed approach to social gerontology – a commitment not just to understand the social construction of ageing but to change it". This underlying commitment has not changed. Rather, the challenges addressed in this book have to do with how best to develop this perspective such that it enables us to provide robust evidence to challenge long-held assumptions and beliefs about ageing, old age and older people.

Our contributors argue that a truly critical gerontological approach must bring together a number of theoretical and conceptual strands. From Peter Townsend, we are alerted to critical gerontology's historical origins in the political economy and structured dependency perspectives in which he himself played such a major part. He now urges us, in this book, to adopt a human rights-based approach as a sound basis for anti-discriminatory work. From our North American colleagues Meredith Minkler and Martha Holstein, Ruth E. Ray and Harry Moody, we learn more about the contributions to critical gerontology from the humanities and from feminist perspectives, and of the need to bring these two strands together to address simultaneously both the problems and the possibilities that ageing presents us with.

As well as extending the theoretical and conceptual basis of critical gerontology, our contributors also highlight the importance of an explicit and underlying value base to our work. This value base plays out in the central concerns addressed here: concerns that extend from some of the more traditional welfare-focused areas and critiques of policy affecting older people, to considerations of ageism, age discrimination and intergenerational justice, especially in the context of a (developed) world in which those over the age of 60 are soon to outnumber those under the age of 16. Whatever our chronological age, discrimination on the basis of age is something that may affect us all at various points in our lives. Yet, although age is relative, as Bill Bytheway and his colleagues show, the negative impact of ageism on the lives of older people is still a crucial and persistent concern for critical gerontologists who seek to illuminate and understand the many and varied dimensions of difference that affect the latter phases of the life course. Alongside the centrality of ageism, the shift towards a life course perspective has also brought with it a concomitant renewal of interest in the notion of intergenerational justice and the ethical and moral questions attendant on the claims that some generations may be receiving disproportionate shares of resources at the expense of other generations. Harry Moody provides an eloquent historical perspective on these debates, while Ruth E. Ray, and Meredith Minkler and Martha Holstein argue that critical gerontology's standpoint – and indeed endpoint – should crucially be focused on bringing about a major transformation in age consciousness and age relations with social justice as its ultimate goal.

Research within a critical gerontology perspective

These shared concerns and goals have far-reaching implications both for how, and why, we do research in particular ways. Between them, our contributors raise important questions about, for example, the role of narrative gerontology; the place of 're-studies' (as opposed to replicated studies) in our research practices; the ethical issues associated with the use of archived qualitative data; the necessity to consider how the details of our research might be opened up to those who follow us; and the importance of reflective scholarship that pays attention to the fact that, as researchers, we too are ageing individuals. In fact, as Ruth E. Ray contends, we must now recognise that we ourselves are 'narrating gerontologists'.

Most importantly, and at the heart of a critical gerontology, lies a commitment to the full and proper involvement and participation of older people in all aspects of research, policy and practice. However, what distinguishes the contributions to this book is the authors' concerns to make this a reality above and beyond the platitudinous claims about simply needing to 'hear the voice' of older people. Although all our contributors share this standpoint, it is the central chapters of this book (Chapters Five, Six, Seven and Eight) that address these challenges most directly. Mo Ray takes us through a detailed exploration of how full participation might best be achieved, while Bill Bytheway, Julia Johnson and their colleagues, together with Ruth E. Ray, show how this translates into the reality of live research. Within the framework of research, these discussions further highlight long-standing issues of concern to critical gerontology including power relations, culturally appropriate practices, the dominance of certain traditions and institutions, and the taken-for-granted nature of much of what we do and how we do it. Importantly, our contributors caution that real participation is fraught with difficulties. Nor can we take for granted that it is inevitably a positive development. A key element of reflective scholarship should therefore include a necessary examination of our motivations for engaging in research of this nature.

Passionate scholarship

Difficult though the practice of critical gerontology might be, it is a perspective that offers us ways of both 'doing gerontology' and 'being gerontologists', whether we consider ourselves researchers, theoreticians or a combination of both. For us, this is encapsulated in Meredith Minkler and Martha Holstein's term 'passionate scholarship'. A reading of these chapters will leave one in no doubt that all our contributors sign up to this view. For us, 'passionate scholarship' is about a number of things: it is about an explicit value commitment; it is about making visible our concerns with the kinds of issues noted above (social justice, challenging discrimination, understanding the varied dimensions of difference etc); it is about engaging in good 'science' (whether that be, for example, close policy analysis or detailed empirical research) while also being reflective; and it is about challenging – and hopefully changing – the long-standing decline and loss paradigm encapsulated in the opening quotation. Along with Peter Townsend, who has always espoused the need for research to effect social change, our contributors are advocating for a 'passionate scholarship' in which, in Ruth E. Ray's words, we should be "willing to move out of the comfort zone" and take the kinds of risks that are needed to bring about lasting partnerships between academics, practitioners, policy makers and older people.

In the chapters that follow, leading proponents of the critical gerontology perspective from the UK and North America both review and update our understanding of how the field has developed over the past 25 years. Together, these original chapters explore current and future concerns and offer suggestions for how we might best address the conceptual, methodological and policy aspects surrounding population ageing in the 21st century.

Overview of the chapters

In Chapter Two, Martha B. Holstein and Meredith Minkler set the stage by examining the origins of critical gerontology and mounting a challenge to the decontextualised and tacitly normative ideal of 'successful ageing', the presumed neutral concepts of post-modern/post-traditional ageing and conventional notions of autonomy and empowerment. Throughout, they stress the necessity of the particularistic lens that feminism and the humanities more broadly rely on, to reveal the hidden sources of values and the effects of these values on different groups. They link this to the political economy framework that informs our understanding about structural sources of difference and highlight the significance of 'standpoint' and 'perspective' in defining problems and in determining how to approach them. They conclude by presenting a new approach to 'bringing elders back in', not as objects of study but as partners in exploring their realities and working to promote change.

In Chapter Three, Peter Townsend turns the focus on the evolution of social policy and its corresponding institutions and makes a powerful plea for human rights-based approaches to addressing ageism and the structured dependency still experienced by many older people around the world. He argues that by the late 20th century, older people were perceived and treated, according to accumulating research evidence, as more dependent than they really were or needed to be, and that this had been fostered by the emerging institutions of retirement, income maintenance and residential and domiciliary care. Forms of discrimination against older people had become, or continued to be, as deep as forms of discrimination against women and minority ethnic groups. Although hopes were invested in anti-discriminatory policies (and in the UK the new legislation relating to age discrimination came into force as this book went to press), the globalisation of the market and affiliation to neoliberal policies, together with the simultaneous passage of various instruments of human rights, have changed the nature of the problem, and therefore the debate, in the early years of the 21st century. Townsend argues that human rights-based approaches offer a framework of rigorous analysis and a sound basis for anti-discriminatory work. However, success will depend on good operational measurement, and the incorporation internationally, as well as nationally, of institutions and policies that reflect those rights.

Continuing with the theme of challenging policy thinking, Robin Means draws on both historical and contemporary perspectives to highlight the ways in which present government policies are creating a re-medicalisation of later life that is to the detriment of older people (Chapter Four). He argues that recent policy developments have ignored the findings from research about how best to respond to the needs of those older people in the community with extensive health and social care problems. Rather than building on work that has pointed to the emphasis placed by older people on quality of life issues and their desire to retain independence and a sense of their citizenship irrespective of their health and social care problems, the dominant driver of recent policy has been to revert to a medical model in which the major desire of health seems to be to cost shunt onto local authority social services. This chapter takes the recent Green Paper on *Independence, well-being and choice: Our vision for the future of social care for adults in England* (DH, 2005a) as a case study and shows that what is most striking are the continuities with the past rather than radical improvements.

Having set the historical, theoretical and policy contexts, the four central chapters of the book (Chapters Five, Six, Seven and Eight) are focused on why empirical research in gerontology is done in particular ways. Drawing on her own ethnographic studies with older adults, as well as the work of other feminists from different disciplines, Ruth E. Ray presents a compelling argument for the need for 'age research' to include the researcher him/herself as a subject of observation, analysis and critique (Chapter Five). Couched firmly within a critical gerontology perspective and the 'passionate scholarship' endorsed by all our contributors, Ruth E. Ray discusses the relationship between personal and social transformation and describes ethnographic methods that gerontological scholars might use to reflect on their position as researchers, their relationship to older adults, the ethics of their research practices, and the value of their studies beyond academe.

In Chapter Six, these issues are picked up again by Mo Ray (no relation) when she explores the participation of older people in mainstream research from the perspectives of both researchers and older citizen participants. She argues convincingly for the real involvement of older people in all aspects of the research process: from conceiving the research topic and research questions, through to developing culturally appropriate methods of conducting the research, analysing and writing up the findings, and ensuring its success in contributing to social action and change. Importantly too, Mo Ray asks us to consider how research should develop in order to redress traditional and long-standing power imbalances between 'researcher' and 'researched'. However, she also cautions that we cannot take for granted that participation in research is inevitably a positive development for older people. Consequently, the chapter concludes by considering some of the implications of developing participation and asks what research establishments may realistically be able to achieve in the frameworks that currently dominate mainstream research agendas.

Some real world examples of the participation of older people in current research, and of the reflections of researchers themselves, are presented in Chapters Seven and Eight. In Chapter Seven, Julia Johnson, Sheena Rolph and Randall Smith provide a fascinating insight into some of the methodological challenges associated with revisiting Peter Townsend's (1962) classic study of residential care: *The Last Refuge*. They discuss the methodological issues related to designing a comparative longitudinal study of residential care provision for older people and draw attention to the benefits and challenges associated with using archived qualitative data. The aim of their study is to find out what happened to the 173 homes Townsend visited: to explore how many of them have survived as care homes and what they are like now in comparison with what they were like in the late 1950s. In addition to the practical challenges that tracing the homes present, they also highlight contrasts as well as continuities between the research instruments used then and now, the nature of the data then and now (including photographic evidence) and the ethical issues attendant on such research. An added dimension to the project is engaging with older people as research collaborators, many of whom had worked in health and social care settings and remembered the homes in question or knew people who had worked in them.

This chapter clearly conveys the excitement and rewards of doing such research but also provides a timely reminder about the responsibilities we as present-day researchers have, both to older people and to the original researchers when we venture to 'pick over' their earlier work.

Chapter Eight shifts from revisiting a classic study to an issue of contemporary concern, namely age discrimination and ageism. Here, Bill Bytheway, Richard Ward, Caroline Holland and Sheila Peace discuss their experiences of coordinating the RoAD (Research on Age Discrimination) project. This UK-wide research project employs the kinds of participatory methods and researcher insights endorsed by both Ruth E. Ray and Mo Ray. In particular, Bill Bytheway and his colleagues reflect on their own roles, asking, "are we simply 'the researchers' or are we 'older people undertaking research'?". They recognise that this project calls into question their own identities as well as raising fundamental issues about how 'old' or 'older' is defined in the context of age discrimination. On the basis of their accumulating evidence, they also caution that policies designed to tackle age discrimination could become overly associated with employment practices and a few other narrowly defined third age issues – echoing the concerns expressed earlier by Robin Means in relation to policies aimed at addressing the needs of older people experiencing health and social care problems.

Picking up the issues raised about critical gerontology in general, and the challenges to gerontologists as scholars and researchers in particular, the final two chapters of the book return us to a consideration of where we now go from here. In their different ways, both of these chapters explore what we can learn about progress in critical gerontology from the developments of the past 25 years, and how this information can be brought together with contemporary understandings to inform the development of a future critical research agenda for ageing. Harry R. Moody's chapter (Chapter Nine) explores these issues from a North American vantage point: highlighting how anxiety about population ageing arises most prominently at times when the fate of future generations appears to be at risk. He draws on historical, environmental and philosophical arguments to show how a focus on justice – rather than competition or conflict – between generations is "an idea that will not go away" and how it can illuminate the policy choices faced by ageing societies during the 21st century. His wide-ranging historical review concludes by proposing a greater attention to the 'late freedom' of old age as a model for generativity and concern for the welfare of future generations around the world.

In the final chapter of the book (Chapter Ten) Tony Warnes and Judith Phillips review progress in (critical) gerontology from a British perspective. Drawing on an examination of the first 25 years of the journal *Ageing and Society*, together with a case study of the interaction between the members and officials of the Welsh Assembly Government and gerontological advisers, the authors clarify who the variety of interest groups now are in the gerontological enterprise (including older people and their perspectives); how gerontology has grown and expanded; and what the strengths and weaknesses of current research are. Like earlier contributors to this book, Tony Warnes and Judith Phillips highlight a number of important challenges for gerontology and gerontologists throughout their review. These include the paucity of theoretical development in gerontology; the persistent tension for gerontologists about whether to commit to gerontology or to their base discipline or research field; and the often difficult relationship between research and policy formulation and the dominance of biomedical and problem-oriented perspectives. Despite this, they also point to the increasingly multidisciplinary nature of research on ageing and later life and its focus on stakeholder involvement generally, and the participation of older people in particular.

Conclusion

Many of the chapters in this book draw, in part, on selected presentations made at the 2005 annual conference of the British Society of Gerontology. This was the third time that members of the Centre for Social Gerontology at Keele University had hosted the Conference (1985, 1995 and 2005) and it also coincided with the silver anniversary of the journal *Ageing and Society*. The long-standing critical gerontological orientation of the host university, combined with the journal's anniversary, therefore make this a particularly appropriate time to reflect on and review our understanding of how critical gerontology has developed over the past 25 years, and where it might go in the future. Distilling the essence of the chapters, it seems to us that, without exception, the contributors to this book have all illustrated both the vitality and potential of the field but without minimising the challenges we still face if our ageing societies are to be societies in which we all wish to grow old.

TWO

Critical gerontology: reflections for the 21st century

Martha B. Holstein and Meredith Minkler

Introduction

Critical gerontology, we believe, must engage in serious but respectful critique of more traditional social gerontology since we assume similar ends but adopt different approaches, sources of knowledge and epistemological stances. In this chapter, we explore where the field of critical gerontology is today in terms of its major commitments and concerns, the way it approaches its multiple tasks, and the opportunities and obstacles it faces as we move further into the 21st century. Although we also look briefly at where more traditional social gerontology is at this juncture, this will be more the backdrop than the central concern of our discussion.

Like beauty, critical gerontology may be in the eyes of the beholder. However, Baars (1991, p 221) succinctly described it as a "collection of questions, problems, and analyses that have been excluded by the established mainstream", while Phillipson and Walker (1987, p 12) characterised it as "a more value-committed approach to social gerontology – a commitment not just to understand the social construction of aging but to change it". Together with our feminist colleagues, Miriam Bernard (2001) and Ruth E. Ray (1996), we also view critical gerontology as an umbrella term that takes as its object the philosophical foundations, epistemological assumptions, and social influences on which social gerontology has been constructed. Furthermore, as philosopher Richard Bernstein (1992, p 162) suggests, "the primary task of the critic is to analyze the present and to reveal its fractures and instabilities and the ways in which it at once limits us and points to the transgressions of those limits". From these various perspectives, and toward the end of exploring where critical gerontology is today, this chapter aims to:

- update observations regarding the two paths along which critical gerontology has been travelling (Minkler, 1996);
- adopt a 'critical' stance that transforms the 'taken for granted' into a problem to be examined;

- expand on the feminist voice in gerontology and philosophy with its focus on standpoint, embodiment and moral perception;
- consider the impact on critical gerontology of those voices beyond feminism that have called out for far greater attention to the meaning and significance of racial/ethnic and other forms of diversity in our increasingly heterogeneous ageing societies; and,
- look ahead.

Social gerontology and its limitations

Before we turn specifically to critical gerontology, it is helpful to consider briefly where more mainstream social gerontology is at this point in our history. On both sides of the Atlantic and in countries around the world, there is strong and growing interest in population ageing and its implications for health and social policy, intergenerational relations, elder care and the like. Efforts in the UK to address institutionalised ageism head on, and in many nations to confront a pension and social security crisis that is part real, part socially constructed, are among the developments that have catapulted ageing as a topic of popular and academic concern.

Yet, as Carroll Estes and her colleagues (2003) point out, despite this growth of interest, "social gerontology as a set of approaches to understanding the nature of growing old might be said to be in a state of crisis and disunity" (p 145). They describe this crisis as an unresolved uneasiness between core social science disciplines and the study of ageing, and the "continued hold of perspectives that fail to acknowledge the profound effects of race, ethnicity, gender and class divisions, as well as intergenerational relations, on the experience of ageing" (p 145). Estes et al further suggest that mainstream social gerontology's "existing conceptual tools and related assumptions, and the scholars working with them, have either not kept pace with the new sets of influences affecting older people, or have uncritically accepted them as unproblematic" (p 145).

The current state of gerontological scholarship in the area of racial and ethnic diversity provides a useful example. Although mainstream gerontology has increasingly addressed racial and ethnic differences in ageing (Bulatao and Anderson, 2004), it has tended to limit itself to individual and group differences, rather than looking more deeply at the power relationships between privileged and oppressed groups that underlie these disparities (Calasanti, 1996; Dressel et al, 1998). As Calasanti (1996) suggests, there is a critical difference between content diversity (group differences in terms of 'race', ethnicity, class and gender) and *approach diversity*, emphasising power and standpoint. While the former is relatively straightforward and can be presented without much theoretical grounding, research in the tradition of approach diversity must, by definition, be rooted within a conceptual framework that stresses "the interlocking sets of power relations that structure social life" (McMullin, 2000, p 517). Although some progress has been made in developing this theoretical base, far more robust conceptualisations are needed that to date have largely eluded mainstream gerontological thought.

The field has tended to ignore, for example, the ways in which the central and interrelated processes of social life – distribution, production and reproduction – "are shaped by interlocking sets of power relations and, in turn, how this leads to inequality for some and privilege for others" (McMullin, 2000, p 528). By failing to adequately address interactions, for example, between 'race', class and gender, we remain hampered by what Andersen (1983) named, more than 20 years ago, "the add and stir approach …: add women [or any other non-dominant group] and stir". Such an approach cannot address the multiple forms of inequality and interlocking oppression as these play out over the life course, nor can it escape from the formative questions that have traditionally shaped inquiry. Finally, as Blakemore (1997) points out, "research at the interface of ethnicity, cultural difference and ageing has been relatively neglected" (p 31) and also is deserving of careful attention with the increasingly multicultural composition of ageing populations in the UK and around the world.

We are troubled as well by contemporary social gerontology's seeming inability to recognise and so acknowledge its tacit value commitments, both methodological and substantive, and to grasp how images shape the lived experience of ageing. Similarly, mainstream gerontology often seems unable, as Cole (1991) observed many years ago, to incorporate the twin poles of ageing – its strengths and weaknesses; its celebrations and pains – simultaneously. It is neither all good nor all bad; we suffer at the same time that we exult. But mainstream social gerontology cannot easily accept such ambiguity, ambivalence and multiplicity, and its inability to 'fix' the 'problem' of ageing. Thus, it does not recognise that the need to impose order and structure can be arbitrary and oppressive (Flax, 1987, quoted in Minnich, 1990, p 155).

The concept of 'successful ageing' reflects the problems these unacknowledged value commitments and assumptions create. In the US, the most widely publicised paradigm of successful ageing is squarely based on the medical model. 'Success' involves three interrelated elements: low risk for disease and disability, maintenance of high physical and mental capacity, and 'active engagement in life' (Rowe and Kahn, 1999), two of which are solely related to physical and mental health functioning and risk factors. The problems inherent in this model, with its universal norms, built on the assumption of equal opportunity to achieve these desired ends, is captured in the story of two elderly men, each of whom wanted to improve his health: suburban retired professor Jim Law and Mario Hermoso, who lived in a small room in a low-rent single room occupancy (SRO) hotel in San Francisco's Tenderloin District. Jim, but not Mario, had every opportunity to 'fix' a lifetime of bad health habits so that he soon was setting world running records for his age group. Mario also wanted to improve his health, but the Tenderloin is a dangerous place; taking an evening walk is neither pleasant nor safe. There are no real grocery stores and SROs do not allow cooking in one's room or facilitate healthy eating. If Mario can barely afford to buy a package of filling, high-fat tortilla chips for a couple of dollars, why would he spend three or four dollars on the fresh fruits and vegetables that he needs – most of which were not available in his neighbourhood anyway? Jim is a model of successful ageing; Mario is a failure. Faulty assumptions about equal opportunity and control doom Mario. Sought-for regularities dwarf the unique nature of Mario's experience, because ageing occurs within a particularistic discursive and normative context that seeks to generalise (Tulle-Winton, 2000). And it also occurs within an environmental context, with place and space relations linked to the kinds of power illustrated in these men's stories.

The successful ageing model thus fails to account for particular life trajectories and environmental realities, and is predicated on reductionist aims for a very large idea – that of success. How would middle-aged people feel if the key measure of a 'successful' middle age was good health? Health is undoubtedly foundational, but it is a means and not an end. After all, what is good health for? Even as a means, this simplistic notion of successful ageing rings hollow to people like a colleague who has been a wheelchair user for many years, yet for whom a rich network of family and friends, and an active life of engagement through political organising or poetry, constitutes a life well lived. Overzealous attention to health as a measure of success and achievement crowds out cultural space to grapple with critical existential questions and devalues people like our colleague, who flourish despite physical limitations. It suggests that one can age 'successfully' in the absence of the ontological security we all crave: the security of knowing that we have a place in our society and community no matter the status of our health. The embracing notion of successful ageing, like the notions of 'healthy' or 'active' ageing, with their implicit normative standards, ultimately devalues those who do not live up to their ideals and offers few representations that might speak to Mario Hermoso and others like him.

In its efforts to eliminate ageism by focusing on the positive features of old age, social gerontology further encounters another profound limitation. It fails to notice the real bodies of old people. Embodiment, when ignored, permits the unproblematic support of positive cultural images and representations that are instrumental – without being deterministic – in shaping our identity and confirming our moral worth. Frida Furman's (1997) study of old women and beauty shop culture poignantly revealed how women could poke fun at their double chins, fat tummies and wispy hair. But, as she noted, they did so in the safety of the beauty shop, not in the outside world – in alternative communities of meaning – where the still dominant male gaze would find them wanting. As Furman suggests, the ageing body dramatically conflicts with cultural representations of feminine beauty, which are developed in the context of power relationships where older women lack power. As the locus of our moral agency, our bodies set limits to how we negotiate the world and how others see us, especially when we do not live up to certain normative conceptions of the desirable body (Dwyer, 1998). The fact that we live within a certain material body that profoundly affects our range of choices, the responsibilities we can assume and the way we see ourselves, gets scant attention in social gerontology.

The assumption that supports the many upbeat positive portrayals of ageing that the new social gerontology favours is that we all have, if not an equal opportunity, then at least a shooting chance of living well in old age – if only we had acted properly earlier in our lives. This assumption erases the constraints on individual agency that difference imposes and blinds us to the choices that are actually, rather than theoretically, available to people across the life span. The underlying value embraces a commitment to individualism and individual achievement so marked in North American society, and to a lesser but still powerful extent in the UK. One result of these assumptions and tacit values is the oppression, rather than the liberation, of old people, especially women. To find a way out of this quagmire – to reverse the decline and loss paradigm without imposing oppressive standards and false expectations – is a task that still lies ahead.

Many of the concerns we have raised about mainstream social gerontology – its failure to acknowledge underlying value commitments; its inability to grasp and confront the twin poles of ageing; its unwitting promotion of a new form of ageism through notions like successful ageing; its reductionism; and its tendency to look superficially at health disparities while ignoring underlying power relationships – were levelled at the field a quarter of a century ago. These concerns helped give rise to critical gerontology, but the failure of social gerontology to come to grips with them in the intervening 25 years is a real cause for concern.

This brief exploration underscores again the need for an alternative, explicitly value-committed perspective as we attempt to further develop critical theory in ageing. A critical perspective is necessary too if older people are to become part of our work, not simply as objects of study (or as ageing gerontologists!), but as co-learners whose expertise about the meaning and significance of ageing we have too long ignored (see also Chapters Five and Six).

Critical gerontology today and tomorrow

So, returning to our central question: 'where is critical gerontology today and where ought it go in the years ahead?'. A decade ago, one of us (Minkler, 1996) described critical gerontology as travelling along two pathways – the political economy of ageing and the humanities – that have occasionally intersected and moved in common directions, but have more often remained distinct. The former path views the problems of ageing in structural rather than individual terms: it owes its existence, in part, to the seminal work of Peter Townsend (1981a) on the social construction of the dependency of the old (see Chapter Three). The political economy perspective reminds us that the phenomenon of ageing and old age cannot be considered or analysed in isolation from other societal forces and phenomena. The central role of the state in regulating and reproducing differential life chances throughout the life course, which in turn help shape how we experience ageing and growing old, remains of central concern in a political economy perspective.

Topics such as globalisation and the changing nature of retirement are among those that have recently lent themselves to examination through the lenses of political economy. It is important to point out, however, as Estes and colleagues (2003) remind us, that the political economy path is premised in part on the notion that social structures affect not only how older people are viewed, but on how they view themselves. In this respect there is an important potential convergence of this path with that of the humanities. For the most part, however, political economy has tended to concentrate on larger sociostructural forces, rather than on how these forces play out on the level of the individual and his or her experience of ageing and its meaning. Agency unnoticed is agency denied.

The humanities, as conceptualised here, are both certain disciplines and a world view or way of thinking, that of engagement across disciplinary and other boundaries (see also Chapter Nine). In its critical dimension, the humanities asks questions about meaning: a perspective that one can understand only from the inside. It has also focused on the intersection of culture and biography – especially as culture represents ageing through images – and seeks to understand how agency is played out within cultural and other constraints. We are neither "trapped nor free" – we always interact with our culture, our times, our realities (Minnich, 1990, p 165). So the humanities would ask questions such as: 'how do old people make sense of the ageing experience and how do cultural ideals – tacit or explicit – shape that interpretation?' and 'How does agency interact with cultural ideals and political realities to shape our experiences of old age?'. To enrich the picture even further, many scholars in the humanities supplement their work with ethnography and other critical social science approaches (see Chapter Five).

Unfortunately, these two approaches – political economy and the humanities – still intersect less often than we might like. As much as we might talk about the interdisciplinary nature of our field and our work, we still function, for the most part, within disciplinary, and methodological boundaries. Although the political economy perspective continues to have outspoken adherents on both sides of the Atlantic, it is not central to professional analyses of old age. The second pathway, the perspective from the humanities, is also marginal. While we see more interest in the voices of older people as expressed in fiction, poetry and autobiography, these voices are add-ons, rarely accorded the status of more traditional empirical and data-driven work. To really 'know' something about old age is to know it quantitatively.

Some historians, some literary scholars publish in gerontology but we rarely, for example, see the work of other critical disciplines like disability or feminist studies in our publication venues. This, we acknowledge, is not necessarily the fault of the journals. In the UK, *Ageing and Society* has been an important source for both the political economy and the humanities perspectives (see Chapter Ten). In the US, one journal dedicated to the humanities and critical gerontology, *The Journal of Aging and Identity*, recently ceased publication; another one, tentatively titled *The Journal of Aging and the Humanities*, is now gestating. It will be interesting to see if this publication gains an audience and survives. Today in the US, however, only the *Journal of Aging Studies*, which has a limited audience, regularly ventures into this seemingly risky terrain. And when mainstream journals like *The Gerontologist* include articles that reflect a critical gerontology stance, they are typically published in sections of these journals with titles like 'Commentary' or 'The Forum', and not as regular (and tacitly more legitimate and valued) academic articles. What is heartening, however, is that when articles that take a critical gerontology stance do appear in our mainstream journals, they often attract substantial interest. Similarly, when sessions reflecting critical gerontology perspectives have been presented at more traditional professional meetings, the audiences are often large and enthusiastic. Clearly then, the interest in such critical perspectives is growing, even as they continue to be marginalised by the arbiters of what constitutes real scholarship in our field.

Moving towards a richer critical gerontology

Moving critical gerontology from the margins it currently occupies to the centre may mean travelling in several directions. The first, we suggest, calls for a deeper understanding of how perception, standpoint and value commitments affect all our work. The second involves encouraging what we are calling methodological bricolage, which requires crossing disciplinary and methodological boundaries so that, thirdly, the different pathways in critical gerontology can together enlarge understanding and systematically challenge the status quo.

Step one: Standpoint and epistemological radicalism

About a decade ago, the then incoming editor of *The Gerontologist* wrote that he hoped to publish the best scientific work that he could. One of us immediately sent a letter to the editor protesting the insistence on 'scientific' work and, of course, received the only response he could give: the journal would certainly publish humanities and related work if it met the journal's standards. But these standards are not as value neutral as he undoubtedly believed. It is hard to see one's epistemological assumptions if they are taken as universally valid by one's peers.

Almost at the same time, Cole (1995) observed that the "growth of an intellectually rich social gerontology depends on the continued willingness to foster greater interactions between empirical research, interpretation, critical evaluation, and reflexive knowledge" (p S343). This endeavour means accepting that research cannot occupy a value-free realm: it means acknowledging that we all view the world – and do our research – with a view from somewhere. The view from nowhere – above the fray – does not exist any more in gerontological research than it does, for example, in physics.

Perhaps a simple example will suggest how our standpoint affects our thinking.

Our colleague Harry R. Moody adopts a very different stance toward such rubrics as 'successful' or 'productive' ageing (see Chapter Nine). We see the problems; he sees the value. It might be that he is an optimist and we are pessimists, but we do not think the explanation is that simple. He is acutely sensitive to context and cannot be faulted for assuming that self-creation is *the* most worthy project of old age, or that all have equal opportunities even to engage actively in their communities. Harry Moody is a philosopher by training, committed to spiritual and other non-material dimensions of our lives, and has been a dedicated caregiver to an old and dear friend and mentor. So what's the problem?

Perhaps it is because we see the world from different standpoints, and that standpoint affects what we see and notice. Feminist scholars have noted that women, for example, see differently not because of our sex, but because material and historical conditions have given us a particular vantage point from which to view the world (see also the examples in Chapter Eight). To take but a single powerful example, in the US today, older women are significantly more likely than older men to live in poverty (12% versus 8%) (FIFARS, 2004), and in the UK, two thirds of those pensioners on low incomes are female. Although the British case is explained in part by technical ways of treating household income, substantially higher poverty rates in older women remain even when these measurement factors are taken into account (DWP, 2005a, p 98). Consider then how this reality influences what we see and notice in, for example, debates about old age pensions or 'informal' caregiving. Perspective is morally relevant because what we notice, and how we notice it, becomes the grounding for what we choose (or do not choose) to act on. What we don't see can "camouflage social ills and thwart critical moral reflection" (Meyers, 1997, p 197). Gender, class, 'race' and ethnicity all influence our moral perceptions: the key instigator for action.

Two other examples help demonstrate this problem. One of our male colleagues once referred to women who provide care to older relatives as "saints". While this may be true, most women probably would prefer basic financial and other supports, including a partnership with their male counterparts, to sainthood. Women give care, most often willingly and even enthusiastically, not because they are inherently better at it than men, but because someone must do it and their unequal position in the labour force makes them the strongest candidates for the job. Emphasising the productive contributions of women as carers does nothing to relieve their burden. Similarly, when one views 'productive ageing' through a gendered lens, one can see that women's lives are already filled with what are often unchosen obligations: caregiving, 'kin-keeping', general maintenance of home and hearth, and jobs that pay little and yield few satisfactions. Further, with pension plans already highly discriminatory toward women and minorities because of their role as carers and the gaps in their paid work history, continued paid work is very often a necessity rather than a choice. These perceptions inevitably challenge commonly held notions about autonomy or productive ageing.

Eliding these gender-based differences creates problems with a hypothesis like the one Gilleard and Higgs (2002) put forth about the third age: that it is a generational rather than a cohort or class phenomenon. In noting the greater affluence and individual assertiveness of the 'baby boom' generation, they conclude by saying that this generation will not be the pensioners of the past. This claim may be true but not necessarily for the reasons they offer. As Phillipson (1998), Polivka (2005) and others (Estes et al, 2003) have observed, we might instead be witnessing the deinstitutionalisation of retirement: a consequence of the dismantling of welfare state provisions making work essential for many elders rather than work being the result of active choosing. It has become a truism that the baby boomers will be less well off than their parents and, in the US at least, class distinctions are hardening. If, in Great Britain, 75 per cent of retirees have pensions that, added to the public benefit, will give them the leisure to live decently and creatively in old age, one must ask – from a feminist standpoint and also from a political economy perspective – how are those pensions distributed? Who will get them and for what amounts of money? How protected are they? And does a modest income, even if safe, give men and women the same opportunity to live as third agers?

In the US, private sector pensions, which never were distributed equally between men and women, are fast eroding if not disappearing, and social security is threatened. The latter has historically worked to the disadvantage of women. Service employees in particular – the fastest growing sector of the US economy – and women, will need to continue working not because they want to but because they must. The proverbial rising tide does not lift all boats. Time will prove if our scepticism is warranted.

Thus, standpoint is important politically. Since what we see or perceive is the foundation for problem definition, whether it is social welfare policies or battles against terrorism, the people or groups who have the power to have their perceptions define problems, and hence structure subsequent solutions, have considerable influence over what actually takes place. People who are on the margins of society rarely have this power; they do not get to define need based on their own knowledge of their communities and so they cannot configure social action (Fraser, 1989; Young, 1990). Hence, as Bernard and Phillips (2000) point out, progress along the road to social justice through more equitable policy must be accompanied by a belief in the value of, and a firm commitment to, "notions of empowerment, citizenship and voice" (p 43). To be heard in a way that influences actions is a critical, but often neglected, element in a just society (Young, 1990).

Critical gerontology can take the lead in insisting that value commitments and standpoint be explicitly affirmed and recognised in all our work. Often, for example, feminist scholars will affirm their identity and speak in the first person, an approach that effectively says, "I come from somewhere and so may see and think differently than one who comes from elsewhere".

Step two: Methodological bricolage

A second way to integrate the two paths in critical gerontology is through what we are calling methodological bricolage. We adopt this expression from philosopher Jeffrey Stout's (1988) concept of moral bricolage, which he defines as: "The process in which one begins with bits and pieces of received linguistic material, arranges some of them into a structural whole, leaves others to the side, and ends with a moral language one proposes to use" (p 294).

In our adaptation, we propose starting with questions, particularly redefining what count as questions worth asking. And to answer our questions, we look to multiple 'bits and pieces' of research strategies and approaches, as we broaden what we consider acceptable forms of knowing (see also Chapters Six, Seven and Eight). When we do this, we may find that the fit between political economy approaches and the humanities is snug and comfortable. Methodological bricolage means not ruling out knowledge that is gained from personal narratives, fiction, poetry, film, qualitative investigations, philosophical inquiries, participatory action research and any other method of inquiry we may discover that yields insights into fundamental questions about how, and why, we experience old age in very particular ways. We need to worry less about large-scale generalisations and more about getting the story right. What does it mean to inhabit a 68-year-old body that does not work as well as it once did? For an old woman, how does it feel to be both invisible and hyper-visible almost simultaneously? How do cultural representations of old age affect those people whose lives are radically different than the norms these representations tacitly uphold? How do we symbolically reorganise our lives as meanings change and old roles disappear (Rubinstein, 2002a)? How might a poem or essay by an older woman yield insights about her recognition that she disturbs the visual field of the young by her very presence? And why should we care about this disturbance? We who are approaching old age know this first hand. Please check with us in 10 years to see if we have achieved our practice of the oppositional gaze, a stare down technique that black writer and poet bell hooks (1984) recommends for people so often made to feel 'other'.

So the first task of integration is to take methodological risks – both in choosing the questions to ask and the forms of knowing we welcome. This task has a further requirement: that we do not demand broadly generalisable data. As critical theorists pointed out long ago, what we seek is understanding and not control. No matter how hard we may try, we cannot take away all the hurts of old age, but we can mitigate them through an understanding of how we, as professional gerontologists, may contribute to them. We can, of course, also help mitigate them by vigorous efforts to prevent the continued devolution of social welfare policies (Phillipson, 1998; Estes et al, 2003), a danger that unrelentingly positive images of ageing unintentionally supports.

One approach to gaining this understanding, and using it as the basis of action for social change, involves using participatory approaches to inquiry that equitably involve all partners in the research process and recognise the unique strengths that each brings (Israel et al, 1998) (see Chapters Five, Six, Seven and Eight). These participatory approaches, which in the UK are called action research and in the US community-based participatory research, begin with a research topic that matters to, and ideally comes from, the community itself, and involves members of the community – in our case older people – in the research process. They are not simply objects of study but co-contributors to knowledge and understanding (Green and Mercer, 2001; Minkler and Wallerstein, 2003). Finally, and consistent with Phillipson and Walker's (1987) observations about critical gerontology, participatory approaches are committed not just to studying the status quo, but to changing it. For applying what is learned to help address inequities and improve how things are, is an integral part of the participatory research process – not something others do with the study findings after the fact. In short, this participatory approach 'turns on its head' more traditional research paradigms. In the words of Hall (1992), it is fundamentally about "who has the right to speak, to analyze, and to act" (p 22).

An example of this participatory research approach suggests how it can contribute to critical gerontology. The Grandparent Caregiver Study (Minkler and Roe, 1993; Roe et al, 1995) involved academic researchers, two community-based organisations, and a community advisory board (CAB) in helping to study and address the problems and strengths of African American women who were raising their grandchildren as a result of a major drug epidemic. CAB helped develop the research approach and carefully word questions so that they were culturally sensitive – and more likely to be answered truthfully. They helped in the interpretation of study findings and worked with study participants to plan an elaborate luncheon where the role of these caregivers could be celebrated, preliminary study findings discussed, and decisions made about how best to use the study findings to bring about change. The team worked with the women, for example, to start a church-based respite centre for grandparent caregivers, as well as regional and state-wide coalitions to seek policy level changes (Roe et al, 1995). The action component of this research lasted for many years, and concurrently, the study findings were published in mainstream medical and gerontology journals to help shed light on this issue, place it in a broader political economy context, and enable a 'telling of the story' through the voices of the women who were living it.

In the UK, as in other parts of Europe and North America, there is increasing interest in engaging older people in focus groups, interviews and other venues in which they can give voice to their views. Yet such involvement is almost always heavily circumscribed as we ask about important, but narrow matters such as how service provision could be improved. In saying this, we are in no way disparaging the excellent work going on in this regard by Tozer and Thornton (1995) and others, but merely suggesting again that we need to go much further, by actually involving older people in setting the research agenda and in helping collect, analyse and use the findings to promote change (see Chapter Six).

As we have suggested, participatory research with older people themselves constitutes one as yet little explored way in which we can integrate the different forms of knowing into a richer critical gerontology. Another approach, however, may simply involve the use of focus groups to reveal otherwise hidden features of growing old, especially for people who are poor. As an example, one of us (Holstein) conducted a focus group on the West side of Chicago with 10 Latinos and Latinas. The goal was to have them tell us what they wanted the state of Illinois to do to make life a little easier for them. These men and women, often monolingual, lived either in government-subsidised housing or in low-rent apartments in dangerous neighbourhoods, where they stayed because there is such a long waiting list for affordable housing. One man – on his $500 (roughly £268) social security cheque – was taking care of his two sisters – one with Alzheimer's disease and the other with Parkinson's. After working for over 40 years hanging metal doors, he had no pension. These people live at the edge: social security goes up $3, the rent $47; one earns a little money and loses his or her health coverage. With cuts in the government's subsidised housing budget and proposed changes to Medicaid (government health insurance for the poor and disabled) this situation promises to worsen.

All of the people who participated in this focus group were neatly dressed and eager to talk. Two left early to pick up grandchildren from school. One had to take two buses and it was a raw, wet day – Chicago's finest. The contrast between this group, and one conducted in an affluent Chicago suburb, is instructive. No one in the wealthy group rushed off to take two buses to pick up a grandchild from school, and no one locked themselves in their apartments at night for fear of what was going on in the empty apartment next door. No quantitative study could have captured the power of these differences. Nor could it have elicited the excited commitment of Anita to join us as we work with our state legislators, or that of Jose who accepted his responsibility for his two sisters because, if he did not, who would? Or of the grandparents who left to pick up their grandchildren at school. These obligations are unchosen but necessary to keep the family going, and they have no real place in a system that emphasises rational, self-interested choice as the most important moral virtue. Absorbing, indeed living the values of their community, these older people accepted responsibility as elemental: care is not optional. This understanding of autonomy, agency and accountability is marginalised in consumer-oriented societies where self-interested choice is an acceptable moral stance.

Step three: Integrating the two pathways

One immediate task for us is to write and speak as often as we can from the two paths in critical gerontology, so that they become what Estes and colleagues (2003) have called "a creative amalgam" that includes "experiential, humanistic and personal approaches" (p 147), as well as a deep and careful look at social forces and movements. Collaborative work is both a humanistic approach and a good way to achieve such integration. Like the focus group just described, work across boundaries can render visible in very human terms the effects of the structural problems that political economy so ably analyses. Yet, as Estes et al (2003) point out, "without an understanding of social structure ... an overly humanistic approach to ageing is isolated from context and history. These two factors, experiential realism and the effects of material realism, lie at the centre of a critical understanding of later life" (p 147).

Two fictional accounts about old women – one by the Australian writer Patrick White and one by British author Pat Barker – viewed through the filter of political economy, suggest a way to bridge the approaches (Holstein, 1994). These novels, both about women who have strokes – Elizabeth, who is very rich and Alice, who is very poor – reveal the power of social location while bringing the reader intimately into the life world of seriously impaired older women. Such intimacy permits us, perhaps the currently healthy, to bridge the phenomenological gap between the well and the impaired. Such narratives make distancing much harder than more familiar research on strokes. One is able to imagine oneself into bodies that would otherwise be unknown to us, knowledge that can lead to greater understanding and better practices. As we see each woman struggling to make meaning in the life the stroke bequeathed, we see the power of agency set against the background conditions of culture and class, and the ways in which the past infiltrates the present. Elizabeth is bemused by her helpless self and observes that "old people aren't quite human for those still capable of moving about..." (Holstein, 1994, p 823). But, she is surrounded by luxury and can afford – both financially and emotionally – to play at her new roles. Alice, on the other hand, has but one choice: to cling to the remnants of self-respect with little or no help from others. She thinks to herself, "They [her son, the social service workers] were sorry for her, but she made them uncomfortable. It was difficult for them to believe that this slobbering, glugging thing that could not make its own wants known was a human being" (p 824). Both women are proud; both have a sense of self-worth; yet, although Elizabeth's choices far exceed Alice's, both fail to 'age successfully' in the contemporary, medicalised sense of that term.

Merging the two approaches, political economy and the humanities, with the collaboration of other critical social sciences, reveals the complexities of individual lives and allows us to see the workings of agency, against all odds. Political economy defines the context, the humanities exposes its intimate effects and offers a plurality of ideals and ideas about how old people create morally coherent lives. As such, working from within the two pathways is critical. Participatory action research and the critical social sciences round out the multiple ways the experience of ageing can be clarified and perhaps made better. Diversity of approaches, methodological bricolage and a broad understanding of what constitutes the 'subject' of our research are keys.

Conclusion

We hold out this hope for those of us committed to critical gerontology – from whatever direction we come at it, since we are as different from one another as people in any other group – that we do whatever we do with passion and a belief that our scholarship can make a difference: that is, move people to action. 'Passionate scholarship' does not aim for control or domination, nor even for certainty, but for the freedom to pursue questions, to challenge assumptions, to hear and respect a multitude of voices, and to take engaged critique as a long-term commitment. For many of us, we take this as being as much a part of our lives as morning tea and the newspaper, as we watch so much of what we have fought for slip away.

With Bernard and Phillips (2000), we believe passionate scholarship must also be passionate about "ridding ourselves of the divisiveness" of concepts like the third age and adopting, instead, an intergenerational, life course perspective. In this way, we do not separate the sick from the well, the very old from the less old. This perspective "would help us move away from seeing particular groups simply as burdens on the state or as 'problems to be solved'" (p 44) – and having this attitude reflected in our discriminatory social policies.

We must find new ways of bringing different pathways together for a richer whole. Actively involving elders as genuine partners in our journey, and not merely as objects of study, is one way. Undoing traditional sources of knowing and authority means listening to the voices of older people and other marginalised individuals who are increasingly finding a voice to speak out about our policies and policy-related research (Bernard and Phillips, 2000). Another approach involves seeking to publish and present our work in those traditional forums that reach those gerontologist and other scholars who may otherwise not be confronted with the alternative perspectives we offer, and the hard questions we raise.

Finally, critical gerontology means challenging what has long seemed obvious in the dominant paradigms. In particular it means unmasking the hidden methodological and substantive value assumptions. Unpacking, rendering visible, challenging questions and methods, transgressing accepted narratives, as our colleague Ruth E. Ray (1999) called on us to do, are all part of the agenda for critical gerontology (see also Chapter Five). Steps in this direction have already been taken in the persistent exposing of the situatedness of what 'we have always known' whether the 'subject' was women, blacks or old people. Critical gerontology must therefore engage in permanent critique, always challenging what we know and how we know it, trying to look beneath and beyond the taken for granted, the unproblematic, asking the 'yes, but' questions. Being a gadfly was good enough for Socrates, why not for us?

THREE

Using human rights to defeat ageism: dealing with policy-induced 'structured dependency'[1]

Peter Townsend

Introduction

New reports always provide good copy for long-standing theoretical and policy disputes. A recent review from the King's Fund (Wanless Report, 2006) found very serious shortcomings in social care provision and funding arrangements. Too little of the national income was committed to the social care of older people, and the cost of any system in meeting needs was set to rise. The current means-testing funding system in England, which was found to discriminate unfairly against many people on the borderline between free National Health Service (NHS) care and payment for community care, and which provokes widespread confusion, anger and distress among frail older people and their families, should be scrapped and replaced with a 'partnership model'. A minimum of two thirds of the cost of a care package, the Wanless Report (2006) concluded, should be guaranteed free at the point of delivery with every £1 of subsequent cost being matched by the state or paid from benefits.

This is clearly a compromise with government intentions to restrict public costs, and to encourage private services and the private replacement of public services at paradoxically greater cost than the measured expansion of public services. There remain immense problems in influencing whether 'care packages' are determined by need or individual cost, and how amount and standard of service are to be made available universally. Consequential reduction of disability benefits is also highly debateable. But at least the review accepts that "the system needs to be more universal with broader eligibility criteria" (Wanless Report, 2006, p 208).

An obvious alternative would have been to urge the government to implement the recommendations of the Royal Commission on Long-term Care (Sutherland Report, 1999), the only Royal Commission to have been appointed since the Labour government came to power in 1997. Its key recommendation, that personal care should be free, was rejected. The recommendation has been implemented in Scotland, and is of course an object lesson for continuing comparison. In its

2006 report, the King's Fund has weakly set aside the force of the Sutherland Commission's argument (Wanless Report, 2006) (see also Chapter Four).

Such examples of contrasting policy reports, dealing with the future services, incomes and occupations of older people, arise with increasing frequency. One report is found to be relatively compliant to government, and the next relatively independent of government. The variability provokes expert consternation and public confusion. The examples nonetheless provide opportunities to stand back and assess the 'big picture'.

Most of us are assaulted by the day-to-day pressures of finding our way, and we look down at our desks or our feet rather than over the rooftops and fields or at our immediate and far away social surroundings. We come to learn that the here and now is a fragment in an awesome sweep of life before our birth and after our death. We can be lucky to capture some sense of what shapes social and not just individual life; and convey, even if only to a few, and to them for only a few weeks or years, a reasoned account of predestination, so that they may join in the difficult and usually unsuccessful task of putting continuing and emerging wrongs right.

Good specialist work depends less on slavish adherence to the latest government report than on making constructive use of layers of professional investigatory history. That of course can depend on regress as well as progress, or underdevelopment as well as development. Reasoned correction and re-direction of specialist work is difficult, but is something of which most of us are very conscious. Ordinarily it lurks behind our specialist practice. This chapter, initially prepared to celebrate many years' work of British social gerontologists, provides an excellent opportunity to stand back and assess the 'big picture' and to review not only previously influential ideas, but also ideas that may not yet have found a place in the sun.

Rise of social development policy

What is the nature of the problem? The volume of research studies, pamphlets and media programmes about the maltreatment of older people grew steadily after the war of 1939-45. A number of social and economic historians (see, for example, Macnicol and Blaikie, 1989) have traced the commissioning of surveys explicitly on old age, the emergence of geriatric medicine after the inauguration of the NHS, the looming prospects of population ageing and so-called 'dependency ratios', and the way in which state pensions were given new priority in the political interest generated after the 1939 war. Because of the respective histories of sociology and social policy, as newly arrived major disciplines, the shock-horror of the most extreme conditions, rather than cause, attracted greatest attention. Theories or explanation of poor conditions and maltreatment were over-weighted towards the demographic, or supposedly naturalistic, on the one hand, or fragmented into the convenient sub-divisions of policy subject-matter

– housing, mental or physical health, education, institutional or family care, and social insurance and social assistance, on the other.

Where theory had a part, and that part summary or undeveloped, it occupied a middle level designed to be immediately practical to the locations and individuals immediately at issue. Larger statements about the record of governments and of policies as instruments of cause were not much attempted. The connections between themes or subjects, and their possibly common antecedents, were not seriously addressed. The achievements of the welfare state in the early years of the 20th century and then again in the immediate post-war situation of 1945, were not hammered home, and the theory of success sustained by continuing political education. The door of public service accessible to all was not slammed shut on interlopers and thieves. In Harold Macmillan's famous comment on one of Margaret Thatcher's privatisations, assaults on public ownership and public service could be likened to 'selling the family silver'.

The gains of 'welfare' could be expressed in many ways. Certainly collective, or universal, interests, public service, interdependence and redistributive rights and responsibilities would figure largely. The recent language of 'reform' from the critics has in some measure found the advocates of welfare embarrassed or defenceless. I would want to suggest that the critics have gained ascendancy mainly because defence has been neither multidimensional nor multinational. When Friedrich Hayek published his far-right book *The Road to Serfdom* (Hayek, 1944), Barbara Wootton comprehensively dismembered it less than a year later in her book *Freedom under planning* (Wootton, 1945). The post-war influence of Keynes prevailed for nearly 20 years, as did the European forms of advanced or undeveloped welfare states, but then Hayek's ideas made a comeback, supported by Milton Friedman and many successor economists. In the UK senior intellectual figures began to lend themselves to the seemingly vacuous ideas of people like Lord Harris and Arthur Seldon, who set up the Institute of Economic Affairs in 1955. For two decades most social scientists dismissed the ideas as unrealistically extreme and poorly supported, and they were not taken seriously until the 1980s.

Several European Union countries have put up a steady defence of welfare. Many have maintained substantial levels of social transfers on behalf of social services, measured by percentage of Gross Domestic Product (GDP). Redistribution of income to pensioners remains considerable in all member countries. However, discussion of the European social model has become heated, and some individual governments have sought to curtail expenditure on pensions. In the UK, in particular, schemes with final salary pensions are declining rapidly, plans are being put in place to raise retirement and pension ages and comprehensive state second pensions are being phased out. The battle both to preserve, and to raise to a reasonable level, basic state pensions continues.

Formulation of theory: 'acquiescent functionalism'

Twenty-five years ago I was one of those trying to make sense of the poor conditions being experienced by many older people. By good fortune I had worked on different national and cross-national projects before that time in residential homes (see Chapter Seven), hospitals and nursing homes, and in private households (much of this work reflecting conditions in the US and Denmark as well as the UK). It became inevitable that I should reflect on the wider as well as immediate causes of the problems that were recognisably severe in particular locations as well as scattered more widely across the general population (see Townsend, 1981a, 1986). Connections had to be made.

What could then be called the 'liberal-pluralist' tradition, now referred to as the 'neoliberal' or even Washington Consensus, was dominant. There existed a 'family' of theories – like neoclassical economics, democratic pluralism, sociological functionalism and certain theories in social psychology – that not only reflected but tended implicitly to approve the staged development of the capitalist democracies into and through the processes of industrialisation. By accepting as givens the changing structural inequalities of a competitive market, this 'family' reinforced individualistic and not social values and gained spurious authority. The continuities of economic individualism within classical economic theory, neoclassical theory, monetarism and neoliberal economics, and on the way even Keynesianism, had to be traced to reveal better what came to be built into social policies.

This 'family' of theories came to be applied to the emerging conditions of rapidly increasing numbers of older people. This can be followed in the wake of many of the social gerontologists of the earliest generation, including Donahue and Tibbitts (1957), Parsons (1942, 1964) and Cumming (1963) (see Townsend, 1986, pp 16-19). Their work, I considered, could be characterised as 'acquiescent functionalism'. This was a body of thought about ageing that attributed the causes of the problems of old age to the natural consequences of physical decrescence and mental inflexibility, or to the failures of individual adjustment to ageing and retirement, instead of the continuing as well as new exertions of state economic and social policy partly to serve and partly to moderate the play of market forces. Social inequality was thereby 're-configured' in the language that is now being applied to universal social services.

At that time, individual characteristics tended to be treated as:

> [The] necessary accompaniments of market forces, technological change and democratic process.... Public and state perceptions of the functions and capacities of the older population may now be completely at variance from properly independent scientific evidence about those functions and capacities.... Institutionalised ageism may be becoming a major feature of modern social structure. (Townsend, 1986, p 19)

And still today there are features of that institutionalised ageism that have to attract our primary attention if, along with other forms of discrimination by gender, 'race', class and disability, it is to be radically reduced and dispersed so that our whole attention may be turned to the more practical fine-tuning of policy.

Alternative theory: structured dependency

In demonstrating the value of new policies in the 1970s the consequences of conventional theory had first to be exposed. I came to understand the debt I owed to social anthropologists like Radcliffe-Brown and economic sociologists like Marx and Weber (especially Weber's *Theory of Economic and Social Organisation*, 1947) for putting concepts of social structure, class and economic and social change at the heart of scientific analysis of society and therefore of ageing and the conditions experienced by the third, and fourth, generations[2]. Retirement, poverty, institutionalisation and restriction of domestic and community roles are the experiences that help to explain how the dependency of older people came to be artificially structured or deepened. Each of these required extensive investigation and assessment.

A great deal of evidence relevant to these forms of dependency emerged in the 1960s and 1970s. There were the examples of: a fixed age for pensions; the minimal subsistence afforded on the state pension; the substitution of retirement status for unemployment; the near-compulsory admission to residential care of many thousands of people whose faculties were still relatively intact; the enforced dependence of many residents in homes and of patients in hospitals and nursing homes; and the conversion of domiciliary services into commodity services. By the 1980s "an artificial dependency [was] being manufactured for a growing proportion of the population at the same time as measures [were] being taken to alleviate the worst effects of that dependency" (Townsend, 1986, p 43). A critical view has to be taken therefore of welfare – weeding out elements that had at the time infiltrated the concept, like parsimony and coercion. But a critical view cannot be allowed to become dismissive or override the massive evidence for extensive national, and now international, 'welfare' action.

Historically, planning as a determinant of social structure and therefore of 'welfare' had seeped into the consciousness of generations in the mid-20th century. This was the end-result of the work of theorists like Marx but also of policy advocates, like Sydney and Beatrice Webb, in European countries. I became acutely conscious of the events leading up to the establishment of the British welfare state after 1945 and understood policy as cause. I was influenced too by early 'planning conscious' social gerontologists like Yonina Talmon, who wrote revealingly about the experimental collective settlements, the *Kibbutzim*, and their value to older people, then being set up in Israel (Talmon, 1961). She understood the importance of maintaining extended family relationships in a new society struggling to introduce egalitarian values, and was especially sensitive about the values of reciprocation and location, as well as organised support for severely disabled people (Talmon, 1961, pp 288, 290, 294).

What we now accept as the long-established institutions *of* welfare and the traditional positive arguments *for* welfare may, at first sight, seem contrary to more recent developments around citizenship agendas and human rights. However, in the next step of the argument, I will try to draw together these two institutions. Because this bridging is historical, international and scientific it represents the core of what I want to say.

Human rights and welfare

First, some general arguments. The language of human rights has particular virtues of *moral obligation*. Each of the rights is 'universal'. Non-fulfilment is a 'violation'. Rights are 'human' and not only civil or political. Rights are multiple and interdependent. Corrective anti-discriminatory measures have to be directed not at the separate existence of racial, religious, gender, disability or ageist discrimination but in a comprehensive, connected and proportionate manner against all forms of discrimination.

Second, the *methodology* of human rights is in its infancy. The operational definition of rights and therefore violations demands imaginative and sustained quantitative, but also qualitative, methods of investigation. The violations are not those only that end life, or involve extreme abuse, the scale of which have to be assembled in statistical handbooks, but those that represent affronts to human dignity and identity. For older people, the Quality of Life research studies carried out in the UK under the auspices of the Economic and Social Research Council's (ESRC) Growing Older Programme offer rich contributions to this objective (see, for example, Walker and Hennessy, 2004; Walker, 2005). In operationalising a definition of rights for people of all ages perhaps there has been too much readiness to adapt familiar indicators of human development or health, or economic growth, as single indicators of sometimes complex conditions or entitlements rather than build requirements for survey data about extreme conditions from scratch.

The 'indivisibility' of human rights seems to have deterred some social scientists – I include lawyers – from developing *multiple* indices of certain general conditions or priorities. And the seeming inflexibility in defining a threshold or line between satisfaction and non-satisfaction of each right listed in the Articles of rights – either the individual has a right or she or he has not – creeps into the use of a single indicator testing whether that right has or has not been fulfilled (because selecting multiple indicators raises a lot of questions about multiple criteria in agreeing a threshold when different individuals are in reality on a point in the scale from extreme non-fulfilment to generous fulfilment).

Only in recent years have serious efforts been made to organise operational definitions in a form that allows multiple non-realisation of rights to be measured reliably and relatively unambiguously. Energetic use can now be made internationally of the Demographic Health Surveys (DHS) and the Multiple Indicator Cluster Surveys (MICS). Similar use can be made regionally of cross-national panel survey data on material and social deprivation among older people. Again, statistical data about limiting long-standing illness, or disability, can be adapted for research into violations of rights in later age – in Europe and more widely in the less economically developed world.

Third, the *politics of rights*. This is crucial in the choice of methodology, investigative priorities and persuasive assessment of needs and policies. As many as 191 nations have ratified the Convention on the Rights of the Child (CRC) and numbers of signatories are almost as high for the original Universal Declaration of Human Rights and still impressively high for other human rights instruments. Access to rights plays a crucial role in public discussion about economic and social developments – for example in responses to conflict, anti-terrorism measures and different types of discrimination. Acknowledgment of the influential role of human rights has spread rapidly among campaigning organisations, departments of state and international organisations of every kind. To base both research and action on human rights instruments is to apply the leverage of accepted authority and democracy.

To traditional positive national arguments for welfare can therefore now be added the perceptions as well as revelations of cross-national agreed rules of a quasi-legal kind – a growing number of which have been and are being incorporated into domestic laws. Knowledge of that process can now enthuse those concerned with domestic disputes of a familiar kind that affect older people, and not only inflame those like Hayek and his successors who have been attached to an older, and inevitably more discriminatory, ideology.

Human rights from a UK and European perspective

I am arguing that a new analytical framework has evolved very rapidly, with which social scientists must necessarily engage. A good witness is David Feldman, author of *Civil Liberties and Human Rights in England and Wales* and until late 2003 the legal adviser to the UK parliamentary Joint Committee on Human Rights (JCHR). Based on the European Convention on Human Rights (ECHR), the Human Rights Act of the UK dates from 1998. The rights are not guaranteed against repeal or amendment by Parliament, and the courts cannot strike down incompatible primary legislation. Nonetheless, following precedents elsewhere, the expressed rights are beginning to have a substantial impact on the law, and also on the activities and thinking of administrators, lawyers and politicians.

To give only one example there has been a transformation among solicitors in the past 10 years in the number professing expertise in human rights (Chambers, 1998; Feldman, 2002, p 1088). The number has grown rapidly. Lack of the guarantee of rights is not proving to be the serious weakness feared, partly because of the manner in which the ECHR is being observed in Europe. There is also the fact that justiciable and constitutionally entrenched Acts do not provide a complete answer to the demands of individuals and groups – as shown by the work of the Court of Justice of the European Community and the US Supreme Court and public reactions to their decisions. Public officials, rights activists, politicians and individual citizens have to share responsibility for acceptance, and institutionalisation, of rights. One of the finest examples of what must and can be done is Jenny Watson's report for the British Institute of Human Rights (Watson, 2002). The problem is how to disestablish and redistribute entrenched powers at the same time. There is a trickle-down but also a trickle-up challenge that can be better organised and followed.

The reports of the JCHR give testimony to the influence both of the Act and the way in which certain of the objectives of new UK legislation can be framed better in accordance with human rights and implemented quickly and effectively without provoking political storms[3]. The Committee came to see and comment routinely on *all* Bills in draft form, which assisted the task of implementing human rights with the agreement of Parliament. The Committee also developed a special programme of work to implement features of the principal Act. It argued successfully for a strategic, rights-based Commissioner for Children and Young People and also for an integrated Equalities and Human Rights Commission to work in a more concerted way than was proving possible with an assortment of separate bodies against discrimination in all its forms[4]. It is now being set up as the Commission for Equalities and Human Rights, and non-discrimination by age will become legally enforceable (see also Chapter Eight).

The UK Act incorporates the ECHR, but the emphasis is on civil and political rights and not also on economic, social and cultural rights. The rights to life, to not being subjected to torture, or inhuman or degrading treatment, or forced labour, to an effective remedy and to non-discrimination raise questions of social protection and reconstruction, and therefore stray into a range of possible social and economic rights, but this cannot be pressed strongly in law. However, the counterpart of the ECHR is the European Social Charter (ESC) (Council of Europe, 2002; Samuel, 2002). As many as 30 of the member states of the Council of Europe had signed and ratified the Charter by 2001. After the Amsterdam Treaty of 1997 came into force the revised Charter has become an integral part of the structure of the European Community. The newly elected Labour government signed the Charter in 1997. Many of the Articles reflect European agreement on the 'European Social Model' and several are relevant to conditions for older people. In particular, Article 4 of the additional protocol of 1988 spells out the right of older people to social protection (see Box 3.1):

Box 3.1: Article 4: Right of elderly persons to social protection

With a view to ensuring the effective exercise of the right of elderly persons to social protection, the Parties undertake to adopt or encourage, either directly or in co-operation with public or private organisations, appropriate measures designed in particular:

1. to enable elderly persons to remain full members of society for as long as possible, by means of:

    1. adequate resources enabling them to lead a decent life and play an active part in public, social and cultural life;
    2. provision of information about services and facilities available for elderly persons and their opportunities to make use of them;

2. to enable elderly persons to choose their life-style freely and to lead independent lives in their familiar surroundings for as long as they wish and are able, by means of:

    1. provision of housing suited to their needs and their state of health or of adequate support for adapting their housing;
    2. the health care and the services necessitated by their state;
    3. to guarantee elderly persons living in institutions appropriate support, while respecting their privacy, and participation in decisions concerning living conditions in the institution.

Source: European Social Charter, 1988

The Amsterdam Treaty represented a significant step towards converting the aspirations of the ESC into 'hard law' applicable in national courts. In particular, the scope of European anti-discrimination law – affecting ageism as well as other forms of discrimination – was enlarged as a result. The European Commission continues to extend access to economic and social rights and integrate these with other, better institutionalised civil and political rights (for example, the proclamation of the EU Charter of Fundamental Rights in 2000).

Violations of the rights of older people in the 21st century

Both the ESC (Council of Europe, 2002; Samuel, 2002) and the ECHR can be widely used in the analysis of conditions experienced by older people and necessary alternative policies. For example, Age Concern and Help the Aged have given worrying contemporary evidence on lack of rights. Help the Aged explained that "older people whose human rights are violated are often not in a position – or do not choose – to take action themselves" (JCHR, 2003, II, Evidence 310). Few staff, and few members of the public were yet informed about the 1998 Act. Older people subjected to abuse rarely complained. A campaign in 1999-2001 by the organisation Dignity on the Ward produced

1,300 complaints, generally from relatives after a death of an old person: "It was very common for the older person not only to remain silent, but to plead with relatives 'not to make a fuss', while relatives themselves often felt that complaining would only put the person concerned at even greater risk" (JCHR, 2003, II, Evidence 314). Collected evidence about allegations made about abuse divided into five forms – physical, psychological, financial, sexual and neglect. About a quarter of the total – a disproportionately large fraction in relation to the locations of the older population – were allegations about institutional settings, such as hospitals, nursing homes or residential homes (JCHR, 2003, II, Evidence 314).

Among confirmed instances is that of an inquest at Eastbourne in 2002 of an elderly woman with Alzheimer's disease dying of dehydration a week after admission to a care home. No one appeared to have understood she needed help with eating and drinking. Another instance was of a man in North London with mild dementia taken off medication despite detailed instructions given by his wife. He deteriorated rapidly and died within a few weeks because, instead of his customary prescription for a heart condition, he was given one for insomnia. Moreover, no inquest was held (JCHR, 2003, II, Evidence 311). These instances are pale in relation to some others collected by the British Institute of Human Rights (Watson, 2002):

- A man in his 80s in a nursing home required use of a catheter and assistance in dressing. He was made to sit naked in a room with five male and female staff while one washed him, another changed his catheter bag, a third was changing his medication. The door into a busy corridor was left wide open. No one spoke to him. In the end he "messed himself and was then rolled over onto his side, whilst they proceeded to put a towel underneath him, and then wash him, on the bed, still with no attempt made to protect his dignity" (p 48).
- A care worker entering a residential home was instructed to get the residents up for breakfast and to seat them on commodes. When she began to help them off to finish dressing for breakfast she was stopped. "The routine of the home was that residents ate their breakfast while sitting on the commode and the ordinary men and women who worked there had come to accept this as normal" (p 50).
- A resident was prescribed morphine as part of her palliative care: "The home did not supply the medication and she died in pain, crying. No resident has their medical needs noted and many residents are not receiving the correct medication" (p 49).

Of course abuse of rights also arises at home and in families:

- A woman of 85 was living with her daughter. For five years social services had been trying to work to remedy a disastrous situation. The elderly woman "was regularly found in her home in just a T shirt, in a house without soap, flannels or towels. Her daughter would take her out of day services after an hour to make her take money from a bank cash machine. She would be taken out of respite care by her daughter in the middle of the night. She had medication withheld by her daughter. The police were called to shouting and slapping incidents in the street when her daughter abused her". Eventually she went happily into residential care: "But her daughter turned up at the home with her husband, and was found by staff to be inspecting her mother's backside by flashlight, saying that she was not clean.... Eventually she was banned from the home because of her disruptive behaviour, after she tried to take other residents to the toilet" (p 12).

In this instance the fact they could use the Human Rights Act had not occurred to the staff and to social workers. Had they done so, this might have helped to engineer a rapprochement between family and social services and might have protected the older woman from five years of abuse.

Unconscious and conscious assumptions or beliefs of a discriminatory kind are held by professionals, including doctors, and by families of the aged, including sons and daughters. Thus, 'DNR' – 'do not resuscitate' – a clear violation now of human rights, was sometimes attached to case notes. Again, the daughter of a woman placed in a residential home in Bristol said the doctor had advised her to sell her mother's house because it was "safer" for her to be in the residential home. One is inclined to ask 'safer for whom?'. When an outsider subsequently visited the elderly resident and looked into her eyes it was evident she had decided to die. And so it proved within a few short weeks. As Jenny Watson concluded her interviews: "Access to benefits, access to transport, and access to good domiciliary care services are all necessary in order to allow older people to make the same kind of choices about their lives that the rest of us simply take for granted" (Watson, 2002, p 45).

Failure to accept Sutherland

Many gerontologists could back up the examples listed above with authoritative specialised evidence. In Britain, perhaps the most authoritative review so far in this century is the Sutherland Commission on Long-term Care (Sutherland Report, 1999). The Commission argued that the long-term costs of care should be split between living costs, housing costs and personal care. Personal care should be available after assessment, according to need and paid for from general taxation; the rest should be subject to co-payment according to means. A National Care Commission had to be created. Private insurance would not deliver what is required at an acceptable cost, nor would the industry want to provide that degree of coverage. The recently evolving private infrastructure of residential and nursing home care had grown rapidly in cost and "the 'market' was shaped in a particular way, driven by what could be paid for rather than what people needed". For example domiciliary care had been discouraged (Sutherland Report, 1999, p 38).

Partly prompted by a querulous note of dissent from two of the Commissioners, the government set aside the recommendations of the Royal Commission. With hindsight it is perhaps unfortunate that the Royal Commission did not strengthen its powerful case by formal reference to human rights generally and the new UK Human Rights Act in particular, and to the rapid developments in the treatment of both the ECHR and the ESC, together with the momentum in Europe and elsewhere in the world in favour of linking current concerns about particular problems of the day that gain wide publicity with human rights. The Sutherland Commission made a feature of the numbers of older people who were disabled. Thus, the Office for Population Censuses and Surveys had calculated there were 4.3 million people aged 60 and over with some disability, 1.1 million of whom had severe disabilities (Sutherland Report, 1999, p 99). The extent of severe disability among older people and their rights to improved services and social security has attracted continuing scrutiny (for example, Townsend, 1981b).

Practicality of human rights

How can the scale and severity of the abuses illustrated above be represented effectively? The question is the same as it might have been 25 years ago. Then, as now, multiple material and social deprivation must be acknowledged and investigation based on identifying and then counting different types of deprivation, or abuse. One type of horror, and the identification of horror in one location, must be placed into a context that is national, multigenerational, applicable to public and private sectors, and international. I have taken the view for many years that specialised research can only carry force if there is generalised research as well, and vice versa. The best national work is that which is also international or cross-national. Of course it is never easy to ride two horses and improvisations and shortcomings will exist. But that is the first necessity. The effort remains crucial and will allow what is truly international and objectively scientific to emerge. It is vital in authenticating priority – in analysis as well as treatment. It is a value that can be lived and rehearsed at every level. One fragment of interpretation is that British social gerontologists will do their best work when that work is also multinational.

Let me give two examples of the methodology. One is old-style multiplication of material and social deprivation. Table 3.1 is drawn from the 2000 Poverty and Social Exclusion Survey, sponsored by the Joseph Rowntree Foundation. After setting aside certain overlapping indices there remain 31 items representing commonly agreed necessities of life. As many as 37 per cent of people of pensionable age were deprived of at least one necessity, but as many as nine per cent deprived of five or more, including a third of these deprived of ten or more necessities. These nine per cent represent more than one million older people. That figure does not include half a million older people who are in hospitals, nursing homes and residential care. Severe multiple deprivation is therefore a common experience, and one that raises acute questions about human rights.

Table 3.1: Levels of material and social deprivation among older people, Great Britain (2000) (%)

Number of necessities of life from which deprived	All pensioners (aged 60+/ 65+ years)	Male pensioners (aged 65+ years)	Female pensioners (aged 60+ years)
0	63	66	61
1	14	18	12
2	5	5	5
3	5	2	7
4	4	3	5
5-9	6	4	7
10+	3	3	3
All	100	101	100
Sample sizes	406	157	249

Note: Derived from the Poverty and Social Exclusion Survey (Gordon et al, 2000), and secondary analysis by Patsios (2005, personal communication).

The measurement of multiple deprivation is also a feature of the work of the Institute for Social and Economic Research at the University of Essex and of the Economic and Social Research Institute in Dublin (for example, Whelan et al, 2003; Berthoud et al, 2004).

The second example arises from indexing human rights. This derives from recent work on children, in which I participated. A research team based in the University of Bristol found that different Articles of the CRC lent themselves to measurement from familiar survey data, graded from extreme violation through severe and moderate to slight and non-existent violation of different forms of material and social deprivation. The problem was to find data of a relatively standardised kind from many countries. Only in recent years have many relatively standardised surveys been carried out in a large number of countries – key examples being the Demographic and Health Surveys and the Multiple Indicator Cluster Surveys. Fortunately, serious material and social deprivation – reflected in a number of the articles of the CRC – could be categorised and measured, including malnutrition, inadequate shelter, no access or poor access to minimally adequate drinking water, sanitation, healthcare, education and forms of information. The results proved more reliable, and certainly less disputable, than the crude estimates of dollar-a-day poverty estimated by the World Bank. The next stage has been to apply Articles of human rights to the measurement of multiple deprivation among adults. For older people we can move in successive stages from the ECHR, through the ESC to the International Covenant on Economic, Social and Cultural Rights. I cannot yet offer the statistical results. What I can do is outline the stages of research.

Table 3.2: Types of violations of human rights (ECHR) and possible indicators

Articles of rights	Indicator
Right to life (Article 2)	Relatively low number of expected years of life/or premature deaths, by location, age and gender
Prohibition of torture or "inhuman or degrading treatment or punishment" (Article 3)	Degrading care practices in residential and home care
Right to respect for private and family life (Article 8)	Wish in disability to stay in own home; access to surrounding possessions of a familiar kind
Prohibition of discrimination "on any ground such as sex, race, colour, language, religion, political or other opinion, national or social origin, association with a national minority, property, birth or other status" (Article 14)	Acceptance for care services, standardised for disability, by minority or gender status

The first is to show ways in which the ECHR can be illustrated. Table 3.2 gives an example. Additional use could be made, of course, with other Articles, like the right to marry (Article 12) and some of the Protocols, such as Articles 1 and 5 of Protocol 7, respectively on safeguards in the expulsion of aliens, and on equality between spouses.

The next step is to do the same for the ESC, which opens the door to a more sophisticated set of measurements. An outline is given in Table 3.3.

A third step in anticipating the growing acknowledgement of economic and social rights, and partly through the slow influence of the ESC on the UK government, is to examine the International Covenant on Economic, Social and Cultural Rights.

One method developed lately of accelerating progress in developing countries with the measurement of multiple violation of human rights, has been to focus on violations representing different features of material and social deprivation so that priorities in policy may be identified (Gordon et al, 2003). Another method would be to focus on the twin rights to social security and an adequate standard of living – Articles 22 and 25 of the Universal Declaration of Human Rights, Articles 26 and 27 of the CRC and Articles 9 and 11 of the International Covenant on Economic, Social and Cultural Rights (Table 3.4). The advantages to be derived from building afresh on these two rights are especially promising.

Table 3.3: Types of violations of human rights (ESC) and possible indicators

Articles of rights	Indicator
Resources adequate for full and active life	Annual subjective/objective survey assessment of amount required to escape poverty/multiple deprivation
Facilities and information to lead an active, participating life	Access to range of public and private services, and facilities providing information
Opportunity to lead a life in a home of their choosing	Type of accommodation by degree of disability and preference
Access to appropriate healthcare	Frequency and speed of utilisation in relation to degree of disability, degree of material and social deprivation and whether and when need for healthcare identified
Freedom of action and quality of living conditions in residential institutions	Subjective expression of opportunities to act freely; objective assessment of living conditions in relation to measured degree of disability

Table 3.4: International Covenant on Economic, Social and Cultural Rights and 1995 World Summit Action Programme

International Covenant on Economic, Social and Cultural Rights (1966-76)	Article 9: The States Parties to the present Covenant recognise the right of everyone to social security, including social insurance	Article 11 (1): The States Parties to the present Covenant recognise the right of everyone to an adequate standard of living for himself and his family, including adequate food, clothing and housing, and to the continuous improvement of living conditions
Copenhagen World Summit for Social Development (1995) relevant decisions by 117 countries	Action Programme 38: Social protection systems should be based on legislation and ... strengthened and expanded ... to protect from poverty people who cannot work ...	Action Programme 8: Equitable and non-discriminatory distribution of benefits of growth among social groups and countries and expanded access to productive resources for people living in poverty

Globalisation and the human rights of older people

In deciding the future direction of the work of social gerontologists, the growing inequality within countries as well as between poor and rich countries must provide the structural context (Townsend and Gordon, 2002). The globalisation of market, technology and communications (see, for example, Walker and Deacon, 2003) affects the organisation of all societies, including the conditions and prospects of older people. Recent failures of privatisation schemes, and even of major transnational corporations such as Enron and WorldCom and parts of the financial services industry, have led to calls for radical new policies. Fresh reports of instances of corporate corruption have paved the way for new calls for collective approaches through law and regulation that go a lot further than the minimal and highly variable expressions so far of 'corporate social responsibility'.

On globalisation, support for a change has come from unexpected sources. For example, the former chief economist at the World Bank, Joseph Stiglitz, has written revealingly about corporate greed (Stiglitz, 2002a, 2002b). Again, in the wake of the $4 billion (£2.1 billion) WorldCom scandal in 2002 Digby Jones, the then Director-General of the Confederation of British Industry, called for new forms of business leadership and for stronger statements about corporate responsibilities in accountancy and administration (Jones, 2002).

Public faith in agreements reached at World Summits to deal with the world's needs has begun to dwindle. Public expectations raised by the announcement of the Millennium Development Goals in 2000 and the closing statements of successive World Summits since then – including those of Monterrey on financial developments and New York on the needs of children – have been disappointed. Some of the earlier international agreements – such as that at the 1995 Copenhagen World Summit for Social Development – had a more lasting impact. The Copenhagen Declaration and Programme of Action followed a coherently organised summit and the recommendations were more specific than in other similar events (UN, 1995). The programme of action has begun to have constructive results and has considerable potentiality for the future, if governments and interest groups, including international bodies, are held regularly responsible – and accountable – for widely agreed objectives in establishing human rights and reducing inequalities and poverty. Compared with diminishing confidence in World Summits, public trust in the charters and conventions expressing human rights has continued to grow. Public support for the values upholding human rights and legally backed action remains strong.

Universal rights

The world has seen only mixed success for the declared objective in the past 50 years of reducing the violations of human rights, including those that address different forms of severe deprivation that were selected earlier in this chapter for special attention. Our findings prompt re-examination of the links between 'universalism' or human 'rights', and both comprehensive public social service and social security. 'Targeting' as a strategy in developing countries to reduce poverty has become highly controversial and the forms of targeting that have been adopted are increasingly criticised. Reports of persisting poverty and deepening inequality in many countries outweigh the modest results that at best reflect the structural adjustment programmes and their successors, including the social funds that were introduced. In developing countries, the Programme of Action to Mitigate the Social Cost of Adjustment was set up in the late 1980s to correct the excesses of structural adjustment programmes, but was criticised for being underfunded and lacking direction (Donkor, 2002). Success for programmes intended both to restrict public expenditure and yet relieve extreme poverty by targeting resources has turned out to be elusive. Action on behalf of children is a priority, but huge numbers of older people will also continue to suffer unless comprehensive, and principled, action is taken on behalf of society as a whole.

Conclusion

The idea of 'structured dependency' helps to explain the box before death within which many older people are placed. Unintentionally, as well as for deliberate reasons of economy and profit or convenience on the part of the state and of other institutions, their dependency is created in market, residential and hospital care and private and public social care policies. There are exceptions from which lessons can be learned about countervailing policies. Many older people themselves also assume the mantle of dependency. They may become resigned to external conditions and restrictions, as well as condescending expectations. Some experience stress in continuing to fight what they see as their enforced dependence. Others become reconciled to a poorer third, or fourth, age. They adjust psychologically to what they believe is not worth the stress to fight, or welcome passivity and low-key self-indulgence.

The various problems of 'structured' dependency persist. And those problems seem set to grow in many parts of the world. Human rights offer a framework of rigorous analysis and anti-discriminatory work. Success depends on good operational measurement – for purposes of producing reliable evidence of violations and monitoring progress – and the incorporation internationally as well as nationally of institutions and policies that reflect those rights. Human rights instruments offer hope of breaking down blanket discrimination and of using resources more appropriately, and more generously, according to severity of need. But investment in human rights is not only a moral and quasi-legal salvation from things that are still going depressingly wrong. Used best, human rights offer a framework of thought and planning early in the 21st century that enables society to take a fresh, and more hopeful, direction.

Notes

[1] This chapter draws extensively on a paper of mine published in *Ageing and Society* in March 2006. I am indebted to the British Society of Gerontology and the editors of this book for the opportunity to re-visit themes that were troubling me, and many others, from the 1950s to the 1970s. Among colleagues at the London School of Economics and Political Science and the University of Bristol, I wish to acknowledge particular help from Sue Brattle (in relation to our support from the British Academy 2004-05), Demi Patsios and Joe Jacob. When at Keele for the 2005 British Society of Gerontology Conference, I gained technical help from Chaz Simpson and Jim Hakim. I would also wish to acknowledge many debts I owe, for indefatigable work on behalf of older people, to Alan Walker, and for instruction about the potentialities of human rights to my wife, Jean Corston, and the former legal adviser to the JCHR, David Feldman.

[2] Among examples of sociological work on organisations that have influenced my thinking are books by Brian Abel-Smith on hospitals (1964) and the nursing profession (1960), and by Joe Jacob on the medical profession (1999). My book on residential institutions for older people, *The Last Refuge* (1962), had also been written at a time when there had been immense interest sociologically in the 'total institution'.

[3] In the first four years of its existence, the Joint Committee published 87 reports, not including subsidiary reports and collections of written evidence (see JCHR, 2005).

[4] "The decision to reorganise the institutional arrangements for the promotion of equality has made it an urgent necessity to consider the institutional arrangements for the promotion and protection of human rights more generally. The Government's decision in principle to establish a new equality commission, which will have to consider human rights issues in the context of its own work, makes it necessary for the Government now to resolve the question of a human rights commission. [..] There is still a long way to go in establishing the culture of respect for human rights, and the momentum from the Human Rights Act is ebbing. If it is not revived, the loss will detract from or adversely affect the conduct and performance of public services, and consequently the well-being of those who use them. [...] We believe an independent commission would be the most effective way of achieving the shared aim of bringing about a culture of respect for human rights" (JCHR, 2003, pp 36-9).

FOUR

The re-medicalisation of later life

Robin Means

Introduction

One long-standing concern of critical gerontology has been to unmask policy assumptions relating to older people and to draw out their often negative practical implications (Townsend, 1981a, 2006). This chapter is located within this tradition by focusing on the recent Green Paper on *Independence, well-being and choice* (DH, 2005a). As suggested in the title, the whole emphasis of the Green Paper was on empowerment through choice with the Preface from the Prime Minister stressing how the proposals were "an important part of our commitment to renew and modernise all our public services so they are centred on the needs and wishes of the individual" (p 1).

However, this chapter challenges the assumption that the proposals in the Green Paper will lead to the type of services in adult social care that older people want. Instead, a mixture of historical and contemporary perspectives are used to argue that the overall direction of government policies towards older people is leading to a re-medicalisation of later life. It concludes by updating the 'story' through an analysis of whether or not the White Paper on community health and social care services (DH, 2006a) is likely to halt this drift to re-medicalisation.

The whole terrain of health and social care continues to change at speed (DH, 2006a; Wanless Report, 2006). However, these new developments need to be subject to a rigorous analysis that gets behind surface platitudes and explores the real implications for older people. This helps us to see that all societies are faced with policy options. Some of these push us towards a holistic and positive approach – such as the vision outlined in the recent work of the Social Exclusion Unit on ending inequalities in later life (ODPM, 2006). However, the central argument of this chapter is that the dominant policy thrust is in the opposite direction and represents a re-medicalisation of later life.

What do older people want?

This chapter is underpinned by a critique of central government in which it is argued that their health and social care policies are leading to a re-medicalisation of later life that does not reflect what older people want. It is, therefore, crucial to begin by exploring evidence about what older people do want and how this relates to medical and social models of disability (see also Chapters Two, Five, Six and Nine).

The first point to stress is that older people do require good quality health care services and the next section on historical perspectives will underline the extent to which this has rarely been the case. Healthcare for older people has too often been a 'Cinderella Service' (Means and Smith, 1998). Therefore, it is important to acknowledge that there are some positive aspects to the present focus on the need to shift resources to community healthcare services (DH, 2006a), as well as to improve the targeting of hospital and non-hospital care to people with specific long-term healthcare conditions (DH, 2005b).

So what is the problem? To begin to understand this requires an appreciation of the fundamentally different starting points of medical and social models of disability and illness. A medical model defines the individual purely in terms of their clinical condition rather than their wider life and potential contribution to society. However, in the mid-1970s disability activists began to challenge the medical model on the grounds that the 'problem' of disabled people was not their impairments, disabilities and illnesses but rather the medical profession's (and the rest of society's) reaction to them (UPIAS, 1976). A widely accepted way of explaining this was that people had impairments but it was society that disabled them (Oliver, 1990; Morris, 1991; Barnes, 1996). This disabling came through being denied work, access to buildings, decent incomes and the right to a normal social life. The focus of the medical model was on treating illness and the focus of the social model was on enabling independence and fostering quality of life. Subsequent writing on the social model has criticised the marginalisation of older people in some of the earlier critiques (Campbell and Oliver, 1996) as well as the tendency to deny some of the realities and limitations of illness and disability for groups such as those with learning disabilities (Deal, 2003) and those with dementia (Gilliard et al, 2005). Nevertheless, the social model remains a very powerful framework against which to assess recent policy changes.

This is particularly true because research on what older people want from health and social care services underlines that they think in terms of their needs from a social rather than a medical model. They emphasise the need for services that start with the person and not the illness or disability and that are flexible, foster independence and self-respect and that include low-level preventative support and not just crisis intervention (Clark et al, 1998; Qureshi and Henwood, 2000; Raynes et al, 2001; Help the Aged, 2002a). Such research has included a research programme funded by the Joseph Rowntree Foundation (JRF), the overview summary of which stressed that:

- Communities, community organisations, family/friends/community networks (often of older people themselves) are the greatest providers of support for older people;

- Definitions of 'quality' need to be driven more by older people themselves; and
- Services need to be more holistic, responsive and adaptable to people's needs. (JRF, 2004, p 6)

The overall message of the JRF programme is that health and social care services are only one part of 'living well in later life' and that "it is often social services directors who are in the vanguard of saying this to chief executives and to those working in housing, transport, health, leisure and community services" (JRF, 2004, p 6). The rest of this chapter is about whether or not recent and proposed policy changes are moving services closer or further away from what older people want. A key element of what is desired is a coherent response to their needs across both health and social care from a social rather than medical model perspective. The next section, therefore, looks at the history of the troubled boundary between health and social care before going on to outline the Social Care Green Paper.

Health and social care divide: historical perspectives

It can be argued that the origins of the health and social care divide in services for older people can be traced back as far as the Poor Law. The early Victorian Workhouse only acknowledged the destitute and made no distinction between those whose destitution had its roots in sickness and those who were in need of such support for economic and social reasons (Crowther, 1981). However, workhouses inevitably attracted large numbers of low-income inmates with major health problems and over time these institutions began to develop hospital 'wings'.

The 1929 Local Government Act transferred all the powers, duties and assets of Poor Law unions to counties and county boroughs, each of which was required to set up public assistance committees. The Act renamed the Workhouse as the Public Assistance Institution (PAI) (for further details of the history of public assistance institutions, see Note 2 in Chapter Seven). However, the 1929 Act failed to carry out any more fundamental reform of the poor law system so that "poor law relief remained poor law relief and pauperism remained pauperism except for a few small modifications" (Gilbert, 1970, p 229).

The classic PAI was a very large institution that contained both hospital and non-hospital provision. Older people tended to be allocated to the non-hospital 'wards' on the grounds that they were 'frail' rather than 'sick'. Elderly 'inmates' were disqualified from receiving a pension unless they were admitted specifically for medical treatment and even then pension rights were lost after three months (Means and Smith, 1998).

A series of PAI and hospital surveys at the end of the Second World War underlined the very inadequate levels of both health and social care being provided for older people in such institutions (Nuffield Provincial Hospitals Trust, 1946; Rowntree Report, 1980). A key complaint of such surveys was the failure to differentiate between types of 'inmate' resulting in "young children and senile dements" being "banded together", along with many elderly patients, for whom earlier diagnosis and treatment might have enabled a return to their homes (Nuffield Provincial Hospitals Trust, 1946, p 16). As argued elsewhere, these findings led to the argument that "older people with health care needs required proper hospital care which ought to be entirely separate from arrangements for supporting those whose needs were primarily social" (Glendinning and Means, 2004, p 439).

The major welfare reforms of the late 1940s did indeed follow this logic that required a clear separation of the services provided for medical reasons and those services provided for social reasons. Medical services for older people were encapsulated by the 1946 National Health Services Act and were primarily provided through the National Health Service (NHS). A more prescribed set of welfare services including the local authority residential home were enacted through the 1948 National Assistance Act. In other words, the post-war settlement for older people saw a much stronger vision of a medical model of service provision than it did of a social or welfare model.

In two studies, the author has tracked with colleagues the almost endless debates from 1948 through to the 1990s about how to define 'what is health care?' and 'what is social care?' and has charted how social care has been consistently re-defined to include even more dependent, frail and indeed sick older people (Means and Smith, 1998; Means et al, 2002). Within the constraints of this chapter it is only possible to make three points. First, almost from the outset, there was recognition from government that older people want to live in their own homes for as long as possible. This in turn led to growing pressure in the 1960s to increase the availability of welfare services (home help, meals on wheels, day care etc) that might enable older people to avoid having to go into hospital or residential care (Means and Smith, 1998). In modern terminology there was a growing recognition that quality of life for older people could not be guaranteed just through the provision of medical services. A social as well as a medical model was needed.

The second point is that older people also need good healthcare, but the NHS has persistently failed to deliver this. The vision of the 1940s hospital surveys was not realised, but rather older people have been a 'Cinderella Group' at the back of the queue for health services investment (Glendinning and Means, 2004) and, even worse than this, older patients have often been the victims of abuse and violence especially in psycho-geriatric hospitals (Robb, 1967; Means and Smith, 1998).

The final point concerns the recommendations of the Griffiths Report (1988) on community care. By the early 1980s, the government was becoming more and more exasperated at the failure of a series of policy initiatives designed to encourage effective joint working between health and social services across a range of groups including older people (Means et al, 2002). This led to Sir Roy Griffiths being asked to carry out a review of community care provision. It had been expected that he would recommend a bringing together of health and social services provision for older people under some kind of health services control. However, instead of this, he recommended that social services authorities should be the lead agency for all the main community care groups including older people and he argued this because he saw such authorities as grounded in the community and accountable to democratically elected councillors. It seemed that the need for a social model of service provision for older people had finally been accepted. Nevertheless, the issue of how to coordinate health and social services remained largely unresolved when the main recommendations of the Griffiths Report and the subsequent White Paper (DH, 1989) came into force on 1 April 1993 as a result of the 1990 NHS and Community Care Act. Indeed, the NHS took the emphasis of the lead agency role for social services as another opportunity to withdraw from continuing healthcare provision (Glendinning et al, 2005, p 247).

Green Paper on Social Care

An initial reading of *Independence, well-being and choice* (DH, 2005a) is likely to have the opposite effect to generating concerns around a re-medicalisation of later life. Rather, the Green Paper is concerned to set out a framework of desired outcomes that is the very opposite to defining older people solely in terms of their medical needs. More specifically, seven outcome areas are identified, namely improved health, improved quality of life, making a positive contribution, exercise of choice and control, freedom from discrimination or harassment, economic well-being and personal dignity (see Box 4.1). With considerable understatement, the Green Paper reflects that "few people will disagree with these outcomes, but delivering them will be challenging" (p 26).

But how are these outcomes to be achieved in practice? The Green Paper stresses the importance of direct payments and individual budgets in order to ensure older people can obtain the services they really want and goes on to stress links with the wider community in terms of the traditional stress on informal carers but also more imaginatively in terms of the local authority well-being agenda. More ominously, the Green Paper goes on to consider how "implementing the vision" can be "managed within the existing funding envelope" (p 40), and concludes with a series of chapters looking at such 'traditional' community care issues as partnership working with the NHS, service improvement, performance assessment and building strong links with the community and voluntary sectors.

However, much of this is still very exciting indeed, especially the emphasis on services tailored to individual need and the stress on the need for a wide vision of community care that incorporates low-level preventative services. Indeed, the main thrust of the Green Paper seems very in keeping with the findings outlined earlier from the JRF research programme on what older people want (JRF, 2004). The rest of this chapter focuses on why this vision is unlikely to materialise and why we seem to be heading towards a re-medicalisation of later life.

Box 4.1: Outcomes for social care

Improved health: enjoying good physical and mental health (including protection from abuse and exploitation). Access to appropriate treatment and support in managing long-term conditions independently. Opportunities for physical activity.

Improved quality of life: access to leisure, social activities and lifelong learning and to universal, public and commercial services. Security at home, access to transport and confidence in safety outside the home.

Making a positive contribution: active participation in the community through employment or voluntary opportunities. Maintaining involvement in local activities and being involved in policy development and decision making.

Exercise of choice and control: through maximum independence and access to information. Being able to choose and control services. Managing risk in personal life.

Freedom from discrimination or harassment: equality of access to services. Not being subject to abuse.

Economic well-being: access to income and resources sufficient for a good diet, accommodation and participation in family and community life. Ability to meet costs arising from specific individual needs.

Personal dignity: keeping clean and comfortable. Enjoying a clean and orderly environment. Availability of appropriate personal care.

Source: Department of Health (2005a, p 26)

Failure to deliver on past promises

One reason for expressing significant doubt about the likelihood of a full implementation of the broad vision for adult social care outlined in the Green Paper is the failure to deliver on past promises. A significant part of this has been the failure of first Conservative and then Labour governments to back social services as the lead agency for community care despite the considerable evidence that social services have proved very effective at targeting intensive care packages at older people with high levels of need (Warburton and McCracken, 1999; Bauld et al, 2000; Glendinning and Means, 2004). More specifically, the NHS has been a much higher priority than social services for service investment and, as already indicated, the NHS has been allowed to cost-shunt onto local authorities by reducing long-term healthcare provision on the grounds that local authorities now have the community care 'lead'.

The story of housing and community care since the late 1980s is especially illuminating in terms of the persistent failure of governments to follow through on the broad perspectives on what should be included under community care policy. As one might expect, given the seven outcome areas, housing features strongly in the Green Paper. The importance of linking local community care needs assessment within the wider assessment of housing needs in any locality is stressed on the grounds that "if people are to be supported to live at home in greater numbers, we need to make sure that local housing stock is suitable, in terms of condition and adaptability and that we make the best use of housing stock already in the system" (DH, 2005a, p 45). The overall shift of emphasis of the Green Paper on prevention leads to a stress on community development, social capital and inclusion by such mechanisms as "providing access to good quality and affordable housing" (p 47). The emphasis on service improvements is seen to include extra-care housing or very sheltered housing as an imaginative alternative to traditional forms of residential care since it "allows people to live in their own homes with a range of facilities and support designed to meet their needs" (p 54).

However, we have seen statements like this for over 15 years. It is true that the Griffiths Report (1988) was criticised for appearing to marginalise housing as just 'bricks and mortar' (Oldman, 1988). Nevertheless, the subsequent White Paper on Community Care stressed that "suitable good quality housing" (DH, 1989, p 9) is essential to social care packages at home, and hence "social service authorities [...] need to work closely with housing authorities, housing associations and other providers of housing of all types in developing plans for a full and flexible range of housing" (p 25). However, the Department of Health's own audit of housing and community care complained that links between community care and housing assessment procedures were rare (1994). The last Conservative government responded to such lack of progress by producing both a circular on housing and community care (DH and DoE, 1997), and detailed practice guidance for practitioners in housing, health and social services (Means et al, 1997). The new Labour government followed up such work by promoting the practice guidance in *Modernising social services* (DH, 1998) while the Royal Commission on Long-term Care stressed the importance of housing and home to older people in general and the potential role of very sheltered or extra-care housing in particular (Sutherland Report, 1999).

It can be seen that the rhetoric around the importance of housing to meeting community care objectives has a long history. However, the reality on the ground has been very different. The government has found ear-marked monies for extra-care housing, although it remains unclear the extent to which it really delivers independence for frail elderly people compared to 'staying put' or moving into traditional residential care (Heywood et al, 2002). It may have invested limited monies in this particular area but it has started to restrict expenditure on other housing and care initiatives such as Supporting People (ODPM, 2005). Many small housing agencies in the independent sector, such as those supporting older homeless people, survive on very vulnerable funding and hence are in constant danger of disintegration (Pannell et al, 2002).

Foord (2005) has recently referred to "the new landscape of precariousness" (p 2) for housing and community care. This is not only because of the extent of cutbacks in the Supporting People programme, but also because of the failure of the Green Paper on Social Care to provide a clear strategic role for housing authorities "leaving community care for the foreseeable future ... built around an axis of social services and primary care trusts" (p 3). The next section suggests that the axis might be even more limited than this, with social services becoming almost as marginal as housing.

Re-medicalisation of later life

Unfortunately, doubts about the likelihood of implementation of the Green Paper go much deeper than the question of resource availability and the level of political will. This section will outline the collapse of confidence of the government in local authorities as the lead agency in community care and how this is leading them to turn to health in a way that might well lead to a re-medicalisation of later life.

The new Labour government of 1997 placed a high emphasis on partnership working between health and social services as the best way to break down the so-called 'Berlin Wall' between them (Hudson, 1999; DH, 2000; Means et al, 2002; Glasby, 2004). However, frustration soon began to develop at the slowness of progress towards partnership working (Rummery, 2003), with the government pointing the finger at local authorities for being responsible for the slow hospital discharge of older people:

> On one day in September last year, 5,500 patients aged 75 and over were ready to be discharged but were still in an acute hospital bed: 23% awaiting assessment; 17% waiting for social services funding to go to a care home; 25% trying to find the right care home; and 6% waiting for the right care home package to be organised. The 1948 fault line between health and social care has inhibited the development of services shaped around the needs of patients. (DH, 2000, p 29)

The above quotation is from *The NHS Plan: A plan for investment, a plan for reform* (DH, 2000), which also announced a new organisational option for improving collaboration between health and social services for older people, namely the creation of new integrated organisations called care trusts, as single, multipurpose legal bodies able to both commission and deliver health and social care for older people (Glendinning and Means, 2004).

Given all of this, it seems an extraordinary case of myopia for the Green Paper on Social Care to fail to address the gradual erosion of the Griffiths Report's (1988) core recommendation that local authorities should be the lead agency in community care and how this erosion relates to the increasingly dominant role of primary care trusts (PCTs) (and potentially care trusts). This is especially true given the parallel developments of government policy towards what used to be called chronic care and is now called long-term healthcare conditions. Long-term healthcare conditions are touched on in the opening chapters of the Green Paper under the need for 'improved health'. However, no comment is made on how emergent healthcare policy and practice towards long-term conditions seems the antithesis of the holistic approach to social care that is articulated in most of the Green Paper.

In further developing this point, it is important to re-iterate that older people with long-term health conditions require and deserve a high quality healthcare response and this has often not been the case. The government should, therefore, be supported for attempting to focus on how to improve healthcare for long-term health conditions even if some believe that the main driver is the high cost of such healthcare to the NHS (Hudson, 2005). The main criticism of this chapter is that this new interest in the healthcare of older people is being pursued within a very narrow medical paradigm that marginalises quality of life issues for the older person. However, it will be seen below that policy statements about developments in this area seem as incapable of making links to social care/community care policy developments as the Green Paper was in making the links in the opposite direction.

In 2005, the Department of Health (2005b) published *Supporting People with Long Term Conditions: An NHS and social care model to support local innovation and interpretation*. This report outlined the discomfort and stress experienced by the 17.5 million people with a long-term health condition but went on to stress that just five per cent of hospital inpatients, many with a long-term condition, account for 42 per cent of all acute bed days. The new model was seeking to embed an effective, systematic approach to the care and management of patients with a long-term condition into local health and social care provision with an overall target to reduce in-patient emergency beds days by five per cent by March 2008 using 2003/04 as the baseline.

Some of the pitfalls of this new approach can immediately be seen from a social model perspective. The document refers to patients not service users. It stresses the discomfort and stress, especially of older patients, but the main target is not the reduction of this but rather a reduction in emergency bed days. In fairness, the report does stress that one of the aims is "prolonging and extending the quality of life" (DH, 2005b, p 7), but this is not then followed through. An improvement in quality of life is seen as coming almost solely through targeted healthcare intervention, organised through a new system of case management for those with multiple needs controlled by a new group of highly experienced nurses to be called community matrons. The report defines the role of the community matron in the following way:

> Community matrons are likely to have caseloads of around 50-80 patients with the most complex needs and who require clinical intervention as well as care co-ordination. They will work across health and social care services and the voluntary sector, so that this group of patients receives services that are integrated and complementary. Whether they work from the PCT, general practice or a hospital, community matrons need to have close working relationships with general practice, hospital wards and local social services teams. (DH, 2005b, p 16)

This new approach to people with long-term conditions has since started to be rolled out with regard to specific illnesses and hence the publication of a National Service Framework specific to those with long-term neurological diseases (DH, 2005c).

Not only is there no discussion of how healthcare intervention can be integrated into wider lives, but there is not even an attempt to cross-reference to parallel developments in social care. Overall, it would be hard to have to come up with a new role title further from the spirit of the social model of disability than the 'community matron'.

Towards the obvious 'solution'?

In early summer 2005, it seemed increasingly bizarre that the government was developing policies for social care and health for what was effectively the same group of older people with only a glancing connection between the two. The absurdity of this seemed to finally dawn on the Department of Health. In late July 2005, it announced that the response to the Green Paper on Social Care was not to be a White Paper, but rather social care was to be included in a White Paper on 'out-of-hospital care', which in the words of the then Care Services Minister, meant that there was an opportunity to explore a "new alliance between health and local government" (quoted in *Community Care*, 28 July-3 August 2005, p 6). It was hard to avoid the conclusion that the new alliance would finally terminate the remnants of the lead agency role of social services in community care by combining assessment and commissioning within healthcare structures.

The resultant White Paper, *Our Health, Our Care, Our Say: A new direction for community services*, was published in January 2006 (DH, 2006a) and failed to 'live up' to the concerns of those fearing a formal termination of the key role of social services in social care. A national system of care trusts is not proposed nor is any clear organisational alternative. Equally, the progressive vision and principles of the Green Paper on Social Care largely remains. However, these apparent commitments are largely obscured by the level of emphasis on healthcare delivery issues.

The White Paper is primarily about 'our health' rather than 'our (social) care'. Four main goals are outlined:

- better prevention services with earlier intervention;
- more choice and louder voice for patients;
- tackling inequalities and improving access to community services; and
- more support for people with long-term needs.

In practice, much of this is to be delivered through general practitioners (GPs) and PCTs, with social services very much as the junior partner. In fairness, references to the role of social care and adult social services are extensive. The importance of direct payments are re-emphasised; recognition is given to the need to integrate health and social care support for people with long-term conditions; integrated health and social care plans are promised; and frequent reference is made to broad understandings of well-being that need to draw in leisure, transport and housing among others.

However, the two dominant agendas in the White Paper are the need to introduce practice-based commissioning by GPs and PCTs within a competitive market of healthcare providers and payment by results for hospitals in terms of the number of patients they attract. Both of these are likely to generate a much stronger element of competition into healthcare provision, seen by some as essential for efficiency and choice (Le Grand, 2003), and by others as a major move to the privatisation of the NHS (Pollock, 2004). Irrespective of which perspective proves to be right in the long run, the short-term dilemma for social services is that they are being asked to work in partnership with health within an environment where the dominant ethos is increasingly on competition and markets. Hence, this requirement to work together is even less convincing than many of the previous exhortations – especially since so much of this requirement is couched in very vague terms, as illustrated by Box 4.2, which draws on the summary of the second chapter of the White Paper.

It is hard to disagree with the verdict of Hudson (2006) that the White Paper "has a disappointing Green Paper feel to it, with too many of the proposals hedged with qualifications and characterised by vague timetables and expectations" (p 35). As an optimist, Hudson believes that the tensions in the White Paper between stressing collaboration at the same time as celebrating choice and competition creates a fluidity that could enable social care to shape the final outcomes of policy direction. Sadly, my own view is more in keeping with the editorial in *Community Care* that stated that "as traditional social services departments are disbanded and their functions subsumed by the health and education leviathans, there is a danger that social care's unique voice could be lost" (2 March 2006, p 5).

Box 4.2: Enabling health, independence and well-being

- Developing an NHS 'Life Check' starting in PCT spearhead areas.
- Better support for mental health and emotional well-being: promoting good practice; demonstrating sites for people of working age, as part of our action to help people with health conditions and disabilities to remain in, or return to, work; access to computerised cognitive behaviour therapy.
- Local leadership of well-being: improving commissioning and joint working through defining and strengthening the roles of Directors of Public Health (DPHs) and Directors of Adult Social Services (DASSs).
- Better partnership working in local areas: a new outcomes framework; aligning performance measures; assessments and inspection; aligning planning and budget cycles for the NHS and local authorities.
- Stronger local commissioning: shifting towards prevention and early support; expanding the evidence base through Partnerships for Older People Projects (POPPs); National Reference Group for Health and Well-Being; re-focusing the Quality and Outcomes Framework (QOF).
- National leadership: stronger leadership for social care within the Department of Health; a new Fitter Britain campaign.

Source: Department of Health (2006a, p 24)

Conclusion

Strong arguments can be made for radical organisational change and for radical new approaches to healthcare delivery for those with long-term health conditions. However, it is unambiguously clear from research that the quality of life of older people in need of combined health and social care responses is defined as much, if not more, by the quality of the response to their social care needs as by the availability of appropriate healthcare. Indeed, older people want the social care response to increasingly focus on how to support them to remain included in their own communities, the importance of which has been acknowledged by the Social Exclusion Unit of the Office of the Deputy Prime Minister (ODPM, 2006). The White Paper does acknowledge some of this, but leaves health even more in 'the driving seat' than before and yet health has a very poor record of prioritising the needs of older people and an even worse record of looking beyond acute ill-health. It is hard to avoid the conclusion that England is seeing a re-medicalisation of later life.

The government continues to claim a radical shift of policy towards meeting the social care needs of older people in which empowerment and choice become the drivers. This chapter has used case studies, namely the Green Paper on Social Care and policy developments on long-term conditions, to argue that what is most striking are the continuities with the past rather than radical improvements.

Part Two
Forms of knowing – participatory approaches

Narratives as agents of social change: a new direction for narrative gerontologists

Ruth E. Ray

Introduction

In their chapter on 'Humanistic gerontology and the meaning(s) of aging', Thomas Cole and Michelle Sierpina (2006) conclude, after surveying the literature of the past 35 years, that humanistic gerontology is still growing and that the "leading edges" in the future will be "research and practice in narrative and creativity", as well as "feminist perspectives, age studies, and performance studies". Cole and Sierpina define humanistic gerontology as the search for meaning in old age. Humanistic gerontologists are those who ask, 'What does it mean to grow old?', 'What makes life worth living into old age?', 'How does the time and place of our ageing affect the meanings we make of the experience, as individuals and as cultures?'.

Cole and Sierpina remind us that, in the 1970s and 1980s, humanistic gerontology was primarily conducted within the disciplinary boundaries of history, literature and philosophy. Over the years, these boundaries have blurred, giving way to interdisciplinary perspectives, including what Margaret Gullette calls "age studies as cultural studies" (2000). Gullette prefers the term 'age studies' to 'gerontology' because it reflects not only interdisciplinarity, but also a grounding in humanistic study that is informed by critical theory. Gullette's particular brand of age studies emphasises that age and ageing are discursively and ideologically constructed, as well as historically contingent. She argues that "aging is a personal residue – of stories we have heard, received or rejected, renegotiated and retold" (p 218), and that narratives should therefore be central to age studies. While cultural critics have been "notoriously sensitive to the stories inherent in mass culture" and have effectively deconstructed those stories in terms of 'race', class, gender, ethnicity and sexuality, they have largely ignored the ideologies of age representation and have shown little interest in age analysis (p 219).

In this chapter, I explore how two of the promising areas identified by Cole and Sierpina – feminism and narrative studies – might work together on the leading edge of humanistic gerontology. I discuss narrative research in terms of its past and future, and I do so from a feminist perspective. My discussion rests on three underlying arguments, which I have made elsewhere and which have become foundational to my thinking about age studies (Ray, 1996, 1999, 2000, 2003). First, it is not enough for gerontologists to write only for themselves and their academic fields; at least *some* of us must also accept the social responsibility of informing the general public about issues of ageing and old age (see also Chapter Three). Statistics clearly show that western culture itself is ageing: according to the US Census Bureau, by 2030, there will be 71.5 million people aged 65 and over in the US alone, making up 20 per cent of the population. This is twice as many older adults as are currently residing in the US. Given the steady growth of the older population in the next 25 years, gerontologists increasingly will be called on to assume the role of public intellectuals, interpreting the ageing experience and its social effects. Narrative gerontologists could be especially influential in changing the public's mind about ageing and old age.

My second argument is informed by the feminist perspective that research on marginalised and under-represented groups (such as old women) should be action-oriented. From this perspective, narrative gerontologists have a social responsibility to function, not just as informants, but as change agents, broadening and deepening public perceptions and providing alternative images and expectations. The ideal end-point of such work is social justice in regards to ageing and age relations. Harry R. Moody, speaking from the perspective of hermeneutics, made a similar argument nearly 15 years ago, asserting the need for a critical gerontology that identifies "possibilities for emancipatory social change, including positive ideals for the last stage of life" (Moody, 1993, p xv) (see also Chapter Nine). As a feminist who conducts narrative research myself, I have observed the social impact of narratives, and I believe that narrative gerontologists can learn to use narratives strategically to effect social change.

My third argument is that individual and collective narratives are closely intertwined. Individual life stories are motivated and inflected by social and cultural stories, and the reverse is equally true. All narratives are deeply 'nested' and never occur in a sociohistorical vacuum; thus, narrative change can, and often does, lead to social change. Both Jacobs (2002) and Richardson (1997) illustrate this connection in terms of identity formation. Based on his research on the mobilisation of social groups, Jacobs (2002) argues that narrative is central to both individual and group identity formation and is therefore an "essential resource for social movements" (p 222). He finds that collective and personal identities work synergistically and that "collective identities are created and transformed through the integration of personal and collective narratives" (p 206). Richardson (1997) examines this connection from the perspective of the individual. She reasons that individuals shape their lives through the narratives available to them. When the narrative possibilities are limited, an individual's sense of his/her own possibilities will be limited. Sometimes, however, individuals deviate from social scripts and in telling their stories offer new possibilities, creating "transformative" and "liberating" narratives (pp 33-4). Hearing their stories helps others "overcome the isolation and alienation of contemporary life and link disparate persons into a collective consciousness" (pp 58-9). When significant numbers of individuals begin to live out these transformative narratives, they change social norms. Richardson reminds us that this is how feminist consciousness-raising groups worked in the 1960s and 1970s. During the second wave of the North American feminist movement, when women got together and told their life stories, they realised that what they thought was 'merely personal experience' was shared by a great many women; it was, in fact, a social experience with political causes and consequences. When individual women broke the narrative mould and began to tell counter-narratives and stories of resistance, those listening began to imagine different narratives for themselves. Over time, an enlargement of individual consciousness became the basis for extending the collective consciousness.

Having rehearsed my foundational arguments, I should now reveal my motives for writing this chapter. I wish to promote social justice, starting with gender justice, in the social construction of ageing and old age, and I believe that narratives and narrative methods are one of the best ways to advance this agenda. I align myself with Margaret Gullette (2004) in arguing for social change through narrative change:"Longing for justice for the life course must drive our writing.... Ultimately, transforming ordinary life story telling will be the best way to comprehend our troubled world and a sign that we are changing it profoundly" (p 158).

I recognise that most narrative researchers do not claim a political agenda, and I am not arguing that they should. I mean to suggest that at least one *strand* of this research be devoted to the cause of narrative-for-social-change. Toward that end, I will consider how this new strand of narrative gerontology might build on previous research to become change-oriented. I review, selectively, the past 20 years of research in terms of five common approaches (allowing that some of these approaches overlap and interconnect): the study of narrative significance; the study of narrativity; the study of older adults' narratives; the study of adult development through narrative; and the reflective self-study of the narrating gerontologist. In my discussion of these approaches, I describe forms of change suggested by each, with the intention of moving toward a conclusion that outlines a sixth approach: the study of narratives as agents of social change.

Significance of narrative

A starting point for much narrative research is Bruner's (1986) distinction between paradigmatic knowing and narrative knowing. The paradigmatic mode of knowledge making relies on observation, description and reason, deriving empirical 'truths', while the narrative mode emphasises people, feelings and relationships, deriving personal or emotional 'truths'. We might say that, where paradigmatic discourse emphasises *sight* and extends our observational powers, narrative discourse emphasises *insight* and extends our sympathies.

Scholars from many disciplines have argued the importance of Bruner's distinction. In writing about emotions and story worlds, Oakley refers us to novelist George Eliot to understand the value of narrative knowing. Eliot recognised in 1856 that "appeals founded on generalisations and statistics require a sympathy ready-made, a moral sentiment already in activity: but a picture of human life ... surprises even the trivial and the selfish into that attention to what is apart from themselves ... it is a mode of amplifying experience and extending our contact with our fellow-men [sic] beyond the bounds of our personal lot" (quoted in Oakley, 2002, p 66). Elsewhere, psychologists Roger Shank and Tamara Berman (2002) draw on years of memory research to explain those human tendencies observed by Eliot. They argue that stories have a far greater impact on human belief, behaviour and imagination than abstract principles and scientific findings, because we process new information in terms of what we have seen and heard before; we constantly refer to our knowledge base of specific cases and stories, grouping together similar cases and experiences to form generalisations (Shank and Berman, 2002, p 292). Further, "we construct and tell stories, in part, to teach ourselves what we know and what we think" (Shank and Berman, 2002, p 294). Most of our knowledge base is constructed of stories, because it is easier to understand and remember a story than a theory, a principle or a collection of facts.

Another relevant aspect of Bruner's work is his characterisation of the socially constructed self (1990, 2002). From Bruner's perspective, human beings reflect culture and history as much as biology and physiology. The self is not an entity unto itself, but the result of a transactional relationship between one's self and an Other (or generalised Others). The self is, therefore, defined and situated within specific social contexts and distributed across multiple contexts; in this sense, each of us has multiple selves, or self-constructs, vacillating between stability and change, and functioning at various levels of development. The proper study of the self, then, *necessarily* involves humanistic, interpretive inquiry. In Bruner's view, change and development entail a continuous, growth-enhancing negotiation between self and culture. Narratives, or 'acts of telling', are the self's primary means of negotiation. The proper study of adult development, then, *necessarily* involves the study of narrative.

Many narrative gerontologists have situated their work in Bruner's theories of narrative knowing and the socially constructed self, as well as other research that deepens our understanding of narrative knowing (Sarbin, 1986; Polkinghorne, 1988); the storied self (Gergen, 1991, 1996); the value of 'narrative truth' (Spence, 1982); and the need for narrative therapies for re-storying the self (White and Epson, 1990; Schafer, 1992). Gerontologists Gary Kenyon and William Randall are most notable for their research on narrative knowing and the narrative self in later life (Randall, 1995, 1996; Kenyon, 1996; Kenyon and Randall, 1997). They use the term 'biographical aging' to argue the importance of storying and re-storying to ageing and development, and to the study of wisdom (Randall and Kenyon, 2001). More than any other gerontologists, Kenyon and Randall have worked to define, describe and exemplify what has come to be known as 'narrative gerontology' (Kenyon et al, 2001).

James Birren (1996a) describes narrative gerontology as a "new look at the inside of aging" (p xi). He argues that, prior to the narrative turn, "something important [had] been left out of our scientific knowledge-generating system in its studies of adult change and aging" (p ix). In their focus on older people's interpretations of lived experience, narrative gerontologists provide the missing component.

A narrative approach to gerontology is especially needed when we consider that processes of meaning making are highly age-sensitive. Researchers from the German Ageing Survey (Westerhof et al, 2003) have been collecting narratives from Germans at various periods in their lives to explore connections between objective life circumstances and subjective interpretations. They have found that older respondents' personal meanings not only differ from the meanings that objective conditions might warrant, but also from the theories that gerontologists advance. As one example, older adults are not as negatively affected by life course transitions and the loss of social roles as some theories would predict. They are also more likely than young and middle-aged narrators to take age into account when assessing the meaning and value of their lives; as a result, they tend to interpret their lives more positively, despite physical ailments, than would younger narrators with similar ailments.

The narrative turn in gerontology is often presented as a corrective gesture, countering previous tendencies to over-emphasise scientific knowing and to ignore or deny subjective knowing. In the case of some researchers, however, it is also seen as a transformational move. Randall (2001) argues that narrative inquiry entails a "perspective transformation": when we "crawl inside the very concept of story and *feel* what life-as-story means", we "experience the shock of viewing [the] world from three feet to one side of everything [we] have learned so far, as happens when [we] first acquire critical awareness of gender or race" (p 34, emphasis in original). To *feel* what it means to be old is to understand ageing from a completely different perspective and to be forever changed by that understanding. We will return to this point in the conclusion.

Narrativity

Narrativity refers to 'that which can be storied', taking into account the personal, social and rhetorical contexts in which stories are (and are not) generated and exchanged. As we know, not every event becomes a story; in fact, most aspects of human life remain inchoate and unarticulated. The study of narrativity helps us understand how, why, to what degree, and under what circumstances people shape their experiences into stories, as well as the circumstances under which their experiences remain 'unstoried'. To understand narrativity, Gubrium (2001) tells us to pay attention to "practical contingencies such as who one's audience is, the audience's tolerance for ambiguity, the occasion's narrative horizons, the narrative resources of storytellers, the storytellers' rhetorical aims, and the concrete course of the experience in question, among other contingencies of storytelling" (pp 24-5). Gerontologists interested in narrativity, search for environments that induce people to tell stories about ageing. Gubrium, for example, has observed and interviewed people in nursing homes and Alzheimer's support groups (1975, 1986, 1993), while other gerontologists have explored narrativity in retirement communities, senior centres, clinical settings, writing and reminiscence groups, therapy sessions and private homes (Myerhoff, 1980; Cohler and Cole, 1996; Ray, 2000; Clark, 2001; Randall and Kenyon, 2001; Chandler and Ray, 2002; Shaw and Westwood, 2002; Rubinstein, 2002b). Randall and Kenyon (2001) use the term 'wisdom environment' to describe narrative occasions in which participants assist each other in telling stories that promote self-understanding and development. In these environments, participants help each other to remember their lives as a whole; identify themes and patterns; distinguish individual stories from family and community stories; identify how individual stories have been influenced by the master narratives of culture and cohort; and re-story accounts that no longer 'fit' the narrator.

In making the case for life story gathering as an important methodology, Wallace (1992) distinguishes between research that focuses on stories per se and that which emphasises narrativity. The researcher's purpose and epistemological stance are key to this distinction. If a researcher is searching for *factual accounts* of the lifestyles of retirees, then methodological issues such as sampling, validity, reliability and accuracy are important. If, however, a researcher wants to know how *meanings* of retirement are constructed and re-constructed over time in the process of talking about retirement, then such methodological issues are less significant. What becomes important is the researcher's process of engaging narrators and eliciting their stories, as well as the social contexts in which the stories are told. For example, the researcher might explore how a narrator's retirement story changes when he is talking to retired friends at the doughnut shop, compared to former co-workers at the company Christmas party who are still employed. The researcher will likely discover that the story changes, yet again, when the retiree and his wife are invited to co-construct the story in a mutual interview. These are the kinds of situations that interest scholars of narrativity.

Anthropologist Mark Luborsky (1987, 1990, 1993) has studied the larger cultural environments in which life stories are embedded, as well as the effects of narrators' mental and emotional states on their storytelling. Luborsky (1993) argues that one reason for the narrative turn in gerontology is that western culture encourages and validates life storytelling. Westerners also privilege certain themes over others. North Americans, for example, "tend to romanticize the realm of personal meanings as a vast resource of adaptation and coping" (p 446), while other cultures encourage the articulation of community values over personal values in telling life stories. Luborsky has also found that mental states, such as depression, significantly influence narrativity and the shape of narratives. Among older adults, depressed informants narrate less of the life course, use fewer details and often fix on a single theme or meaning for their story. Non-depressed narrators tend to elaborate more; to see their lives as still unfolding; and to present multiple, flexible identities across the life course. Based on his studies in narrativity, Luborsky concludes that western ideals about the importance of articulating a coherent life story with a specific 'life theme' – an underlying premise of much reminiscence therapy – is misguided, because it does not allow for a situated understanding of stories as shaped by narrative environments.

An aspect of narrativity that merits further study is the influence of researchers themselves on narratives and narrative environments (see also Chapter Six). For example, Luborsky (1987) considers the effects of his own age, class, ethnicity, gender and geographic background on the life history accounts he received from older adults. He also notes that "a familiar obstacle to understanding the American middle class is that studies of it reflect the white, middle-class researcher's own ambitions and ideals. 'Self-actualization' and personal-moral development are notions embedded in the researcher's own folk models and may subtly refract determinations of what is significant about the informant's talk" (p 378). Presumably, these same factors will affect the questions researchers ask in their interviews, as well as the types of people they feel comfortable interviewing, and the environments in which they seek informants. In my own work (Ray, 2000), I have discussed how my age, gender, class and 'race', as well as my status as an English teacher and published writer, influenced the narrative environments of the writing groups I studied in senior citizen centres.

If narrative gerontologists were to assume the role of change agent, we would envision future research projects in narrativity that address a number of questions. What narrative environments reinforce age identities and negative attitudes toward ageing and age relations? Where and how are these environments created, and for whose purposes? Alternatively, what narrative environments become 'wisdom environments', not just for individuals, but for groups, communities and societies as a whole? How do these environments promote stories of alternative and multiple age identities, flexibility in meaning making, openness to change, and an ability to re-story one's self and one's relationships with others? Is it possible to change negative or limiting environments, and if so, how and to what degree? What influences do gerontologists themselves have on the narrative environments they study? How might we educate the general public about the need for wisdom environments and assist in creating them?

Older adults' narratives

The vast majority of research in narrative gerontology focuses specifically on narratives as texts. Researchers advertise for study participants or find them through personal associations, word-of-mouth or reminiscence groups. They then conduct open-ended or semi-structured interviews in private homes, nursing homes or senior centres, eliciting retrospective accounts of participants' lives, after which they analyse the narratives for themes and organisational patterns (Kaufman,

1986; Sherman, 1991; Koch, 2000). Such narratives, it is argued, give older adults 'voice' in the field of gerontology.

A frequently cited work in this vein is Ruth and Oberg's (1996) study of 37 Finnish women and men, aged 73-83. The researchers selected participants on the basis of former occupation, looking for different degrees of freedom and flexibility in careers and the life course in general. They transcribed each of the taped interviews and produced a summary text for each respondent, condensing the interviews to a manageable length. In analysing the texts, they focused on a central question: what 'patterns of life' were discernable? Ruth and Oberg were primarily interested in how narratives reflected the life that was lived and how gerontologists might better understand the difference between an 'optimal' old age and a 'dysfunctional' old age from a life history perspective. They found six conceptual or interpretive patterns in the narrators' life stories: the bitter life; life as a trapping pit; life as a hurdle race; the devoted, silenced life; life as a job career; and the sweet life. Ruth and Oberg found that some patterns followed class lines. People from urban backgrounds and from upper and middle-class families, as well as those who had held leading positions in their professions, patterned their stories in terms of 'the sweet life' and 'life as a job career'. People from rural or working-class backgrounds with certain upward social mobility, cast their stories in terms of 'life as a hurdle race' and 'the devoted, silenced life'. 'The bitter life' and 'life as a trapping pit' crossed class boundaries. These narratives appeared to be more affected by relationships and health problems than by career or social mobility. Ruth and Oberg found two patterns to be gender-related: the 'devoted, silenced life' was typically a female construction, while 'life as a job career' was typically male. Two patterns corresponded with what the authors call a 'problematic old age': 'the bitter life' and 'life as a trapping pit' were used by narrators who experienced old age as a time of health problems, powerlessness and loss of control over their lives. These narrators saw themselves as sufferers and losers. All the other patterns corresponded with what Ruth and Oberg call a 'good old age': narrators felt they could control their lives and overcome their misfortunes. They were satisfied with themselves, enjoyed the freedoms of old age and continued to engage in new endeavours.

The point of Ruth and Oberg's study, consistent with Gubrium (1993), is that gerontologists gain a much better understanding of the meaning of old age by understanding the meanings informants themselves make of their lives as a whole. Berman (2000) offers the best articulation of this point: "the process of aging is in part a historical process involving not only the history of social customs toward the aged, but, equally, the history of older people's understandings of themselves" (p 282).

Another type of research involves the analysis of older adults' written texts in the form of biography, autobiography, memoir, letters and personal journals. This work and its place in gerontological knowledge making has been thoroughly reviewed by Anne Wyatt-Brown (1992, 2000), but I will focus here on Berman's work as a representative example. Berman (1994, 2000) follows the hermeneutic tradition to show how older writers' self-interpretations can help gerontologists understand ageing. Berman reads the diaries, journals and memoirs of May Sarton, Doris Grumbach and Florida Scott-Maxwell to extend and challenge theories of ageing, such as Erikson's concept of generativity, and to explore the role that self-reflection plays in 'successful' and 'unsuccessful' ageing. Berman finds that the best texts for analysis, from a gerontological perspective, are those that vividly convey the experiences of later life, but which also trace the changes in a narrator's sense of self that accompany those experiences.

Gerontologists interested in using text analysis to help change people's attitudes about ageing would focus precisely on the themes of personal and social change that Berman identifies, and they would pursue the kinds of questions suggested by Ruth and Oberg's (1996) analysis: to what extent do patterns of interpretation in later life continue the patterns established earlier in life? Are there interpretive patterns that are typical of specific periods in the life course – youth, midlife, old age? How might an intervention or 're-storying' during one of these periods affect patterns of interpretation later in life? And, most important, how might changes in interpretive patterns affect the *lived* experiences of narrators? What might gerontologists do to inform the general public of the impact of interpretive processes on their experiences of ageing over the life course?

Adult development through narrative processes

Narrative gerontologists who look for evidence of development in older adults' narratives and narrative processes are already predisposed toward change-oriented research. James Birren's guided autobiography groups (Birren and Deutchman, 1991; Birren and Cochran, 2001) are designed specifically to involve older adults in a systematic review and re-vision of their life stories. Indeed, the overall point of Birren and Cochran's (2001) *Telling the Stories of Life through Guided Autobiography Groups* is that sharing life stories in groups of like-minded peers induces introspection and enhances development, provided, of course, that the group functions as a 'wisdom environment', in Randall and Kenyon's terms. Premised on the same idea is Kenyon and Randall's *Restorying our Lives: Personal growth through autobiographical reflection* (1997). The authors refer to members of writing and reminiscence groups, as well as gerontologists who elicit their stories, as 'collaborators' and 'co-authors', referring to the social, interpersonal and dialogic nature of life storytelling. They provide suggestions for effective story listening and response, as well as ethical guidelines for 'biographical encounters' that ensure mutual trust and consent. Their bottom-line definition of a biographical encounter that fosters development is one that helps another person to "continue on his or her journey and to find his or her own direction" (p 159). Such an encounter is therefore non-directive, non-judgmental and non-coercive.

In my research on development through life storytelling (Ray, 2000), I have focused on the ways that men and women contribute differently to autobiographical writing groups and to the various types and levels of development that occur in these groups. In my observations of senior centre writing groups, I have found that group norms, which differ across groups and are influenced by the age, 'race', class and gender of group members, affect the structure, tone and content of individual members' narratives. I also found that self-directed groups (in contrast with Birren's guided autobiography groups) encourage various forms of self-censorship, indirectness, avoidance and distancing from disturbing aspects of narrators' life stories. However, particularly skilled narrators demonstrate, by their own example, the therapeutic value in narrating difficult life experiences. In the middle-class, suburban groups I observed, the women were more likely to take on an educative role in writing groups, especially in their interactions with men. They did so by asking questions about men's stories, as well as their feelings about the events being narrated. The men also gained a better understanding of their own relationships with women over their lifetime through the narrative examples that women brought to the group. For the women, the men became figures they reacted to and against. In my interviews with them after the group sessions, the women often talked about the men, usually in terms of their early limitations and the changes in their stories over time, while the men never talked about the women in such terms. In other mixed-gender settings, we have found that repeated tellings of the same story get refined and redirected by female group members in such a way that the narrator comes to new understandings of the 'same old events', as well as new possibilities for making sense of them (Chandler and Ray, 2002).

Narrating gerontologist

As I conclude this brief review of narrative gerontology, I am pleased to include a category that I consider most promising for future inquiry. By the 'narrating gerontologist', I mean the age researcher who engages in critical self-reflection and demonstrates him/herself in the process of studying age. In this genre, which is fairly new to gerontology, the researcher tells personal stories about him/ herself *of a certain age*, often interacting with others as they tell their own age stories. Together, researcher and informants try to make sense of the ageing experience. When done well, this kind of inquiry generates significant insights. It also demonstrates the potential of narrative inquiry to generate empathy and compassion, as well as intellectual understanding, and to evoke a change in consciousness on the part of the researcher *and* the reader. Such writing entails a careful balancing between others' scholarship and one's own, others' stories and one's own. The gerontologist integrates thinking and feeling and demonstrates great skill and sensitivity in writing. Two feminist gerontologists who have beautifully demonstrated this form of research are Gullette (1997) and Holstein (2006). Both reveal what it *feels* like to be simultaneously observing (as gerontologists and cultural critics) and experiencing (as women in late-midlife bodies) the phenomenon of ageing. In the end, both argue the need for more autobiographical awareness in the scholarship on ageing.

An extended example of autobiographical scholarship is Manheimer's (1999) *A Map to the End of Time: Wayfarings with friends and philosophers*. What I like most about this book, and the reason I offer it as a stellar example of engaged, self-reflective narrative, is that it demonstrates how story is a means, not an end, in the search for understanding. Manheimer vividly illustrates the concept of the narrative self by narrating himself as he explores and interprets the narratives of others. The range of narratives in the book, from Plato, Aristotle, Schopenhauer, Nietzsche, Buber, Confucius and Cavel, to the stories of ordinary elders in Manheimer's adult education classes, are treated with equal interest and respect. Manheimer seamlessly interweaves his own life story within the larger story of his search for meaning and also reveals how the self – Manheimer himself – is constructed through relationships with people, ideas, places and texts over the course of a lifetime. Manheimer says of his philosophical explorations, "I wanted to feel the weight of history, bear it gracefully, to place my life in the context of generations, to understand that becoming a self, achieving individuality, also meant belonging to the world and to others" (p 51). This is a good description of the narrating gerontologist's credo; s/he must be willing to move out of the comfort zone of academic abstractions and disembodied research and become an integral part of the research. In making the epistemological shift from studying age in terms of 'what it is' (out there) to 'how it feels' (in here), the gerontologist must observe him/herself growing old.

This kind of reflective, engaged scholarship is inherently revisionist and change-oriented. It points to new directions in research that require new skills, particularly self-reflection and self-reflexivity, on the part of gerontologists. Barbara Myerhoff and Jay Ruby (1992) argue that both reflection and reflexivity are important to knowledge making. Reflection means showing ourselves to ourselves or holding up a mirror to ourselves. For example, the gerontologist must be willing to look at her body and examine her own thoughts and feelings about ageing. Reflexivity takes this analysis a step further, requiring a second mirror: we detach from the first image and look at ourselves looking at ourselves. The important distinction here is that someone or something else – an older person, a reminiscence group, a nursing home – holds up the second mirror. To be reflexive, we need an Other to show ourselves *to* ourselves, and to help us develop a self-conscious awareness of the process of self-scrutiny. Myerhoff and Ruby remind us that reflexivity is ancient and universal, found in very old texts of storytellers telling stories about storytellers. Such reflexivity opens the world to an endless regress of possibilities, which is the perfect frame of mind for a change-oriented researcher (Myerhoff and Ruby, 1992).

The importance of self-reflexivity and personal change resonates for me, especially, because it corresponds with the central tenet of feminist scholarship that feminists must work to effect social change and that lasting change – change that results in social justice – occurs *in conjunction with* personal transformation (see also Chapter Two). Activist Gloria Steinem (1992) wrote a book on the necessity of personal transformation as a basis for social change called *Revolution from within.* The same argument has been made convincingly in the academic mode by Fernandes (2003), who claims that social activists need to first recognise and then *dis*-identify with their privilege (in terms of 'race', class, age, gender, etc) in order to understand and take responsibility for how that privilege negates and oppresses others. This happens simultaneously on a personal level, in our daily interactions, and on a cultural level, in our conceptualising of social interactions and their larger meanings. She goes on to say that change-oriented intellectuals, especially, must engage in "a painful and honest confrontation with our own investment in and attachment to power" (p 35) so that we might "confront the deepest sources of our own complicity in the external structures of power we want to change" (p 34). This is a process that challenges the very identifications that shape our aspirations for recognition, success and superiority. Fernandes demonstrates, through her analysis of failed social justice projects, that progressive activists and intellectuals "can benefit from one of the simplest and most powerful teachings that has permeated most spiritual traditions – the need to engage in an honest and continued process of self-examination and self-transformation" (p 39).

There are some drawbacks to research that foregrounds self-analysis and transformation. To make ourselves subjects in our own inquiry leaves us open to the critiques levelled at post-modern scholarship in other fields: narcissism, 'navel gazing' and endless analysis that seems to go nowhere. Yet this need not be the case. As Behar (1996) argues, making ourselves objects of analysis can make us better observers – more inclusive and empathetic. However, we must balance self-reflexivity with careful data gathering and continued emphasis on the material (not just intellectual) consequences of our work. To be responsive to the material needs of research participants and the groups they represent, we will need to develop new writing and reporting practices, addressing larger audiences that include the older people with whom and for whom we are researching. Behar makes the point clear: "for [advocacy research] to matter in a multicultural world, it needs to reach a wider range of audiences both in and beyond the academy" (p 21).

Final thoughts

I have been moving toward a conclusion that now seems obvious (at least to me): as social change agents, narrative gerontologists must not only change the way people *think* about ageing, but also how they *feel* about ageing. This requires that we must first change our *own* thoughts and feelings about ageing. I offer one last bit of evidence to reinforce my argument that narrative research centred on *emotions* is crucial to social change.

In his discussion of emotionality and continuity over the life course, psychoanalyst Wilhelm Mader (1996) argues that emotions co-write the life story; therefore, to change the life story (and the meanings one makes of ageing), one must change the emotional patterns underlying it. The link between emotions and stories is the felt need for continuity within storytellers, which Mader describes as follows. One's biography or life story serves the social and psychological function of lending continuity to one's life. This sense of continuity is a "necessary resource for the behavior, thinking and feelings of people, of interacting and communicating generations and cultures living together, so that ... they accrue confidence in 'generalized others' ... and they find their individual uniqueness" (p 51). The feeling that one needs continuity grows stronger as one ages and finds him/herself increasingly at odds with, or ignored by, the general culture. Emotional states, moods or dispositions "codetermine and survive whole periods of life, indeed the total life span" (p 44) and are fundamental to one's sense of continuity in old age.

Narrative gerontologists, then, must learn more about emotionality, which Mader defines as "the sense of balance, the social sonar for positioning us in the force field of cultural values, norms, expectations and stereotypes. Basic emotionality is like a searchlight in a crowded social twilight" (Mader, 1996, p 52). Emotionality is, in narrative terms, a plot, script or story form. Starting early in life, emotional patterns are acquired, adjusted and reinforced as the individual navigates the social landscape. Over time, these patterns become self-regulating, consciously or unconsciously. They come to "imprint and color lifestyles", as well as life stories, and they are "efficacious right into old age" (p 55).

Drawing on his psychoanalytic practice, Mader argues that traditional beliefs, values and social roles cannot be changed by rational insights and countervailing efforts alone. The basic emotional patterns underlying these beliefs and behaviours must be changed as well; otherwise, existing social relations will remain the same. Mader illustrates this point in regards to gender relations. He finds that, when clients hold traditional emotional patterns of femininity (emphasising connection and care) and masculinity (emphasising autonomy and rights) their real-life gender relations remain the same, even when clients express a desire to change them. Mader finds that educated clients are "curiously unaffected" and continue to follow their "customary mold", "despite all formal equal opportunity acts, and despite all critical-emancipatory enlightenment" (p 56). Having internalised the traditional emotional patterns, the clients have established their gender relations accordingly. As a therapist, Mader believes that emotional patterns can be modified, thereby changing social relations, but he acknowledges that this is a slow process that requires a great deal of concerted effort to change.

Age relations, like gender relations, are based on emotional patterns that have been internalised over time. Important work on the part of change-oriented gerontologists will be to identify the emotional patterns that underwrite life stories and to connect these patterns to larger social patterns, illustrating (to an ever-widening audience) how 'personal feelings' and reactions to ageing are the result of lifelong cultural regulations and reinforcements. The result, for most of us, is an internalised ageism of which we are barely aware. Learning for ourselves and then teaching others that emotions are a "basic component of our understanding of aging" (Mader, 1996, p 60) will be the first step in our efforts to change the meanings people make of age.

SIX

Redressing the balance? The participation of older people in research

Mo Ray

Introduction

Despite the considerable growth of interest in user participation in policy and service development and more recently research, the definition and meaning of participation is a contested and ideologically loaded concept (Braye, 2000). There remains considerable uncertainty as to what does or should constitute participation and what its purpose should be. While there may be significant agreement in the research community that the participation of older people in research is (at least in principle) a good thing, its potential remains significantly underdeveloped as do the complexities of participation. Who should, for example, benefit from research? To what extent should research impact be judged on its success in contributing to positive change for older women and men? What sort of criteria might be used to judge the success or otherwise, in older people's participation in research?

The potential for participation to become the 'big idea', which must be achieved at all costs, carries with it the risk of what Beresford (2003, p 1) has described as a "tick box approach to participation". At its worst, a predominantly superficial approach to participation could trivialise or underplay both its complexities and potential. In reality, a critical and complete analysis of participation in research is absent. As it stands at present, this omission raises a range of complex issues for researchers and user participants within all areas of the research process (Beresford, 2003).

The aim of this chapter is to review critically some of the questions that surround the participation of older women and men in gerontological research. This discussion is set in the context of increased interest in participation across research, policy and practice. An engagement with democratic approaches to user participation in gerontological research has the potential to make progress in a number of areas that are of critical importance to older people. But changes in this direction would imply fundamental changes to, for example, traditional approaches to research; the ways in which research is organised; and the goals and aspirations for dissemination and action from research. The chapter begins by setting participation in research in the context of the wider drives towards citizen participation. The ways in which participation approaches are informed by different ideological positions are reviewed. Traditional approaches to participation in gerontological research have meant that older people are generally confined to involvement in limited and specific areas of the research process. The implications of these approaches are highlighted alongside an attempt to draw out some of the questions that seem critical if participation along more democratic lines is to be pursued. The chapter concludes by considering some of the implications of developing participation and asks what research establishments may realistically be able to achieve in the frameworks that dominate mainstream research agendas.

Participation: setting the context

Participation of older people in policy and practice

The participation of older people has moved up the policy and practice agenda in Britain over the past decade. Citizenship and democratic renewal are ostensibly at the heart of the Labour government's agenda, where the engagement of citizens is seen to be essential to improving public services as well as fostering social inclusion and creating community cohesion (for example, Audit Commission, 2004a, 2004b; DH, 2006a, 2006b). The ageing population and older people have been the focus of national strategic and policy initiatives, including the *National Service Framework for Older People* (DH, 2001) and *Opportunity Age* (DWP, 2005b). A plethora of reports from government and official bodies have highlighted the imperative to engage with older people in the development of strategies and services (for example, ADSS/LGA, 2003; Audit Commission, 2004a, 2004b). Moreover, national policy focused on public issues such as health, housing, social services and social inclusion, has increasingly directed attention towards the notion of user participation (predominantly at an individual level), and involvement in wider issues of policy and service development (see also Chapter Four). The Social Care Green Paper (DH, 2005a, p 27), for example, argues that a reorganisation of social care services would enable:

> ... people to have greater control over identifying the type of support or help they want, and more choice about and influence over the services on offer ... putting people at the centre of the assessment process and creating individual budgets that give them a greater freedom to select the type of care or support they want.

Freedom to secure individual support requirements through direct cash payments to an older person may be welcomed as a means of supporting active participation and maintaining individual rights to self-determination. Nevertheless, it remains the case that moves towards apparently more inclusive policies will inevitably exist alongside policies that are fundamentally residualist, underpinned by aims to distribute finite resources to those people deemed most in need and, increasingly, most 'at risk' (for example, Kemshall, 2002). Older people, particularly those people with complex needs, who require support services and have traditionally been excluded from participation, are especially vulnerable to the consequences of a competitive, resource impoverished welfare agenda where, traditionally, service responses for older people have been poorly developed.

Approaches to participation

Consumerist and democratic approaches to participation are underpinned by contrasting ideological positions and their value base, aspirations and practices are distinctly different. Consumerist approaches to participation are based on market principles (Beresford and Croft, 1993; Braye, 2000). Taken from this perspective, participation focuses on the individual 'consumer'. The level and type of participation or involvement is determined by pre-set managerial agendas defined by the most appropriate mechanisms for participation in order to enhance market competitiveness (Lupton et al, 1998). Participation in this vein may be characterised, for example, by inviting users to meetings or committees dominated by professional workers (and professional agendas) without access to training, support or resources or with no clear idea about goals and aspirations of participation.

Democratic approaches, by contrast, emphasise the importance of collective action and citizen rights. The goals of democratic participation focus on participants being able to influence and control participation agendas. Outcomes would seek to secure positive change in the lives of participants. By implication, democratic participation widens its remit beyond narrowly defined professional agendas (Braye, 2000). The importance of *process* is highlighted in the development of skills, experience and shared perspectives through collective action (Lupton et al, 1998, p 46) and the goal of empowerment.

Empowerment may be identified as an aspiration for participation across both consumerist and democratic orientations to participation. Despite its almost ubiquitous status as a professional aspiration 'for' users in many aspects of health and social care development, delivery and practice, what empowerment means is another contested and inevitably uncritically used term or concept (Bernard, 2000). Empowerment within a consumerist model is more likely to focus on the notion of an individual being 'empowered' through, for example, access to comprehensive information, choice from a range of options and exercise of choice and rights to redress (through, for example, complaints procedures). Consumerist approaches are unlikely to have any significant impact in altering established power relations or challenging oppression. Such approaches might appear to offer the potential for influence, but as Lupton et al (1998) argue:

By channelling interaction to a limited agenda, attention can be diverted from areas of potential conflict that those with power wish to avoid. Seen in this way, participatory mechanisms can serve as a means of social control by preventing challenges to the status quo. (p 48)

This notion of individual empowerment from a consumerist perspective has been criticised by user groups who argue that such an approach is, at best, enabling and, at worst, another form of professional paternalism (Jack, 1995). Moreover, user groups have accused professionals in their wholesale adoption of the term 'empowerment', of colonising theoretical ideas developed through the hard-won battles of the user movement (for example, Morris, 1993).

Empowerment from a democratic perspective emphasises personal opportunities for capacity and confidence building, skills development and training, and opportunities for direct action and collective political activity, thus seeking to alter traditional power arrangements (Lupton et al, 1998). Taken from this perspective:"Empowerment happens not just because powerful people give away power, but because oppressed people engage in wresting it from them, speaking out against abuse and oppression, and for change in systems, demanding a radical rather than a liberal or functionalist form of partnership" (Braye and Preston-Shoot, 1995, p 100). Clearly, the ideological positions and practices underpinning consumerist and democratic approaches to participation in policy and service development map onto, and resonate with, research practices and notions of participation.

Participation of older people in research

Traditional knowledge hierarchies and assumptions about whose knowledge is valued above others are underpinned by deeply ingrained assumptions about the nature of knowledge, hierarchies of different types of knowledge, and established power imbalances between the professional research community and the 'researched'. Approaches to research within traditional frames of reference inevitably preserve and reinforce those power arrangements. Participatory approaches that seek to involve older people fully in the whole research process have the potential to unsettle fundamentally and alter traditional assumptions about what constitutes good research: to shape the research agenda, shift established power imbalances and contribute directly to positive action. Should gerontological research be informed by a moral imperative to direct action as part of the research? How would such changes impact on, or influence the hegemony of, mainstream research?

Historical perspectives on participation in gerontological research

Historically, the visibility of older people in research has been confined to their role as research 'subjects' in the collection of data. Traditional approaches to research reinforce the asymmetry of power relations between researchers and researched and the invisibility of older people in terms of their lived experience, individual biographies and diversity (see also Chapters Two and Five). Research has directed its attention towards the 'problem' and burden of ageing with an emphasis towards biomedical perspectives in ageing. Estes et al (2003, p 100) argue that: "A focus on bodily dysfunction and individualized relations has contributed to a reliance on medical hierarchy and power relations as givens, with a tendency to place professional helpers in active and older people in passive roles". Theoretical developments in early gerontological research arose from a (predominantly descriptive) problem-orientated perspective, and were motivated by a desire to offer insights into the management of the difficulties and challenges considered as inevitable in the experience of ageing. Theoretical advancement rested on a problem perspective and reinforced assumptions about individual dysfunction. Disengagement theory (Cumming and Henry, 1961) highlighted the natural propensity of older people to socially disengage, but, as Baars et al (2006, p 3) argue, this analysis "... ignores the fact that their study population lived under a social regime in which age-graded retirement was a social institution.... Because it deflects attention away from the importance of social and political forces, naturalization can serve as a form of legitimation of a social order".

Feminist researchers sharply criticised systematic scientific investigation with its emphasis on methodological rules and the institutionalisation of expertise and what is defined as valued and valuable knowledge (Ramazanoglu with Holland, 2002). Developments towards a feminist standpoint research sought to challenge traditional assumptions and develop a methodology that consciously examined and made explicit power relations and the exercise of power in the research process (see Chapter Two). Feminist method has focused to varying degrees on the notion of collaboration in research to ensure voice and visibility of women marginalised and rendered invisible by traditional research paradigms (for example, Reinharz, 1992). Browne (1998, p xxxv) writes of a new epistemology on women and age that seeks to make visible the multiple causes of oppression throughout the life course and that critiques and seeks to address the lack of research on older women. Redressing the balance in research on older women includes developing research methodologies that value the importance of women's voices and lives.

The development of a critical gerontological perspective is underpinned – in theory at least – by a value base that appears to bode well for democratic approaches to participation and inclusive research practices. The moral economy perspective (Minkler and Cole, 1999) has, at its root, a commitment to improving quality of life for older people; such a notion would imply social action as a critical component of the perspective. Values that espouse the importance of diversity, commitment to surfacing older people's perspectives and lived experiences, together with conscious and critical exploration of social and structural location in respect of ageing, suggest the *potential* for a fundamental shift in traditional perspectives on the place of older people in research (see also Chapters Two and Five).

What we know

Traditional approaches exemplify the central role of the professional researcher throughout the research process and have dominated mainstream or academic research. In this frame of reference, relatively few people have possession of expert research skills and knowledge. 'Insider–Outsider' boundaries are maintained by possession of specialist and technical language and jargon, access to specialist networks and resources and insider 'know-how' from which older citizens are likely to be substantially excluded. It continues to be relatively rare for older people to be in at the 'ground floor' in shaping research agendas or participating in devising research projects (Hanley, 2005), and to have accessed the resources needed to develop required skills. The Older People's Steering Group (2004) highlighted the often considerable separation that exists between a research (or policy) agenda relevant to the priorities and concerns of older people and the concerns, interests and activities of researchers and policy makers about older people and services for older people.

Older people could potentially influence research agendas and the manner in which projects seek to develop participation, by a variety of means. This might include, for example, membership of research development groups, advisory boards and research proposal steering groups (see also Chapter Eight). Participating in peer review of proposals is another means of influencing the research agenda. Nevertheless, the Toronto Group review (Hanley, 2005) suggests that, at present:

> ... users can feel isolated, or feel they are the token user on a committee. There is little training to take part, and this can lead to users feeling exposed or unskilled for the task at hand. Users often feel they are only expected to comment on 'user involvement' in the proposal and not on the overall aims and purpose of the work. (p 4)

Lack of resource to enhance and consolidate existing skills to participate in research, as well as learn new skills, appear as a consistent theme in the critical literature around participation.

Traditional approaches to participation by older people in fieldwork have been confined to 'shallow' involvement (Kemshall and Littlechild, 2000). In other words, participants are relied on for the collection of data and their involvement ceases on completion of the fieldwork interview. Methodological discussions have directed attention to the issue of power and researcher control:"... shorter, more formal interviews may grant more power to the interviewer, in relationship to the informant, because there is a greater degree of rigidity and control, a more pressing agenda and less chance for the informant to emerge and take charge" (Rubinstein, 2002c, p 139). This sort of participation is generally located at the lowest end of the participation continuum. Older people may feel that they have been involved inasmuch as their views, opinions or lived experience have been sought. But the impact of such involvement is questionable when there is little or no opportunity for participants to have any real influence on the ways in which narratives, interviews or questionnaire responses are treated and ultimately used.

However, many older people have been effectively prevented from participating in research, even at a peripheral level, because of assumptions about the ability of older people to engage 'meaningfully' in participation. Traditional cultures of dementia care, for example, have been dominated by powerful assumptions that people with dementia have inevitably lost the capacity to participate, including communicating their experiences of having dementia or their experience of getting and receiving formal support services. In the past decade, pioneering qualitative research (for example, Keady et al, 1995) with people with dementia both challenged assumptions about capacity to participate and provided the opportunity for participants to tell of their experiences first hand. Research has gone on to find meaningful and creative ways of enabling people with dementia to evaluate and reflect on their experiences of formal services (Allan, 2001). Making visible the lives of older people in this way may be a vital step in the process of developing participation, and is distinctly different from keeping participants at the lower end of the participation ladder because of professional research assumptions about the place of participants. Butt and O'Neill (2004), for example, make clear that older people from minority ethnic groups feel they have been 'researched to death' and that researchers persist in asking questions that either did not reflect the lives of older participants or addressed questions to which answers were already known. Crucially, participants felt that there had been little discernible impact by research on experiences of poor provision, access and the experience of institutional racism.

Dangers of participation

Older people who have given considerable energies to research may feel worn out or disenchanted by the apparent lack of impact or change despite their best efforts: "All the talking has been done and people have lost their voices and don't give an opinion anymore. There is consultation fatigue – if they were not listening the first, second, third time – what's going to happen now?" (Dunning, 2004, p 24)

A developing role for older people in research participation is as researchers. Clearly, there is the potential here for older people to influence and actively participate in research roles that have traditionally remained the preserve of the academic community. But of course, asking older people to, for example, participate in fieldwork as research interviewers does not of itself guarantee any fundamental changes in power structures between academic researchers and other participants. Without attention to the assumptions that underpin the nature of partnership working, academic researchers can still colonise user participants and decide what they do and do not participate in: "I did the training and undertook the [research] interviews and it was great; really good. But afterwards there was no further contact and I didn't know what the outcome of the research was or whether anything had changed because of it." (FACT[1] member, Staffordshire, 2005).

The level of commitment and activity involved in traditionally accepted approaches to fieldwork may create particular demands for some older women and men. Opie (1999), for example, highlighted that in her own research, many of the participants were ill, exhausted and used their personal resources for other activities. She asks: "is it legitimate to expect others to make that which is central to one's own working life a dominant part of theirs?" (Opie, 1999, p 203).

Research dilemmas in power imbalances and interpersonal dynamics between the 'researcher' and the 'researched', are not inevitably altered in a positive direction by simply putting older people into the research process. Is it more likely, at least at present, that older people who are able to participate in training to develop research projects, learn new skills and undertake research interviews within *traditional* approaches to fieldwork, are more likely to have access to more resources than other older people, be in good health and feel they have space from other responsibilities? This may create a potential tension between the 'successfully ageing' older researcher and the research participant if that person requires personal assistance and support. Clearly, given the diversity of ageing, it is erroneous to assume a shared perspective. Moreover, such assumptions carry the risk of essentialism. Cohort differences are likely to have significant impacts on attitudes, perceptions and the experience of ageing. Ageing is a cross-cutting feature in the social and structural location of people, but the experience of lifelong physical disability, sexual identity or experiences of racism may be more pertinent to an individual's identity and lived experience. Empathy, warmth, the ability to engage underpinned by relevant communication and interpersonal skills, as with any other researcher–researched relationship, cannot be assumed. There are too many issues concerning the ways in which older people, not conversant with traditional research methods, can achieve the necessary skills to compete with mainstream research institutions.

The participation of older people in the analysis and presentation of data, beyond participation in fieldwork, remains substantially undeveloped in both qualitative and quantitative research. Professional researchers continue to make decisions about how best to present data, what data to present and what to leave out. Exclusive analytic strategies are informed by attitudes underpinned by notions of the researcher as expert. Unilateral decisions about how to present analysis are often made, at least in part to fit the requirements of the funding body, to address the academic community, and to deal pragmatically with research output requirements. Nevertheless, practice in analysis may be rooted in a conscious and ethically grounded commitment to try to ensure that the voice of older people is presented in a way that gives the best visibility, tells a relevant story or powerfully highlights ways in which older people may be disadvantaged.

If analysis is to engage successfully with powerful institutions, including the academic community, specific skills and abilities are required to address those requirements. Attempts to facilitate participation in analysis have included offering older people the opportunity to check their interview transcripts and perhaps to participate in a discussion about analysis or its outcomes. Researchers may feel anxious that such a step would lead to older people seeking to challenge and change the analysis or research findings of researchers. It leads to difficult questions about who has the most appropriate or pressing mandate to tell the story or present the case; who is the expert and whose voice is the most powerful and carries the most weight? This may mean that this sort of participation (especially when it exists in isolation from participation in other aspects of the research process) is rather than a genuine attempt at participation, effectively a rubber-stamping activity, where a project can confirm that participation happened in this part of the research process:

> ... as is increasingly common scholarly practice, many researchers are returning to their informants for verification of conclusions and to provide feedback on study findings. This type of closure helps to satisfy not only the intellectual curiosity of the participant but also reassures the participant he or she assisted in the creation of knowledge. (Schoenberg, 2002, p 134)

Literature has consistently cited the potential for research effort to focus on data collection, analysis and publication in peer-reviewed journals at the expense of time for fuller or more considered dissemination approaches. Findings from research (for example, Hughes et al, 2000; Hanley, 2005) examining the integration of dissemination activities into the research process and action resulting from research concludes:

• Dissemination activities are usually subsumed within the overall research budget rather than having a specific allocation (time and financial resource).
• Researchers were often moving onto the next project before completing developmental work.
• There is usually little expectation or resource for long-term involvement.

Clough and colleagues (2006) have argued that failure to involve service users throughout the whole research process would ultimately impede dissemination. The key issue that is often overlooked in the research process in general, and dissemination in particular, is the extent to which older participants, who have given of their time and resource, can feel aggrieved or disappointed by the lack of tangible outcome from a research project. Professional researchers may be rather more inured to the fact that making the case for change through research, no matter how compelling or well conducted, does not necessarily fulfil its promise for change. Researchers may not expect change to be an outcome of their research and are likely to be very well aware of the extraneous variables that affect the ways in which research is perceived and received. Moreover, research communities may feel that their research, while not immediately changing policy or practice, contributes to the pressure for change or improvements. But people who are less frequently involved may have high expectations and feel very disappointed by its failure to deliver. Alongside the need to argue for resources dedicated to dissemination, there is an implication in respect of the way we – as researchers – talk about the possible outcomes of research and what older people and their participation may or may not achieve. Crucially too, there is a need to consider the extent to which mainstream research currently includes goals for change and action specifically aimed at improving the lives of people on whom the research focuses.

Developing participation in research?

Research grant-awarding bodies increasingly articulate a requirement that proposals include some form of user participation strategy. Evidencing a transparent discussion about the nature of participation relevant to the purpose and aspirations of each research proposal seems a more appropriate and fruitful path than assuming a standard level of participation, particularly if it errs towards a superficial accounting of the participation process. Increasingly, discussions about participation highlight the importance of developing principles or standards around participation (for example, Older People's Steering Group, 2004; Hanley, 2005). Such a move would seem to require a considered assessment of the current state of participation in research, the need to surface examples of good practice and work with older people, funding bodies and research communities in the development of standards.

Mainstream researchers and their research communities also need to consider their own attitudes, perceptions and understandings of participation. To what extent, for example, is participation on the agenda for discussion, research training and activity? How visible are different opinions and attitudes towards participation? Beresford (2003) has argued that these questions are critically important if superficiality is to be avoided, where an ill-conceived nod in the direction of participation might suffice to secure funds. Increasingly, awarding bodies encourage interdisciplinary research proposals that may contribute to reflecting the diversity of perspectives on ageing. Nevertheless, researchers grounded in different disciplines, research traditions and methods are likely to have divergent or diverse views about the role of participation in research, or even whether participation is an idea worthy of consideration. Time taken to explore these differences across disciplines proposing to work together and considering participatory research is vital. How does or should an interdisciplinary research project combining the biomedical and social sciences, for example, seek to resolve potentially divergent perspectives on the role of participants?

The importance of developing participation at all stages of the research process is highlighted by older people involved in research or in evaluating research (for example, Butt and O'Neill, 2004; Older People's Steering Group, 2004; Clough et al, 2006). To what extent do traditional research establishments seek to develop ongoing relationships with local communities in which older citizens keen to participate in the full range of research may be located? Clough et al (2006) observe that involving older people in research is a valuable part of universities' involvement with local communities. These developments might facilitate an exchange of ideas and interests of concern to older community members and researchers. They may build relationships that develop over time for their own sake rather than artificially created for the duration of fieldwork or a research grant. Clough and his colleagues (2006, p 61) comment that: "Universities are the core repositories of research expertise. In their role of widening participation and encouraging life long learning they could play a major part in both training in research methods and support in research activities". Such sharing of expertise could enable older men and women to, for example, develop capacity, confidence and skill to participate actively in research, develop partnerships in research projects, commission professional researchers to undertake user-defined research, or to seek advice on securing funding to undertake their own user-led research. Godfrey et al (2004) highlighted the ways in which support for new older research participants and the insights older people brought to their particular research project enhanced the reciprocal nature of the relationship. The evolutionary process of ongoing learning and development was a key contributor in sustaining relationships over the course of the project.

Participation should, I think, also include sharing what we (as researchers-practitioners) know. Older people are inevitably disadvantaged if they do not have access to information about gerontological research and the state of the current knowledge base. Academic communities are familiar with the rules of communicating with each other, policy makers and formal organisations, but may be less familiar with engaging with, and sharing research information with, older people and wider communities. Older citizens who attended the annual conference of the British Society of Gerontology in 2005 were amazed by what they perceived as an overwhelming and unanticipated level of research interest about older people. Ways to communicate about research and its outcomes and findings to a wider audience may contribute to older people feeling better informed and more involved in a community they have traditionally been excluded from.

Carter and Beresford (2000) highlight the time and resources required to build capacity and to provide resources for ongoing training and support. Research with older people about their experience of home care services (Raynes et al,

2001) highlighted the importance of the time needed for researchers, planners and operational staff to actively listen to the experiences and views of older service users. Moreover, making user-led changes to the service required considerable commitment from all participants. This is an issue for many older citizens unfamiliar with research or who may have particular requirements that must be taken account of (for example, hearing impairment, chronic pain or family commitments). But it is a critical issue for older people considered to be 'hard to engage' or impossible to include by virtue of their complex support requirements. Lupton et al (1998) argue that socially marginal communities that may be most likely to attract empowering projects, are precisely those where members' resources are extremely limited. The intricacies of participation with people with complex needs may lead to developing relationships with older people who are more visible or perceived as 'easier' to engage with. These approaches run the risk of further obscuring people traditionally excluded from participation in mainstream research by virtue of the complexity of their requirements and the resources associated with it. Older people from black and minority ethnic groups have commented on how essentially they remain excluded from participation that moves beyond providing information to actively participating in developing ideas into practice (Butt and O'Neill, 2004). Older people with communication difficulties have also been significantly excluded from expressing views and opinions in interviews about their lived experiences (for example, Allan, 2001). Clearly, additional thought, preparation, time and money are needed to invest in participation of older people with complex needs (Steel, 2003). It is imperative that we are able to learn from good practice in developing resources, skills and translating values of inclusive practice into reality (for example, Allan, 2001; Murphy et al, 2005).

The rhetoric of policies and services for older service users consistently highlights the importance of individual and person-centred assessment, planning and intervention. One size does not (or should not) fit all. A similar message seems relevant to the discussion and practices around participation and research. Approaches should reflect the diversity of older people, their aspirations and commitments to participation. There is no single type of involvement and, clearly, not all older people want to engage in the whole range of research activities and processes (for example, Clough et al, 2006). Chambers (2005) reflected in her research on older widows that participants were not seeking to be empowered through participation in research. The research/er came to them and they wanted to contribute their narrative accounts of widowhood in older age. What is crucial is that participants can make choices about the ways in which they may participate, and feel that their involvement has the potential to make a difference. Moreover, it seems imperative that research establishments are transparent about the ways in which they might seek to develop more participatory approaches to research.

Older people have given much of themselves in contributing to the knowledge base derived from research. It is true to say that there are significant areas in gerontological research where the evidence base is now well rehearsed, but nevertheless has had little actual impact on the lived experience of older women and men. This applies, for example, to the significant occupational poverty of people with dementia, especially those people with complex needs in collective care settings (for example, Perrin and May, 2000), the challenge of providing appropriate support to people with dementia in acute settings (for example, Archibald, 2003), and the potential for admission to a care home because there are no appropriate community facilities (for example, Handcock et al, 2006). Rather than trying to conduct more research that confirms what we already know in these areas, it seems more fruitful to engage in democratic approaches that seek to impact positively on the lives of the older people that this research concerns. Active involvement of older people with direct and personal experience would contribute to a more compelling discourse about what are or are not acceptable standards for older people. The participation of older people geared towards more emancipatory approaches requires us to question whether research is done at all, what issues are explored, which research designs are adopted, and what actions are taken following the research.

Implications

The complexities of participation in mainstream research highlight the importance of uncovering and debating these issues more fully. The experiences of older people who have participated in research suggest participation must reflect diversity to accommodate to the interests, aspirations and commitments of individual people. This must include older men and women having better opportunities to lead on research, commission research and to participate in the full range of research activity.

Participation strategies employed in individual research projects will reflect a similar diversity and be influenced by a range of factors. Decisions about the ways in which participation was incorporated (or not) into a project should be transparent. Moreover, participation in research should be accompanied by a commitment to evaluating the experience and outcomes of participation and sharing lessons learned. Building participation into the infrastructure of a research organisation would seem to offer at least the potential to ensure that issues around participation are visible. If relationships with older people as partners in the research agenda are part of the picture, this offers the potential to make more democratic decisions as to what is researched, why it is researched and the ways that participation may be a part of that research. The Social Care Institute for Excellence (SCIE) includes user participation as a key component in its infrastructure. In a recent systematic review of qualitative research on hospital discharge for older people (SCIE, 2006), the report made clear their rationale for user participation and acknowledge:

> ... the process of systematic reviews includes some highly technical
> tasks ... And it is questionable whether users and carers would see
> this as the first call on their time as a way of influencing services ...
> the question may be more how to generate proper accountability to
> users and carers as stakeholders, than to ensure that the time of users
> and carers is spent in the technical processes of the review. (SCIE,
> 2006, p 7)

An advisory group comprising older people who had direct and recent experience
of hospital discharge was formed to highlight critical issues borne from their
direct experiences. These insights had a direct impact on the way researchers
undertook searches, informed decisions about outcomes and provided
opportunities to debate and discuss key findings and categories with the group.

Incorporating the issue of participation into the infrastructure of a research
organisation would have major implications for the organisation and its researchers.
This would include seeking to develop relationships with local communities
that were ongoing rather than relationships that were defined by the duration of
a research project. This would clearly have major resource implications as well as
be difficult to achieve in a climate in which the need to secure funds for new
research projects in order to maintain research status and keep short-term
researchers in employment might appear more pressing.

Grant-awarding bodies have a significant role in shaping participation. Awarding
bodies should make visible the ways they have worked in partnership with older
men and women to develop research themes and research topics. Funders can
ensure that applicants clarify their participation strategies and the rationale for
them as well as developing standards in their own practices (for example, Older
People's Steering Group, 2004). If participation is to be developed appropriately,
it is essential that funding acknowledges factors such as the:

• resource implications of participation; this includes finance, time, expertise
  and access issues (for example, Carter and Beresford, 2000);
• importance of evaluating participation strategies as well as the outcome of the
  research;
• implications of proper dissemination strategies;
• increased attention to the importance of action-based research; and
• role of user-led or user-commissioned research.

How, on the one hand, the complex agenda for participation is achieved when,
on the other, the pushes and pulls of traditional research appear to mitigate
against genuine participation, remains open to question.

Conclusion

We cannot take for granted that participation in research is inevitably a positive development for service users (Beresford, 2003). Any plans for participation might include the question 'Who stands to benefit?'. If older participants' involvement is a means to achieving a research objective, then we must be cautious in our assumptions that participation is a good thing (for the participant). Mainstream research cannot simply adopt the notion of participation without consideration and exploration of fundamental questions. Failure to do so will run the risk of older people feeling colonised or perpetuating the lived experience of a lack of real involvement, influence and power. Alternatively, there is a risk that participation with some people or some types of participation become the norm. Older people who are traditionally excluded from participation may remain so. Ultimately, research will suffer the consequences if it persists in colonising older people or perpetuating constructions of older people as biomedical time bombs, passive recipients or apolitical beings. The requirements placed on mainstream researchers may mean that emancipatory research in traditional research settings is an unlikely outcome. At present we do not know what is or is not, may or may not be possible. There is a need to learn from the experience of others and to evaluate the current state of play in participation.

Note

[1] The Fifty and Counting Team (FACT) is part of Age Concern, Stoke-on-Trent. Its aim is to participate and consult on a wide range of community issues. The membership is made up of retired citizens from diverse backgrounds who live in local communities.

SEVEN

Revisiting *The Last Refuge*: present-day methodological challenges[1]

Julia Johnson, Sheena Rolph and Randall Smith

Introduction

When Peter Townsend "had to leave his university rooms on his retirement" (Thompson, 1998, p 173), data from his lifetime's work were deposited in the National Social Policy and Social Change Archive at the University of Essex. As Paul Thompson has commented, this is "very likely the most in-depth documentation that will ever be collected of the conditions and experience of old age and poverty in Britain" (Corti and Thompson, 2004, p 338). Our research is reusing the archived data from *The Last Refuge* that was first published in 1962 (Townsend, 1962), and this chapter focuses on some of the methodological challenges that revisiting a study, which was carried out in the late 1950s, involves. Before discussing these challenges, however, we briefly introduce *The Last Refuge* and why we are revisiting it.

The Last Refuge reported a study of residential care provided under the 1948 National Assistance Act in England and Wales. More than 40 years later, it continues to leave its mark, both positive and negative, on the provision of care for older people. Townsend's fundamental research question was: "Are long-stay institutions for old people necessary in our society and, if so, what form should they take?" (1962, p 3). With its focus on institutions, *The Last Refuge* complemented his earlier community-based study, *The Family Life of Old People* (Townsend, 1957), and it had a major impact on how he subsequently theorised the position of older people in Britain (Townsend, 1981a; see also Chapter Three).

The research for *The Last Refuge* was conducted in 1958-59. Townsend carried out a national survey of residential care provision in all the 146 local authorities in England and Wales. He was surprised to find that, despite the promises of the welfare state, a substantial proportion of older people were still being accommodated in homes that, between 1930 and 1948, had been known as Public Assistance Institutions[2] (PAIs) (Townsend and Thompson, 2004; see also Chapter Four). The fieldwork included visits to a stratified random sample of 173 local authority (publicly owned), voluntary and private residential care homes.

Although a majority of the homes visited were judged to be of poor quality, the research uncovered gross inequalities in provision for people with the same needs.

Townsend also found that people were in residential care as much for social as for physical reasons. He concluded that residential care as an instrument of social policy for older people should be abandoned. Those who were seriously incapacitated, he argued, should be in hospital or small publicly owned nursing homes. All others could live in private households provided their housing was appropriate. These conclusions generated widespread interest in the development of sheltered housing in the 1970s and 1980s (Butler et al, 1983). However, residential care for older people has continued to be a major plank of provision and expenditure in the UK.

Revisiting *The Last Refuge*

The aim of our study is to find out what has happened to the 173 homes Townsend visited. In particular we want to find out how many of them have survived as care homes, how they have managed to survive and what they are like now in comparison with what they were like in the late 1950s. We also want to find out what has become of the homes that did not survive, when (and if possible why) they ceased to function as care homes. By focusing on a particular cohort of homes, we are examining care policy for older people through a different lens, one that might open up new insights into the history of residential care for older people. As Charlotte Davies has observed: "The principal strengths of longitudinal studies of all sorts lie in their greater sensitivity to change, the increased likelihood of being able to distinguish fluctuations from fundamental changes, and the greater depth of ethnographic understanding achieved from the multiple perspectives that such research facilitates" (Davies, 1999, p 175). In addition, we hoped to contribute to the development of methodologies relating to the use of archived qualitative data, a topic that has been attracting growing attention among sociologists in the past few years (Heaton, 2004).

Townsend's sample of 173 homes[3] was stratified as follows:

- 39 former PAIs;
- 53 other local authority homes;
- 39 voluntary homes; and
- 42 private homes.

The archive at the University of Essex contains a substantial amount of qualitative data on these homes that includes home reports, some completed interview schedules, diaries and photographs. It also includes reports of interviews with 65 chief or deputy chief welfare officers[4]. These data, we decided, in conjunction with the data contained in the appendices to *The Last Refuge*, would enable us to conduct an over time comparison, one of six approaches suggested by Corti and Thompson (2004) to reusing such data.

Through the archived material, we managed to assemble a complete list of the 173 homes and, as far as possible, their locations. Very few included addresses but we were able to put together enough information from Townsend's original list together with the home reports. Our preliminary research identified 20 of these homes as currently registered care homes (what we call the surviving homes). It seemed likely that the remaining homes would no longer to be registered as care homes (the non-surviving homes).

On the basis of this, we designed (and obtained funding to carry out) two discrete but related longitudinal fieldwork studies:

- a tracing study of the non-surviving homes
- a follow-up study of 20 surviving homes.

Tracing study

In order to trace the history, over the period 1959-2005, of the non-surviving homes, we have engaged older people across England and Wales as local volunteer research investigators. Through their local knowledge, local contacts and local archives, they are investigating when and why the homes ceased to be residential homes and (if applicable) the current purposes of the buildings on the same site. An added dimension to the project, therefore, is engaging with older people as research collaborators, another area of growing interest to gerontological researchers (Peace, 1999, 2002; see also Chapters Five, Six and Eight).

At the time of writing (in 2006) approximately 65 volunteers have already been recruited, mainly through the University of the Third Age (U3A) but also through local history associations, the Older People Researching Social Issues (OPRSI) consortium[5] and the British Association of Social Workers' retired members group. Many of them used to work in health or social care. Some remember the homes in question or know others who worked or lived in them. For example, a local historian has memories of one of the homes that was near to where she had lived as a child and that her mother used to visit. She herself used to pass by the home every day:

> It was off Foxhouses Road at the junction with front Corkickle. There was a pillar box and a seat at the junction of the roads where people from the home used to sit in the sun. As a little girl passing by I would stop to say 'hello' as we had all been brought up to do. I think it was a very happy home. (quoted in Rolph, 2005, pp 3-4)

Each volunteer has been provided with an information pack that includes details (from the archive) of specific homes, guidance on how to search out relevant information, and a standard form for completing their report. Standard data relating to dates, building works, demolition, changes of name, use and/or ownership and changes of residency will be abstracted from these reports. A year-by-year analysis should reveal a changing pattern of attrition that we can relate to changes in social and public policy.

We are also interested in finding out what kinds of usage surviving buildings have been put to and what changes in ownership have occurred. Have new buildings containing new services replaced the old ones, such as sheltered or extra-care housing? Reports coming in are revealing a variety of outcomes. For example, one of the homes is now a museum, another is a hotel, one is a doctor's surgery, another a veterinary practice. One is now a day centre for older people and others provide respite care. In addition, through the tracing study, a further 13 surviving homes have been identified and added to the original 20.

When the tracing study investigations have been completed, a random, stratified sample of the non-surviving homes will be drawn, matched for size and tenure (as in 1959) with the surviving homes. This will enable us to draw some conclusions relating to how and why different kinds of homes have adapted to changes in policy and practice. It will reveal different ways that homes survive and successful and non-successful aspects of residential care provision.

Follow-up study

This is a longitudinal study of the surviving homes, what Wadsworth refers to as an "accelerated prospective" study (2002, p 104). Our purpose is to compare these homes then with now. For this reason, we intend to replicate Townsend's method, but with some modification in order to accommodate not only historical and cultural changes in policy and practice but also changes in methods of social inquiry. We expand on this later in the chapter.

As mentioned earlier, the archive includes the original reports on these homes. Those that agree to participate will be visited and the same procedure as that adopted by Peter Townsend in 1959 will be followed:

- available demographic data on staff and residents will be collected prior to the visit;
- the manager or deputy manager of the home will be interviewed (and audio recorded) about how the home is managed and run;
- a tour of the home will be made and facilities and equipment noted;
- supplementary information, such as brochures, copies of menus etc will be collected;
- four residents admitted within the previous six to twelve months, subject to consent, will be interviewed;
- staff and residents will be asked if they are willing to keep a diary for a minimum period of one week;
- a report will be written on each home, replicating the format of Townsend's home reports; and
- photographs will be taken of the exterior buildings and, with consent, of interiors, staff and residents.

All this will generate detailed comparative data relating to the built environment, staffing and routines, the characteristics of residents and reasons for admission, and their daily lives. Overall the comparative analysis will explore not only continuity and change in the care regimes, in the quality of care provision, and in the conduct of social research, but also in cultural constructions of, and responses to, old age.

Some methodological challenges

Of course this design raises a host of interesting methodological challenges. As Bell (1977) pointed out 30 years ago when reflecting on the Banbury re-study[6], in undertaking a re-study it is important to understand the context within which the original study was designed and undertaken and how that context has changed in the intervening years.

It is easy to underestimate the extent to which the demographic, sociocultural, technological, policy and academic contexts have changed in Britain over the course of the past 50 years. It would be inappropriate in the space available for us to attempt to summarise these changes. Rather, we want to focus on some specific challenges these changes have created for us in designing and implementing the follow-up study. How do we accommodate change?

First, and perhaps most fundamentally, are the objects of our research: the 173 homes. A key challenge, one that is central to the whole research design, is deciding what constitutes survival as opposed to non-survival. In other words, which homes should be included in the follow-up study?

Objects of study: then and now

This may seem at first sight to be a simple matter. Our initial criterion for including homes in the frame for the follow-up study was that the home was currently registered as a care home for older people with the Commission for Social Care Inspection (CSCI) or the Care Standards Inspectorate for Wales (CSIW). This seemingly straightforward criterion proved almost immediately to be problematic. Some of the homes that were still registered were, for example, providing respite or short-term care only. It would not be possible to replicate Townsend's method in such homes because it assumes a relatively stable resident population. Another problem was that several of those still registered were due for closure in the very near future. To conduct the research in these homes was not appropriate because it might cause unnecessary distress to people facing change. Consequently, two further criteria were added to our initial one:

- the home provides long-term accommodation and care for older people;
- the home is not to our knowledge, or that of the provider, due to be closed in the near future.

These basic criteria, however, did not resolve the issue of what constitutes a 'home' in the context of our follow-up study. Care homes are a mixture of people and bricks and mortar that together form an identifiable entity. The question is: are the homes we plan to visit today the same ones that Townsend visited in 1958 and 1959? Of course all have changed over the past 50 years. But what kinds of changes are compatible with the notion of survival? For example, should we include the former PAI that has been demolished and replaced by a home, carrying the same or sometimes a new name, on the same site? Should we include the home that not only moved into a new building (taking its name, the staff and the residents with it) but also moved to a new location some 25 miles away? And what of the homes that were publicly owned and run by local authorities that now belong to an 'independent not-for-profit company' or a large private for-profit one?

We were faced with the question of whether to include or exclude for all these examples. We resolved that all are examples of the continuities and changes that we are exploring. Indeed, it is through these kinds of adaptations that homes have managed to survive. Nevertheless, we also decided that the notion of a 'discrete identity' should be retained and not lost. For example, one former local authority home was demolished and the site sold for private development. The residents of the home were moved across the road to its 'sister' home which, in advance, the same authority had substantially extended and refurbished. We decided that this home was a non-survivor. It had, we argued, lost its 'discrete identity' when its population was subsumed into that of its sister home that was contained in another building, with a different name, on another site: a home with a pre-existing identity of its own.

So we decided that, in addition to our basic criteria, for a home to be considered a survivor, at least one of the following factors should have remained the same: the building, the site or the name. Of the 33 homes currently in the frame, 27 are in the same building, 31 on the same site and 26 have retained their original name. Whether these factors will prove to be sufficient determinants of survival remains to be seen.

Having established what our basic study population is, the next set of methodological challenges relate to our methods of investigation. How do we accommodate change in the design of our research instruments?

Research instruments: then and now

Our aim is not to replicate Townsend's study. That could be done with a new sample of residential care homes, addressing the same 'grand' question that Townsend did. What we are doing is following up his original sample, thereby creating a longitudinal study, so that we can compare then and now. In order to do this, it is important that we generate comparable data and we are using Townsend's research instruments and procedures as our starting point.

We have followed the lead of Charlotte Davies and Nickie Charles who recently revisited the community study of Swansea conducted by Colin Rosser and Chris Harris in the early 1960s (Rosser and Harris, 1965): "the research design is replicated where meaningful and altered after careful consideration of social analytical changes where necessary" (Davies and Charles, 2002, p 13). Such an approach, they suggest, is likely to "increase our understanding of both the original object of study and the sociological account of it, as well as the contemporary object of the re-study and the intervening processes by which one was transformed into the other" (Davies and Charles, 2002, p 13). Our study draws on the research instruments used by Townsend but modified, where necessary, in the same reflexive manner as that proposed by Davies and Charles.

The main research instruments that Townsend used when he visited his sample of homes were:

- a census of all residents at the time of the visit;
- a schedule for interviewing the 'warden' or 'matron';
- a schedule to be completed while touring the building;
- a schedule for interviewing 'new' residents; and
- instructions for completing a diary.

On the basis of the originals, we have designed schedules so as to cover the same topics as well as making an allowance for new issues to emerge. The amendments we have had to make in order to accommodate change to the existing content of Townsend's schedules are relatively minor. By way of example, in asking a resident about family contacts, we took into account reconstituted families and the increased use of telephones as a means of personal communication. A few items on the questionnaire have become inappropriate over time, for example a direct reference to 'basket-work' as a potential form of occupation. Should we find residents who still do basket-work, it can be specified under 'specialist hobby or pastime' or 'organised activities'. Similar amendments have been made to some items listed on the schedule to be completed while touring the home, such as the number of bedside mats in a dormitory. Townsend did not collect that many diaries but we have designed 'an informant diary' (Johnson and Bytheway, 2001) that can be used by residents or care staff to record daily life in the home.

Townsend used the information he collected to give each home a quality rating. His quality measure included 40 items that cover physical amenities, staffing, means of occupation, freedom of daily life and social provision (Townsend, 1962, pp 477-91). We intend to use this measure as it stands to compare the homes then and now. But we will also use a current quality measure such as that used by the CSCI to assess each home now (for example, Dalley et al, 2004). Using two different measures in this way will reveal changing standards over time.

At the time of writing we are piloting these research instruments in three follow-up study homes. It is helpful that we are able to explain to our participants that we are attempting to replicate what Peter Townsend did in 1958/59. He was a pioneer in researching residential care and the methods he devised have had a lasting impact on subsequent research. During the 1970s and 1980s, a great deal of work was done on developing ways of evaluating and measuring quality of life in care homes and of eliciting the views of those living in them (Hughes and Wilkin, 1980; Willcocks et al, 1987; Kellaher and Peace, 1993; Peace et al, 1997). The challenge for us at present is how to accommodate these important developments in social research into our design without jeopardising our original purpose. We will take heed of Harris et al's finding in their attempt to replicate that: "Valid comparison between the data collected at two time points could not be guaranteed by mechanically following the procedure adopted in the original study" (Harris et al, 2004, p 3).

Data: then and now

Townsend's interest in residential care was triggered by a visit he made to Southern Grove, a large PAI in London. He was shocked by what he found (Townsend and Thompson, 2004) and realised that the situation of older people living in institutions required investigation. He also realised, as mentioned earlier, that theorising old age purely on the basis of those living 'in the community' was insufficient. There is little doubt that Townsend was, and indeed as his own chapter in this collection demonstrates, still is, a social reformer and that in carrying out the research he did for *The Last Refuge* he was on a mission. In an interview for the Social Policy Association News, he reflects on the influence of his colleague at the London School of Economics and Political Science, Brian Abel Smith[7], on his work:

> Brian was very helpful in regard to my study of old people's homes. The project was very ambitious. It involved visiting 200 homes across the UK and living and working in some of these places. I was chewing over how we would handle the huge quantity of information. Brian in his usual gung-ho way said, "Come on Peter, what is your conclusion? What do you think you're going to say?". I said, "I suppose I'm trying to work with the idea of whether residential homes for old people are the right solution or not?". He said, "That's it. You've got to take a view. You think they shouldn't exist, don't you?". "Well, I don't know. It's for me to find out but maybe I should take that as a hypothesis".
>
> Having that single question in my head for all the interviews was like saying 'Let's test this single point to destruction'. This is what research should be about as I've learnt since in many different ways. To test to destruction some new contribution or new conclusion is far better than trying to assemble a huge range of information at the end of five years or three years in the hope than you can put together something new. (SPA News, 2002, p 5)

A close reading of *The Last Refuge* and of the research instruments used indicates that Townsend was intent on producing hard evidence that something needed to be done. He devised two research tools: one measuring the quality of homes (Townsend, 1962, Appendix 3) and the other the degree of 'incapacity' of residents (Townsend, 1962, Appendix 2). These measures ultimately produced evidence that (a) the majority of homes were of poor quality, and (b) a majority of the residents did not need to be cared for in an institution. However, it was his qualitative data that really brought the message home. In addition to his 'scientific evidence', Townsend also produced the most eloquent descriptions of 'being there' (Geertz, 1988) in the homes he visited. His prose is enormously evocative and persuasive. Much of the qualitative data reproduced in the book come from the reports that were written on each home, which are a summary of what was found out from the interviews with staff and residents and what was observed during the visit to the home. We will likewise produce reports on the homes we visit to set alongside the originals. But qualitative research has moved on, and replicating the reports is not without its problems.

Townsend's reports were produced in the positivist tradition prevalent at the time where the distinction between the 'known and the knower' (Lincoln and Guba, 1985) was retained and the method of inquiry was regarded as value free. Fifty years on, we are inclined to take a more reflexive approach, not only to the origins of the primary data, but also to the production of our own reports. In effect, in comparing our reports with the 1958/59 ones, we will need to adopt a form of documentary analysis that contextualises both sets of data. We will be comparing reports produced in the main by two young male sociologists (Townsend and his researcher conducted 80 per cent of the fieldwork) in the late 1950s with reports written by three 'mature' academics in the early years of the 21st century.

Those familiar with *The Last Refuge* will also know that the book included 38 photographs, most of which were taken by Townsend himself (and there are more in the archive that did not appear in the book). The photographs in the book, like the prose, are extremely powerful. Becker has identified the early 1960s as the site of a renewed belief by social scientists in the importance of visual material (Becker, 2004). By giving prominence to photographs in 1958/59, Townsend was, arguably, on the cusp of a new generation of sociologists interested in social reform who once again saw potential in visual material – the use of photographs 'in the interest of rhetorical persuasion' (Dowdall and Golden, 1989; Dimock, 1993).

As indicated earlier, we would like to replicate the photographic data. This of course raises the question as to whether Townsend regarded the photographs as data. And this in turn raises the question 'Why did he take photographs of the homes, and why did he include them in the book?'. In a recent conversation with us, he spoke of photographs as "a neglected source" and said he wished he had taken more. He emphasised their importance in "telling a different but complementary story, one that would make the text come alive" (British Society of Gerontology Conference, Keele University, 14 July 2005).

The photographs are placed together in the centre of the book. One might be tempted to regard them, therefore, as 'naturalistic' as opposed to 'non-naturalistic' data (produced and structured through the research process). The latter, however, appears to be the case. The photographs are carefully organised into four subject groups: exteriors; entrances; matrons and staff; and residents. They seem to have been selected to illustrate particular contrasts between one type of home and another. For example, in the group of photographs relating to matrons and staff, the staff of both the former workhouses and the local authority homes appear in uniform, including the male charge attendant, while the matron of a voluntary (Methodist) home wears a cardigan and pearls and appears to be warm and friendly towards the resident in the photograph, holding her hand and smiling. The resident is smiling too, also wears pearls and is obviously in her own room, with washbasin and bed. She is wearing a hearing aid. The message of this photograph appears to be that she is cared for in a good environment, with no hierarchies of dress or power in evidence. Interestingly, however, the majority are scenes from former PAIs and there are no photographs at all of the private homes.

Townsend did not refer to his photographs in the text of his book, except to say (in the introduction) that they were not 'necessarily' the homes he visited. Nor did he simply let them 'speak for themselves' – a disputed concept in any case (Jordanova, 2000). Instead they were not only accompanied by captions, but were also an accompaniment to the text, the one being intended to illuminate the other. His captions were not just informative, but also interpretive. Although brief and reticent, they were telling in their choice of words. For example: "Dining-hall in a former workhouse, with recess used as dormitory for 56 men"; "Day-room with no floor-covering in a former workhouse"; "Apathy in a day-room". This latter caption can be placed alongside the following description of life in one of the former workhouses:

> This ward seems to be cut off from the world, cut off almost from its nearby surroundings. Only 6 of the 40 men go out, though many more could.... A member of staff bound on some errand would provoke a slight ripple of interest, but this quickly subsided. Half the men seemed always to be asleep, some of the others were staring at the windows, and about four or five were reading newspapers. One was huddled over a newspaper with a small magnifying glass tucked in one eye writing figures in the margins – 'mental' I was told. A woman attendant went up to one man slumped with his head between his knees. "Lift yourself up, love, you'll fall and crack your head open". "A bloody good job if I do". (Townsend, 1962, p 105)

So, as Townsend intended, the photographs powerfully complement the text. Like him we also aim to reveal contrasts between types of homes. In addition, however, we wish to highlight historical change – the contrast between residential care in 1958/59 and in 2005/06 – as well as continuity. One issue for us, therefore, is the extent to which we use the composition of the photographs from *The Last Refuge* as a baseline.

A further issue is the extent to which we are able to replicate the kinds of photographs he took because of the ethical issues they raise. How, for example, would we negotiate taking a photograph of a group of residents in a lounge or dining room? Some might be asleep, others might not be aware of the implications of their agreement. We might also need the consent of a relative or advocate. And how would we preserve their anonymity if the photograph were to be published? Our consent forms, both for individual residents and for the home manager, include permissions relating to photographs. Using a digital camera, we are able to show the photographs we have taken to residents and the home manager and to delete any they are not happy with. But what if Townsend had been able or required to do this?

Ethical issues: then and now

In planning to revisit Townsend's homes and replicate what he did, we have had to grapple with a variety of issues relating to confidentiality and consent. Currently, there is ample guidance on these issues from many sources (for example, ESDS, nda; Social Research Association, 2003; DH, 2005d). We each have clearance from the Criminal Records Bureau[8] to undertake research involving older people living in care homes and our research procedures have been scrutinised and approved by the Human Participants and Material Ethics Committee at The Open University. Nearly 50 years ago, such matters were treated rather differently.

Townsend's research was funded by the Nuffield Foundation and was, therefore, independent of government. In talking with him he has pointed out how important this was and how useful in gaining the confidence and cooperation of the participating homes. He was able to offer assurances to the wardens and matrons he interviewed that nothing would go to 'the council', that his findings would be generalised and anonymised (British Society of Gerontology Conference, Keele University, 14 July 2005). It is perhaps important to realise that his research was the first major study ever conducted of residential care for older people in Britain and that academic researchers, particularly in the social sciences, were much more of a rarity than they are today. As such he carried considerable authority and many of the homes, particularly the local authority ones, had no choice but to cooperate. It is interesting, although perhaps unsurprising, that of the 180 homes he sampled, only seven were not visited and none of these were because they had refused (Townsend, 1962, p 9). Of the 173 visited, none of the 92 local authority homes were in a position to refuse; only four of the 39 voluntary homes and six of the 40 private homes refused to fully cooperate during the visit and in some cases access to residents was denied.

It is certainly not our intention to make judgements about the way in which issues relating to informed consent and confidentiality were dealt with in the late 1950s. The point is that the context in which Townsend's research was conducted was very different to today and this means that our actions are (quite rightly) constrained in a way that 50 years ago they might not have been. In many ways this simply means that we need more time to accomplish our research: to ensure that everyone in the home knows what we plan to do and why, that people have a choice about allowing us into their home and about being interviewed.

In regard to publications arising out of the research, Townsend anonymised the homes and the people in *The Last Refuge*. To make doubly sure about confidentiality in relation to the photographs, he wrote the following proviso: "The photographs included in this book ... do not necessarily indicate the institutions that were visited in the course of our research" (Townsend, 1962, p 16). However, in more recent years, there has been substantial debate about the issue of anonymity versus ownership (Gluck and Patai, 1991; Finnegan, 1992; Yow, 1994; Summerfield, 1998; Walmsley, 1998, Rolph, 2000). While there is a need to guarantee anonymity so that participants are able to entrust us with their views, there should also be the opportunity for people's contribution to be valued and acknowledged. We have designed our consent forms for both residents and managers so as to offer them the opportunity both for personal acknowledgement and acknowledgement of the home by name in any publications.

Apart from these fairly familiar ethical issues related to the conduct of our fieldwork, there are also ethical issues related to the use of archived data. There are two categories of archived data: first, Peter Townsend's dataset that is now contained in the National Social Policy and Social Change Archive at the University of Essex; and second, the data emerging from our own research that will be deposited in turn in the same archive at the end of the project. There are ethical issues associated with our use of both that concern the anonymisation of the data.

As already indicated, the data on *The Last Refuge* that are currently in the archive contain the names of homes visited, sometimes with their addresses, and also the names of the managers and owners who were interviewed. If this material had been anonymised, it would not have been possible for this present study to take place. David Jordan has noted with regard to longitudinal studies that "subsequent researchers should have access to names so that they can restudy the data and challenge data, methods and conclusions" (Jordan, 1981, p 416). Although we would not wish to adopt this kind of critical approach, Jordan makes the point for us that the anonymisation of data can reduce opportunities for valuable future research. So the obvious question for us is the extent to which we anonymise the material we deposit. The Economic and Social Data Service (ESDS) suggests that research participants should be given a choice on this matter (ESDS, nda) and, over the matter of the home's identity, we have incorporated this choice into our consent form for home managers. To safeguard participating homes, one possibility might be to place restrictions on the use of the archive, or even put a closure order on it for a number of years.

The original research participants in Townsend's study did not have the opportunity to consent to information about them being deposited in an archive. Today, this raises issues about data protection and access to personal information. It also means that we have to be extremely careful about what information, if any, we reveal to third parties. Our tracing study volunteers, for example, need to be briefed. In briefing them we are releasing the identity of homes that Townsend visited but we are not releasing any further information contained in the archive about them. In addition, some of the managers and residents of the homes in the follow-up study may, understandably, be curious to know what was in the original report on the home they now manage or reside in. It is part of the end users licence with the University of Essex, however, that the confidentiality of information "pertaining to individuals or households" is preserved unless it is already in the public domain (ESDS, ndb).

Connected to the use of the archived data is our responsibility to the original researcher, Peter Townsend. We are extremely fortunate to have him as a consultant to the project. Already he has provided us with valuable insights into his approach to the research, and his views on the use of data such as photographs. He has also transcribed for us his appointments diary for 1959 and this has been enormously helpful in identifying some homes, the location of which was proving elusive. It has also given us a flavour of his punishing timetable, his journeys to many far-flung parts of England and Wales, and the way in which the interviewing was divided between himself and the other researchers. Despite all this, he has made it clear that he does not want his involvement and cooperation with us to inhibit our approach to his data. We appreciate this of course, but we are very aware that we have a relationship of trust: there is no formal contract between him and us. Just as he reassured his respondents of confidentiality, and we are reassuring ours likewise, so we have a duty to treat Townsend's words and deeds with care. This does not preclude us, however, from looking critically at his work.

Conclusion

We would support the view that there is a great deal to be learned from revisiting past research and from looking again at archived qualitative datasets. As this chapter demonstrates, revisiting *The Last Refuge* is presenting us with all sorts of exciting methodological challenges. At a recent seminar about reusing archived qualitative data, Dennis Marsden explained how reluctant he had been to deposit his data on the seminal study he conducted with Brian Jackson: *Education and the Working Cass* (Jackson and Marsden, 1962). One of his reservations was the thought of researchers 'picking over' his data. We are conscious of the fact that researchers who deposit their data are in a vulnerable position and we intend to respect that position. Like Dennis Marsden, Peter Townsend has generously opened up his lifetime's research to other researchers. This in our view is something for which we should all be grateful.

Notes

[1] This chapter arose out of a paper presented to the 34th annual conference of the British Society of Gerontology, 'Ageing Societies: Critical Perspectives on the Past, Present and Future', held at Keele University on 14-16 July 2005. The research on which the chapter is based has been funded by the Economic and Social Research Council (Grant reference: RES 000-23-0995). We would like to thank both Professor Peter Townsend and Professor Joanna Bornat for reading and commenting on an earlier draft of this chapter.

[2] Under the 1929 Local Government Act the responsibility for the relief of the poor was transferred from the Poor Law Unions to the Public Assistance Committees of county boroughs and counties in England and Wales. The old workhouses, hospitals and other forms of indoor relief were included in this transfer. The workhouses were renamed Public Assistance Institutions (PAIs). Under the 1948 National Assistance Act the former Poor Law system was replaced and residential services became the responsibility of the Welfare Committee of local authorities, but the inherited buildings did not finally disappear until the 1970s. They became known as former PAIs.

[3] Townsend drew proportionately larger samples of homes with more than 100 residents (mainly the former PAIs) because, although they only represented four per cent of homes in England and Wales, they accommodated 25 per cent of all residents.

[4] In 1958/59, services for older people were the responsibility of local authority welfare departments that were set up under the 1948 National Assistance Act. The chief welfare officer was in charge of the department.

[5] OPRSI is a consortium of older people who have set up a Private Limited Company in order to undertake research. The founder members undertook a Certificate in Research Methods sponsored by the University of Lancaster and the older people's charity, Counsel and Care.

[6] The first sociological study of Banbury (a town in central England) was undertaken between 1948 and 1951 (Stacey, 1960). The re-study (Stacey et al, 1975) was the first of its kind in Britain. It was undertaken by different fieldworkers but with the same research director.

[7] Brian Abel Smith was at that time a lecturer in social science at the London School of Economics and Political Science.

[8] Criminal Records Bureau disclosure certificates indicate whether or not a person has any recorded convictions, cautions, reprimands or final warnings and whether any information about them is recorded on the Protection of Vulnerable Adults (POVA) list (DH, 2004). This list was set up in England and Wales under the 2000 Care Standards Act and care providers are required to obtain disclosure certificates for those who will be working with their clients.

EIGHT

The road to an age-inclusive society

Bill Bytheway, Richard Ward, Caroline Holland and Sheila Peace

Introduction[1]

Over the years, 'the scrap heap' has been a popular motif in campaigns against mandatory retirement. For many older people it has represented the reality of being excluded from the labour market: thrown on the scrap heap, no use to anyone, next stop the workhouse. In the 1950s and 1960s, how to adjust to retirement was the subject of extensive research (Phillipson, 1993). Success was represented in part by evidence of contentment and in part by that of activity. The concept of 'disengagement' was much discussed. During the 1980s and 1990s, attention turned to 'early' retirement and the structured relationship between age and the labour market. It was evident that workers in some industries were being forced out through redundancy programmes and others were 'induced' into an early exit (Bytheway, 1986).

Now, at the time of writing (2006), as the government pushes through anti-discriminatory measures[2], attention once again is heavily focused on employment and how older people, alongside other disadvantaged groups, are excluded from the opportunities and rewards of paid employment. The White Paper *Fairness for All*, for example, introduces the situation of older people with the comment: "Older people – who already experience discrimination in the labour market – will need choices and opportunities to continue in work and save for their retirement" (DTI, 2004, p 14).

Although the UK government is seeking to promote 'equality and human rights' in many areas of public life (see Chapter Three), there is a growing risk that legislation could become overly associated with employment practices and a few other, narrowly defined, 'third age' issues. If this were to happen, such attention could be construed, paradoxically, to be discriminating against people in their 'fourth age', and the ways in which they are excluded from education, housing, citizenship, travel and the like will be overlooked.

This chapter is based on our experience of coordinating a participative UK-wide research project aimed at uncovering evidence of age discrimination against older people. We first describe how we have defined age discrimination, 'older people' and participatory research. Then we go on to detail our methods and, in particular, the use of diaries. We then present a preliminary analysis of some evidence, discussing questions relating to age identity and the experience of discrimination. Finally we turn to the challenging question of what is involved in 'being older', how we manage this and how this places participants in relation to the project.

The title of the project is 'Research on Age Discrimination' (RoAD) and the tagline is 'the road to an age-inclusive society'. The aim is to undertake participative research with older people, and to point to ways of achieving a more age-inclusive society. At the present time, as older people, we are excluded from many areas of life, either by formal regulations or by informal pressure. Such exclusion is one particular aspect of the general phenomenon of discrimination, and various sections of the population experience it. There are similarities, for example, in the experiences of older people and those of women, disabled people and people from black and minority ethnic communities. At its most polite, older people are excluded with: "Sorry, but you're not allowed in. You're too old". The specific aim of RoAD is to reveal such bars, to describe the experience of meeting them, and to identify ways in which they might be challenged.

How do we define age discrimination?

We think of age discrimination as an interpersonal act in which one person makes the claim that another is 'too old'. The older person is in effect threatened with exclusion. The challenge may take many forms, ranging from bureaucratic regulation to physical aggression. It may be written, verbally articulated or expressed through subtle body language or gesture. It may be unambiguous or it may involve more complex messages. The challenge may be directed at one particular older person or at older people collectively. Similarly it may be articulated by one individual or it may be evident in the writings of a 'faceless' bureaucracy. It may relate to such aspects of social life as place, activity, services, benefits and club membership. The claim may be challenged, ignored or accepted by the older person. Whatever, the challenge is one that can be interpreted personally as A telling B that B is 'too old'.

The intention behind this definition is that it should be narrower than the more general concept of ageism and in particular that it should focus the research on actions more than on attitudes: that it should be a study of acts of discrimination that threaten exclusion rather than expressions of prejudice. We realise of course that this is often a difficult distinction to draw (Bytheway, 1995; Peace, 2002; Thompson, 2005).

Who are older people?

In planning the project, and in particular the involvement of 'older people', we decided that we would not implement age bars ourselves. Excluding people on the grounds that they were 'not old enough' is, arguably, an unacceptable form of age discrimination. We opted for a simple subjective definition. Older people are people who feel able, and are willing, to adopt the identity of 'older person' and to recount and compare experiences of being judged by others to have been 'too old'.

This, however, immediately raises questions of identity that we, the researchers, have been forced to address: are we simply 'the researchers' or are we 'older people undertaking research'? As the project has unfolded, we have attempted to maintain both identities. In some respects, we have aspired to rigorous methods of data collection and analysis and, in doing so, have exercised our past training and experience as 'researchers'. However, we have also adopted the latter identity, drawing on our own lived experiences as 'en-aged' people (sometimes younger, sometimes older). We appreciate that this might be thought presumptuous: for many of those we have recruited we are 'younger people' who are undertaking the research. But they too can be challenged: 'you may think of yourself as an older person, but you too are younger than others engaged in this project'. Age is relative and all of us have had experience from time to time of being judged 'too old'.

At the same time, we appreciate that this relativist approach to defining 'older' might shift the focus of the project away from the oldest generation (Andrews, 1999, p 316). It is critical that we do not neglect the current experiences of those born in the early decades of the 20th century and, in particular, that we avoid the possibility of the project being dominated by the experiences and concerns of 'third agers' (Laslett, 1989). We are tackling this risk by building age into a strategy for maximising diversity. In addition to ensuring that we learn from older people in minority ethnic groups, for example, we have also specifically sought evidence from people in their late 80s and older, and from residents of care homes.

What do we mean by participative research?

We could write at length about our individual experience of working on this project. However, in coordinating participative research it is rather more important to critically and systematically examine the experiences of *all* participants and, in particular, the identities they claim in the course of being recruited to the project and what this reveals about age-related processes of inclusion and exclusion.

Not only has participative research become increasingly common but there is a growing literature on methods (Peace, 1999; Reason and Bradbury, 2001). Whereas it has often been seen as an approach which, in promoting collaboration, preserves the distinction between researching and being researched (Oliver, 1992; Mercer, 2002), we have sought to blur the distinction and have actively encouraged all participants to engage in the process of 'doing research' (Beresford and Croft, 1993; see also Chapter Six). For example, we have fed evidence back to participants and asked "Does this experience ring any bells with you? Do you think this is an example of age discrimination, or is there some other explanation?". In this way all participants have had the opportunity to discuss the emerging evidence and to write about the issues raised (see also Chapters Two and Five).

The RoAD project was planned so that 'older people were involved at every level' and at every stage. They are participating in a number of roles:

- *The project team.*
- *The project advisory group.*
- *Members and officers* of participating *Older People's Forums.*
- *The mailing list:* people who, through the Forums and other groups of older people, are contributing accounts and opinions about age discrimination.
- *The panel:* older people who will amplify and comment critically on the outcomes of the data analysis.
- *The fieldworkers:* older people appointed and trained to support the diarists and carry out interviews.
- *The diarists:* older people invited to keep one-week diaries and to discuss specific experiences that they record.
- *The focus groups:* groups will be set up to discuss and comment on findings.

In this chapter we focus on three of these roles: mailing list contributors, fieldworkers and diarists. As we write, the project is still ongoing. While most of the fieldwork has been completed, the material we have collected has yet to be analysed systematically. For this reason, what we offer, drawing on a reading of a range of accounts and some illustrative examples, is a discussion of some of the issues that the experience of age discrimination raises.

Mailing list contributors

The project is based on two broad strategies. One maintains a traditional approach to research aimed at collecting data systematically and analysing it rigorously. The second opens up the project to receive input from whatever source. To this end, we circulated the Help the Aged network of Older People's Forums with an invitation "to join a project that challenges age discrimination". We indicated that we wanted to be contacted by "people who know what it feels like to face discrimination because of age". We made it clear that participation was open to anyone who had relevant experience, regardless of age. The invitation did not exclude, for example, those who had witnessed age discrimination experienced by their parents. The invitation made no mention of being interviewed and did not ask about age. It was simply inviting readers to express an interest. There was an immediate response to the invitation and, as a result, we set up the RoAD mailing list.

To date we have produced six editions of our newsletter, writing in an inclusive style, encouraging feedback and participation, and distributing it widely through the participating Forums. We have specifically invited people to return (in accompanying reply-paid envelopes) accounts of their experiences of age discrimination. In this way we have made the project 'open' to the submission of evidence from all sources. This has been supplemented by our website (http://road.open.ac.uk), which similarly solicits comment and accounts of the first-hand experience of age discrimination.

In assessing the significance of the contributions we received, an important consideration is how the people we reach might be influenced by the information we give out: how it comes to them and how it invites them to contribute as 'older people'. In particular we are aware that some will refuse, and that some will contribute but not as 'an older person'. What we receive are responses from people who are 'doing older' or, in other words, either performing the part of 'being an older person' or reporting on how they see others performing that part. According to traditional research values this is a major weakness: what we are being told may be what the contributors imagine we want or need to hear or what we ought to be told. Thus there is a danger that what is offered is the 'received wisdom' rather than the evidence of those who have witnessed acts of discrimination. That said, these contributions constitute a serious exercise in emancipation (Mercer, 2002) and, having issued the invitation, we take seriously what they represent and reveal.

Fieldworkers

Being a national study we needed to recruit fieldworkers from across the UK. We aimed to recruit two in each of six areas: the south, midlands and north of England, Northern Ireland, Scotland and Wales[3]. We made it clear that there were two primary requirements: to have some relevant experience of fieldwork and to be an 'older person'. In the further details, we explained that we were not implementing any age bar but nevertheless expected the fieldworkers to be willing to identify themselves as 'older people'[4].

The 12 fieldworkers who attended the 24-hour induction meeting in York in January 2004 included one man and eleven women, and ranged in age from 44 to 71. Five were recruited through research networks. Contact with most of the other seven was through Older People's Forums and similar groups. There were two who had some prior involvement with such groups but whom we contacted through personal networks. There were two who had previously undertaken research together. Similarly there were two or three who were acquainted through other networks but, overall, the 12 were strangers to each other. The meeting was planned and managed by us, the research team.

At the outset we explained our definition of 'older people' and how they, the fieldworkers, had been appointed as 'older people who had relevant skills and experience'. Also we discussed participative research and how, although we, the research team, had the basic responsibility of ensuring that the project was completed satisfactorily, we took their particular interests and concerns seriously. Despite the differences between their contracts and those that we, the team, had with The Open University, we saw the fieldworkers as 'co-researchers' and the working relationship as collaborative rather than one of 'them working for us'.

It was particularly interesting to observe how age figured in the ways in which the newly acquainted fieldworkers introduced themselves. Perhaps what was most significant was that, despite age being central to the whole project and the fact that some account had been taken of their own age in their being there, there was comparatively little explicit reference to age. Ann[5], at 44, was 10 years younger than the next youngest and was, we felt, a little self-conscious of the fact. Rather adeptly she claimed an identity as an older person on the basis of having recently become a grandmother to twins (somehow the fact of twins seemed to doubly qualify her). She was able to describe the experience of clarifying her relationship to the twins (for example, "No, it's my daughter who's the mother") and the pride she had in her family in a way which presented generational seniority as a positively valued identity.

The next two youngest fieldworkers were in their fifties and what was distinctive about their situations was that both were still pursuing careers based on salaried employment. The opportunity to be a fieldworker came at a convenient period when they did not have full-time contracts. The participation of these three, coupled with the standard contract that all 12 had signed with The Open University, meant that, at the induction meeting, the fieldworkers established a shared 'double identity' as 'older person' and 'employed fieldworker'.

The main task of the fieldworker was to support and interview three older people living in their area who had agreed to keep diaries for the project. In describing the plans for fieldwork with diarists, we stressed the importance of focusing on 'real' experiences. In the course of the concluding interview we indicated that we hoped that detailed accounts would emerge of up to four specific experiences. Having obtained these details of 'things that had happened' in the course of the diary week, the interview would then move into a less structured phase when fieldworker and diarist would discuss more conversationally the issues that had been raised, exchanging accounts of similar experiences of 'things that had happened'.

To prepare for this, the fieldworkers undertook some role play at the induction meeting, where each took the part of interviewer and then diarist. We wanted them to engage with the diarists as 'older people too', with their own distinctive experience of age. Intentionally we offered little direction or guidance on how they should go about interviewing and conversing with the diarists. Neither did we offer any indication of the nature of the events that we expected our fieldworkers to select and focus on, other than that they should be examples of, or raise issues relating to, age discrimination. Our hope was that these would emerge 'naturally' in the course of the interview.

In the role-playing session and, more generally, over the course of the 24 hours of the induction meeting, several of the fieldworkers recounted examples of age discrimination that they had experienced at first hand. Reflecting back on the event, we concluded that the induction had succeeded in helping the fieldworkers become familiar with the two roles of 'older person' and 'fieldworker', and we felt confident that they were equipped to enter the field. One further task was the production of a brief report on each interview. We gave them written guidance on how they should compile this.

Diarists

In order to study how age discrimination features in the everyday 'lived' experiences of older people, we recruited a UK-wide sample of older people willing to keep a one-week diary (Bytheway and Johnson, 2002; Bytheway, 2003). Each fieldworker was asked to recruit their first diarist through their own networks[6]. Subsequently diarists were chosen from older people who had been recruited by the participating Forums. In our recruitment leaflet we appealed for volunteers: "to keep diaries of their experiences over a seven day period". We indicated that diarists would be supported by trained fieldworkers.

Through selection, we endeavoured to ensure that the diarists were a diverse group and to that end we were guided by a principle of inclusivity. But translating this into practical measures is not straightforward and requires some prescience as to possible factors that might prevent or hinder certain groups from volunteering. Anticipating that some potential diarists may have sensory impairment or limited dexterity, or may be people whose first language is not English, we indicated that they could ask someone to act as a 'scribe', writing entries into their diaries. We also offered a small payment to diarists.

Nevertheless, even allowing for the support of fieldworker and scribe, our approach implies a degree of literacy and we recognised that some might still be discouraged from participating. Potential barriers take very different forms and this was a concern to our advisory group. For example, one member suggested that older people using mental health services may not see their experiences as relevant, not least because of a personal history of being excluded.

At every turn it seemed there were older people just beyond our reach, whose experience of age discrimination might be critical to our aim of achieving a broad understanding of how older people experience age discrimination. However, as the project has progressed, we have realised that the goal of 'representativeness' opens up complex questions of how identities are lived, experienced and expressed, and the importance of understanding how different aspects of identity – of who we are and are judged to be – overlap and intersect. The process itself, of recruiting older people to participate in the project, has revealed the impact of age discrimination in addition to other forms of exclusion and disadvantage.

To date, a total of eight men and 29 women have kept diaries, ranging in age from 60 to 97 years. For the most part, they were unknown to the project prior to volunteering. Thus they were freely identifying themselves as 'older people', sometimes seeing their role as that of searching out evidence of age discrimination as it affects other older people. It is important to recognise, however, that they do not represent people who, for whatever reason, choose to deny or resist the identity of 'older person'. This must be borne in mind in interpreting what they have written and said about age discrimination.

The fieldworkers delivered the blank diaries to the diarists, explaining the format and answering any questions. For each of the seven days there are four pages in the A4-sized diary. The first page is a summary of the events of the day. It provides boxes relating to each hour from 7.00 am through to 11.00 pm. The second page provides two half-page boxes for notes on 'Encounters with people while shopping or doing business, on the 'phone or in person', and then on 'TV, newspapers and the media'. The third page similarly has boxes for notes on 'Discussions with friends or family' and 'Times and places', and the fourth page provided space for 'Any further comments'. At the end of the diary, there is a page for general comments on the week.

In designing the diary, our intention was to provide sufficient space for those 'with a lot to say' or with complicated experiences to recount, while at the same time indicating that all we wanted was a record of things that 'actually happened'. We did not ask the diarists to search out evidence of age discrimination, or to check that specific criteria were satisfied before including notes on a particular experience, and the fieldworkers explained that we would not be disappointed if spaces were left blank.

Having explained the purposes of the diary, the fieldworkers made arrangements to return to review and collect the diary. They sought permission to record the interview/conversation on tape. As explained above, we gave the fieldworkers only two specific instructions regarding the interview. One was that they should select up to four incidents recorded in the diary and endeavour to obtain further information or comment on these. The second was to follow this review of the diary with a more open conversation about age discrimination.

Evidence of age discrimination

A priority in the planning of the project was on acquiring 'good' evidence. The informal criterion for this was 'hard evidence that would stand up in court'. We wanted accounts of 'real' experiences rather than generalised descriptions of 'what happens', and we specifically asked that accounts be located according to time and place.

As accounts came in through the mailing list and the website, we began to recognise familiar accounts of age discrimination. An early example is the following from Mr Craig:

> My most blatant experience of age discrimination ... was when I, together with all other 'over 50s', was summoned to the Chief Engineer's office, one by one, to receive a letter that detailed what monetary terms we could expect if we applied for 'voluntary severance' (redundancy). This was not a ploy to mitigate any compulsory redundancies at the time since there were no proposals for such, but

was a new policy to bring 'new blood' (that is, younger blood) into the company.... The underlying, if less blatant, feeling within the company was of a pro-youth and age discriminatory culture.

In this account, there are unambiguous echoes of the public debates of the past 20 years regarding ageism in employment practices (Glover and Branine, 2001; Platman and Taylor, 2004). Although a common experience, it is significant that Mr Craig describes this as his "most blatant experience of age discrimination" and as evidence of an "age discriminatory culture". We are convinced that this is an account of a real experience that Mr Craig shared with others and not just an imagined or dramatised version of a familiar complaint. Nevertheless, in his references to employment practices and the language of management there is evidence that he knew he was recounting a common experience. He considered himself to be in a position to explain how older workers such as himself are 'eased' out of the workforce; in effect he felt able to 'theorise age' (Gubrium and Wallace, 1990).

Some of the diarists provided similarly unambiguous accounts. We have selected two to examine in some detail. First, here is how Mrs Brown described a series of incidents and how they were recounted by the fieldworker[7]. On the first day she wrote: "Local walk with spouse on canal path. Encountered 3 cyclists who showed no consideration – eg no bell or voice in spite of my white stick. Riding at great speed" (12.1)[8]. Three days later she visited her sister in a nearby seaside town and enjoyed another walk:

> After lunch Husband, Sister + Self walked on the coastal path. We jumped a number of times, as cyclists whizzed by. Me because I cannot see properly, my husband because he is deaf, my sister because she is 73 [and] of a nervous disposition. I ask myself have bicycle bells been abolished (same thing on canal path near our home). (12.4)

Back home on the following day, they were walking again on the canal path (in her notes she added: "We try to walk every day", 12.5), and she commented once more on the threat posed by cyclists.

Regarding the first day's encounter on the towpath, the fieldworker commented:

> This was particularly upsetting for her husband who is now deaf. [Mrs Brown] said that she had at least heard them. However, she thought that they should have rung bells or shouted to signal their presence. When asked whether she thought that the behaviour of the cyclists was deliberately ageist she responded affirmatively, going on to say that younger people do not appear to have respect for older people these days. This comment was illustrated by an account of how she is sometimes treated by motorists when crossing the road near her home. [Mrs Brown] remarked on the ambivalence of drivers

who have the courtesy to slow down and wave her across the road when they see her at the roadside with her white stick but, when she is slow in crossing the road because she cannot see the driver's gestures, they appear to become very impatient, and sometimes make rude and inconsiderate remarks such as 'silly old bag'. When asked if she thought that the driver's behaviour was particularly ageist, she replied that she did not know as in her opinion drivers were impatient generally.

This is a good example of how the diary, interview and the fieldworker's report worked in combination to produce a fuller understanding of specific experiences. First, Mrs Brown notes a specific experience in her diary and then notes similar experiences over the course of subsequent days. This is discussed in the interview, during which Mrs Brown confirms that, in her view, the behaviour of the cyclists is an example of ageism: it represents a lack of respect for older people. She then amplifies this with a broader, less specific, account of her experiences as a pedestrian crossing the road with a white stick. The details of this suggest that this too relates to one particular, possibly recent, experience even though she generalises it to drivers as a whole. In particular, it is not clear whether or not the remark that she cites ("silly old bag") was spoken on a specific occasion or whether it is simply an example of the kind of remark to which she has been subjected.

The contrast between cyclists and drivers suggests that Mrs Brown is more inclined to interpret the behaviour of cyclists as discriminatory against older people than that of motorists. Whereas she sees the speed of the former as inconsiderate and dangerous, the rude remarks of the latter are explained as evidence of impatience. In this way, the written accounts of this particular incident help to illuminate some of the complexities of identifying age discrimination. It would appear that Mrs Brown views the prospect of being knocked into the canal, unlike a few rude remarks from impatient drivers, as a serious threat to her well-being.

The second example we have selected from the diaries illustrates how the selection of four incidents from the diary helps to uncover distinctive aspects of how everyday events are experienced. After interviewing Mrs Davidson, the fieldworker produced a report that included considerable detail on four selected incidents:

• *Being treated like a non-person.* The relevant diary entry reads: "The barman ignored us & when challenged said 'Let me serve the young lady first'" (44.4). Mrs Davidson then made notes in her diary on her discussion with her friend: "We deplored the pub man's attitude, but it happens all the time – I am [writing] this because, having queued at Boots' counter, when it was my turn, the shop assistant looked over my shoulder as if I didn't exist and asked the man behind me what he would like – I had the satisfaction of reducing her to tears & the supervisor removed her for retraining" (44.4).

- *Disabled parking spaces.* On the day Mrs Davidson went shopping she entered this in her diary: "I felt infuriated that mothers and children get the best parking, there is nothing for the old" (44.2). She expanded on this experience in the interview, arguing that "there are many older people who, while not disabled, face more physical strain from a long walk across the car park than do children" (fieldworker's report).
- *The rough behaviour of younger people.* The relevant diary entry reads: "4–5pm, I felt uncomfortable in [...] town centre – too many people pushing and jostling" (44.5). In the interview, she explained how public behaviour in various public settings deterred her from venturing from her home.
- *The exploitation by authorities of the weak position of older people.* This is a comment on a newspaper story headed 'Police under orders to "get tough" arrest woman of 79 in 4am raid' (44.2). Mrs Davidson felt that the police did not act to protect older people in public places despite the evidence produced by CCTV cameras. Moreover, she concluded from the evidence of the newspaper story, coupled with her own experience of passing through customs, that officers see older people as easily intimidated and unlikely to make a fuss when they, the officers, are attempting to achieve their performance targets.

Here is what the fieldworker concluded:

> She has a strong feeling that, as an older person, "the world isn't for you". Among [my] interviewees, she stands out as someone who seems strongly affected emotionally by incidents like those described here. Sometimes her emotion is [fury]. Sometimes it is fear or a sense of great vulnerability. The incidents selected from her diary week are fairly low key instances of types of situations which repeatedly cause her much distress....
>
> The tone of [Mrs Davidson's] written diary communicates something of her anger and sense of vulnerability. But neither her diary nor the details given here convey [the fact] that on the 'phone she is actually very pleasant, chatty and enjoyable to talk to....
>
> A theme running through the four selected incidents is how, on account of her age, she feels treated as someone to whom the normal rules of courtesy, human fellow-feeling or even the law no longer apply. You get ignored in queues for service, pushed off the pavement, people push past you in queues – and no one will lift a finger to help you.

In short, Mrs Davidson used the diary to describe different ways in which older people experience age discrimination: being ignored, excluded, threatened and picked on.

Mrs Brown and Mrs Davidson have given us powerful evidence of how, in the course of their everyday lives, older people can experience age discrimination. Any one incident seems comparatively minor, but when they occur repeatedly, they constitute a major form of discrimination, one that can easily lead to a form of forced voluntary self-exclusion.

There is a difference between 'real' experiences and 'hard' evidence, and as the project has progressed we have come to understand the limitations that a request for hard evidence places on what can be recounted. It became clear that, unlike unsolicited accounts such as Mr Craig's, the diaries and interviews tend to be sites for expressing uncertainty and ambivalence rather than making unqualified claims. In this respect, Mrs Brown and Mrs Davidson were exceptional. Several of the fieldworkers concluded that with some diarists it was difficult to identify incidents that were unambiguous examples of age discrimination. Rather their interviews generated unresolved discussions, often centred on the diarist's failure to 'see' age discrimination. This was most evident when diarists (voluntarily) set out to raise the issue with other older people. One fieldworker, June, reported on two such diarists.

First, Janet Simpson raised age discrimination with friends and colleagues at a drop-in centre. In her diary, she commented: "Most people I spoke to feel that what concerns them is medically related. Long waiting lists, etc" (21.3). Two days later, she tried again at a tea dance: "The only person who appeared anything like interested in what I was talking about complained she got on a bus full of students who let her stand with two bags of shopping" (21.5). This is what June wrote in her report:

> I thought there might have been a wealth of information with her colleagues and friends ... but they were surprisingly silent. No, no, they didn't see any discrimination, didn't want to talk about it. "I think it was apathy", [Janet] said. "Or perhaps it was the wrong time to ask. We were all pretty busy". Apathy to me means hopelessness. Perhaps if these people had been drawn out slowly, we would have learned more, as was true with [Janet]. Still, I think the clear unwillingness to speak about discrimination is important, particularly since [Janet] says everyone experiences it. Why?

June had a similar experience with her second diarist, Mrs West. Having discussed a number of encounters recorded in Mrs West's diary, June turned to the following entry:

> Asked mature friends whom I met in the street "What do you think about older age discrimination?". "Usually felt by people who have a life time of discrimination" – not a reply I'd considered. "Discrimination? Rubbish. It just keeps getting better" added his wife. (22.7)[9]

June reflected on this as follows:

> The friend went on to say that age discrimination worked against people who have felt that way all their lives. In other words, once a victim, always a victim. Mrs West wondered aloud with me if this were true. I sensed she'd been a bit embarrassed with her friends. Had she been showing weakness by even bringing up a topic that they dismissed so quickly? (Too quickly, I thought.)
>
> I disagreed, saying that maybe some insecure people imagine slights where none exist, and perhaps the meek do invite abuse sometimes, but age discrimination is not a state of mind. And even if this were true, why should only the bold be free of unfair treatment – as if age discrimination only exists if you acknowledge it.

Another diarist, Jo Smith, was particularly interested in film and how older women are portrayed. She described the discrimination against older women as 'terrible'. In the course of the diary week, she discussed this with her husband. This is what she noted:

> Discussion with husband about portrayal of an older woman in film without ageing issues being raised. We do not seem to understand each other. I say that ageing issues are different from being portrayed as a person who is older. For example, the Queen. No agreement. (4.5)

She expanded on this in the interview when she asked: "When we look at the Queen, do we see an old lady?". No, she answered, we see what she's wearing and we might wonder how long she will be Queen. What enrages her is how films portray older women as stereotypical older women rather than as particular people (such as the Queen) with a unique identity and biography. She can see this as a kind of age discrimination whereas her husband cannot.

Discussion

Reporting age discrimination

Many older people recognise age discrimination as something that must be uncovered and challenged (and to this end, a large number have enthusiastically accepted our invitation to participate in this project). Nevertheless some have difficulty in identifying particular experiences as unambiguous examples. There are a number of possible explanations for this.

First there is embarrassment. This was discussed at a meeting we organised at the 2005 British Society of Gerontology conference, when we described the difficulties described by some diarists in uncovering evidence of age discrimination. John Miles, of the Older People's Advocacy Alliance, argued that "if you are going to people saying tell us about discrimination, you are in a sense saying tell us about your experience of the power of humiliation". It was not surprising, he suggested, if this made them uncomfortable. He argued that it is not that they don't necessarily recognise discrimination. Rather our actual approach was not giving them much room to start "from where they were themselves".

We have since reflected on this valuable comment. June felt that Mrs West may have been embarrassed. Perhaps, in addition to being humiliating, recounting experiences of age discrimination means claiming the mantle of 'old age', a socially unwanted status. Note how Mrs West describes her friends as 'mature', and how she asked them about 'older' age discrimination. If she felt embarrassed to be raising such questions, it is hardly surprising if negative experiences are then explained more ambiguously, as Janet Simpson found, invoking illness and long waiting lists as well as age.

Secondly there is blame. Being slow in crossing the road, Mrs Brown was prepared to tolerate the offensive language of motorists. Age is to be blamed, not the prejudices of the younger generation. Mrs West's friends similarly, older people themselves, were quick to blame the victims: older people who start to moan have only themselves to blame.

Such inconsistency raises the troubled question of whether there exists a stable notion of what age discrimination actually is. Perhaps the deceptively simple definition with which we set out belies the wide-ranging and contested constructions of age discrimination offered by our many contributors. We have come to question whether our original definition stretches to touch on the more complex, embedded and indirect forms that age discrimination takes. The evidence we have gathered tests the limits of our plain and simple notion of age discrimination and we have recognised that, in setting out with a simple definition, we may have obscured some of the complexities of age discrimination and blinkered ourselves to the subtleties of a far greater and more pervasive social phenomenon.

What is involved in 'being older'?

The diary interviews were an occasion for the discussion and negotiation of ageing identities. A striking theme, given the topic at hand, was the negative construction of 'old' embedded in the reflections of both diarists and fieldworkers. For us, these passing references to old age as a negative state, whether drawing on popular idioms such as a person 'looking young for their age', or 'feeling young on the inside', were themselves important signals of an ageist culture. Andrews (1999, p 309) writes "Why is it that so often attempts to speak about ageing in a positive light result in a denial of ageing?". So, even as the topic of discriminatory treatment of older people organised the interviews, so our diarists and fieldworkers drew on negative constructions of old age to portray both themselves and others.

For example, here is how June described a series of embarrassments following her interview with Mr Martin:

> I left behind my jacket after the second interview, and Mr Martin 'phoned me to tell me so. I felt quite embarrassed, because earlier that day I had mistakenly gone to the block of flats adjacent to Mr Martin's. I was sure I was at the right place, but I couldn't find his name and number on the outside door. I 'phoned him on my mobile. "You're having a senior moment", he told me. Later, when he recounted to me his fears of the "beginning of the end", I realised I had had a similar feeling. "I hope you find your way back to your car", he said jokingly, as I left. So when he 'phoned me to tell me I'd left my jacket, I felt doubly mortified. He brought my jacket to me in a carrier bag to my place of work in town (he was passing there anyway). When I got home I found an unknown umbrella in the bag. To my shameful pleasure, I 'phoned him back to tell him. "Oh yes, I'd brought an umbrella with me because it might have rained. Please keep it as a gift". We both had a laugh. But I woke in the night, worrying about the whole business.

This is a powerful account of how we are liable to interpret minor incidents as failures of age, and to recognise that this interpretation is available to others – and, as a result, to lose sleep at night. It highlights the dissonance between age discrimination, the topic in hand, and the ways that old age is reproduced in discussion as unquestioningly negative. Arguably it illustrates how ageism is woven into the fabric of daily experience and discourse.

The diaries and subsequent discussion have also revealed the relational basis of establishing ageing identities. How, for example, the vulnerability of older people is constructed through shared perceptions of the threat of youth: the 'new blood' replacing Mr Craig, the disrespectful young cyclists threatening Mr and Mrs Brown, the young people who jostle Mrs Davidson in the town centre, and the students June Simpson was told about who remained seated on the bus. In this way older people are, inadvertently perhaps, constructing 'youth/young' as a homogeneous and stable category while, simultaneously, attempting to reject the categorisation of 'old' and all it implies.

Conclusion: is participative research revealing a road to an age-inclusive society?

In developing strategies that might generate a more age-inclusive society, much can be learned from developments in the study of other forms of discrimination: disablism (Oliver 1992; Mercer, 2002), racism (Mac an Ghaill, 1999; Gunaratnam, 2003; Sin, 2005) and sexism (Naples, 2003). Sin (2005) for example, argues that "understanding the experience of racism requires much more than just asking questions on the experience of racism" (p 112), and we would agree that this applies equally to understanding ageism. Current debates surrounding the establishment of a Commission for Equality and Human Rights are stimulating exchanges regarding all forms of discrimination (Age Concern, 2005; see also Chapter Three).

We would also agree with Sin (2005) when he argues that: "we can learn as much by focusing on the process of research as on the products" (p 112). Accepting that we too are older people, along with our co-researchers and other participants, has generated a different perspective on the experience of age discrimination. Nevertheless, even among older people, age is associated with important differences. There is a growing risk, as we argued at the beginning of this chapter, that policies designed to tackle age discrimination could become overly associated with employment practices and a few other narrowly defined third age issues. People in their 80s and 90s may feel excluded. Help the Aged (2002b) have recognised this, and the hope is that through RoAD a much more comprehensive understanding of age discrimination will emerge, one that reveals 'the road' to a society that is more inclusive for people of all ages.

Notes

[1] We would like to register our appreciation of the contribution of many older people to this project. In particular this chapter draws heavily on the writing of fieldworkers and diarists. The fieldworkers who worked with diarists were: Diana Findlay, Nicola Humberstone, Val Jarrett, Sue Jones, Nell Keddie, Anne Kelly, Elizabeth O'Dell, Andrea Russell, Charles Patmore, Diane Smeeton, Lynda Spencer, Anthea Symonds and Ruth Waitt. We are also indebted to the RoAD project secretary, Irene Paton. We are working closely with colleagues in Help the Aged and our advisory committee. The project is being funded by the Big Lottery Fund. The project began in July 2004 and finished in January 2007.

[2] At the time of writing, the 2006 Employment Equality (Age) Regulations were still in draft and out for consultation.

[3] In advance of the induction meeting, we managed to recruit fieldworkers from all areas except Northern Ireland. Subsequently we succeeded in appointing a fieldworker for Northern Ireland and another based in London. We also intended to appoint at least one fieldworker from a black or minority ethnic community but did not manage this prior to the induction. We have since appointed Jenny Sleight, Zara Farsi and Ulfat Riaz as fieldworkers undertaking projects in the African-Caribbean and Irish communities in Leeds and the Pakistani community in Bradford.

[4] An immediate complication was that they would be offered up to 15 days employment at the standard Open University associate lecturer rate, and this entailed them being formally appointed and contracted. The requirement that they should be 'older people'

appeared to contradict the university's policy of equal opportunities. By an unexpected coincidence, we had to negotiate a solution to this at a time when the university was promoting a code of diversity. The accompanying handbook featured age discrimination and attempted to make a clear distinction between positive discrimination (not permissible) and positive action (permissible).

[5] The names of fieldworkers and diarists used in this chapter are pseudonyms.

[6] This decision was forced by our tight schedule. There were advantages in that these pilot diarists became an extension to the fieldworkers' induction. Moreover, in the light of this phase, we made some minor modifications to the design of the diary.

[7] Mrs Brown has little sight and she kept notes for her diary separately on small sheets of yellow paper. Although the fieldworker transcribed these into the diary, what we include here is transcribed directly from Mrs Brown's notes. This is a good example of how some diarists were enterprising in overcoming problems in participating with the project.

[8] For purposes of cross-referencing, diaries are numbered. These numbers, along with diary days, are included at the end of quoted extracts: 12.1 refers to day 1 of diary no 12. Where extracts have been edited for purposes of anonymity or clarity, this is indicated by square brackets.

[9] Like many of the diary entries, this is somewhat cryptic. The 'mature friends' are Mr and Mrs Thompson (pseudonyms). The question comes from Mrs West; the first response is from Mr Thompson, followed by a comment from Mrs West. And then the second response, questioning discrimination, is from Mrs Thompson.

Part Three
Future considerations

NINE

Justice between generations: the recent history of an idea

Harry R. Moody

Introduction

In the 1980s a debate erupted that was greeted as a policy nightmare for ageing advocates: namely, a claim, from conservatives as well as some prominent liberals, that older people were gaining too many resources at the expense of the young. This 'generational equity debate', as it was called, has not disappeared, but it has assumed new forms in different countries. Like 'The Terminator', justice between generations is an idea that will not go away. It is therefore the purpose of this chapter to explore both the recent history of this idea, and how it has come to shape contemporary political discourse in the 21st century.

In the 21st century, the challenge of justice between generations is not limited to competition between age groups but extends to a range of challenges that appear to put future generations at risk: how will pay-as-you-go social insurance systems adapt to rapid population ageing? Will the human impact on earth's environment permit future generations to enjoy a life comparable to our own? Are governments allocating resources and establishing modes of taxation for sustainable economic prosperity in the future? Debates over generational accounting, global warming and demographic change are part of a larger history, dating back to Thomas Malthus and Edmund Burke, later revived by philosophers like Daniel Callahan and Norman Daniels, and posed again in the 21st century as we contemplate prospects of population ageing in planetary terms. In devising global policies for an ageing society of the future, the challenge of justice between generations assumes unprecedented importance on an historical scale, and encompasses both social expenditures for an ageing society as well as policies for environmental protection and fiscal integrity. Above all, the problem of justice between generations must be framed in terms of broad social values concerning 'duties to posterity' and our 'image of the future' (De-Shalit, 1995). Together, these ideas are conditioned by attitudes about optimism (progress) or pessimism (decline) with respect to things to come. These attitudes and assumptions become the basis for our concept of obligation to those generations, born and unborn, who will come after us.

The idea of progress

The prevailing ideology of the modern world, since the Renaissance, has been rooted in notions of optimism or faith in the future (Nisbet, 1994). The Renaissance understood its own time to be a 'rebirth' from what would become called the 'Middle Ages'. The 16th and 17th centuries witnessed exploration of the New World, followed by the 18th-century Enlightenment, events that brought wide celebration of the idea of progress in human affairs. By the 19th century, capitalism manifested an idea of progress through Victorian morality and the economics of the Industrial Revolution, both based on restraint and delayed gratification for the sake of a better future. Progress for posterity could be taken for granted.

By the 20th century, this idea of progress received decisive blows. The Second World War, the Holocaust, and then the spectre of nuclear war promoted pessimism about things to come. Yet the idea of progress itself has flourished in the lives of today's older people. For instance, the so-called 'Greatest Generation' (Brokaw, 1998) – the generation born between 1911 and 1924 – survived the Depression and the First World War; they could have few doubts that, whatever their struggle, their children would enjoy a better life. Indeed, the life course of the 'Greatest Generation' seemed to conform to the 'Master Narrative' of progress. Yet since the 1970s, the idea of progress has begun to collapse on a far wider scale. It is precisely at this moment, with eclipse of the idea of progress, that the ethical problem of justice between generations becomes acutely felt.

The ethical challenge of justice between generations is not experienced equally by all birth cohorts. For example, the lives of today's older people witnessed progress illustrated by rising life expectancy, increased home ownership, the spread of pension coverage, and the benefits of modern medicine, ranging from antibiotics to organ transplants. The conditions of older people, in particular, improved markedly in the past generation. In the US, for example, poverty rates among those over 65 declined since the 1970s. In short, the lived experience for today's older people demonstrates decisive progress in comparison to old age experienced by their own parents. Whatever theorists may say about the decline of a 'Master Narrative' of progress, the lived experience of today's older generation seems to uphold the idea of progress that has been fundamental to modernity from the Renaissance up to the present day.

Furthermore, the notion of justice between generations becomes prominent at those times in history when the fate of future generations appears to be at risk. In the 1960s, for example, fears were expressed that older people in charge would put at risk the prospects for progress shared by the post-war generation of baby boomers. The post-war generation had led a charmed life of growing peace and prosperity. Those born after the Second World War had no experience of the Depression or military struggle. Those who grew up in the prosperous 1950s came to believe that economic progress and expanding social justice were a condition they could count on in the future. Moreover, young people in the

1960s had come of age in a time when government and other dominant institutions of society were granted a high measure of legitimacy and trust.

The sense of future generations at risk grew more acute in the 1970s with the impact of environmental crisis and economic stagnation. No longer could a master narrative of progress be taken for granted (Lyotard, 1984). The 1970s witnessed oil embargoes and stock market declines. As the world faced the prospect of diminished natural resources and economic decline, it became proper to ask about the rights of those still young. But in the 1970s older people were not explicitly blamed for this condition. On the contrary, this was a time when old age itself became understood as a 'social problem' and age-based entitlements were expanding. Environmental ethics, not generational equity, was the watchword of the decade.

By the 1980s previous assumptions about ageing and the welfare state began to be challenged. The idea of justice between generations was applied to thinking about obligations toward different age groups and cohorts. Journalists and ethicists took up the cry of 'generational equity' and advocates for older people responded in defence of older people. By the 1990s the idea of justice between generations had become applied to both environment and ageing policy. Anxiety about 'sustainability', whether of environmental resources or age-based entitlements, had become an ongoing theme of public policy and public consciousness, not only in the US but also in Europe and elsewhere.

For younger generations, this master narrative of progress, and the shape of things to come, is now far less clear and filled with more foreboding. Those who are concerned to promote intergenerational solidarity, therefore, must think deeply about normative questions concerning justice between generations. The place to begin thinking is in understanding how the recent history of this idea has come to shape our political discourse in the politics of ageing and in other domains.

The 1960s: conflict between generations

The 1960s was a decade dominated by optimism and conflict between generations. It was a time of high hopes for the future and the worldwide youth rebellion reflected a revolution of rising expectations (Farber and Bailey, 2003). But the ideology of progress, of social justice and economic growth, also had a downside. The question may be asked, what stands in the way of progress, either material or social? The answer could be those who are old, and here, precisely, lies the origin of the conflict between generations. 'Don't trust anyone over 30' was the conclusion of those with great expectations: namely, young people. The youth culture of the 1960s set itself in opposition to adult values, as portrayed for example in films like 'Wild in the Streets' or 'The Graduate'. Of course, one might argue that during the 1960s it was not older people themselves who were to blame but rather a system that gave preference to seniority, to the old over the young. But in the mood of the 1960s, claims for justice between generations became linked to opposition to anything old and established, inspiring elements of ageism that have been persistent to the present day.

In the US, these sentiments were strengthened by opposition to the War in Vietnam. The War was a supreme example of generational injustice where old men sent young men abroad to die for a cause in which older people made no sacrifice. Thus, protest against the War in Vietnam became not merely a generational revolt, but a protest cast in terms of justice between generations: that is, age groups. Elders make decisions but young people make the sacrifices. We should note, too, that generational conflict was not limited to the US. It was felt in France, for example, in the events of 1968 as well as in the upheavals of the Cultural Revolution in China. The mood of the 1960s, fuelled by intergenerational conflict and claims of justice, became imbued with a motif Habermas would call the 'Legitimation Crisis', which would only grow stronger in the 1970s and continue in the decades that followed (Habermas, 1975).

The 1970s: the rise of normative ethics

There are no simple demarcations between decades and the early 1970s maintained many of the themes of the late 1960s. But the souring of expectations in the new decade led to a mood that would prove decisive in politics, economics and culture: namely, acknowledgment of limits. The awareness of limits was critical for the rise of the environmental movement and of normative ethics. Environmental consciousness achieved the status of a social movement with the first celebration of Earth Day in 1970 and, throughout the decade, the movement gathered strength. Expectations of progress through material prosperity had ended.

The growing sense of limits and pessimism about the future had its roots in the 1960s. For example, Rachel Carson's book *Silent Spring* (1962) was an early warning about the environmental danger of pesticides such as DDT. Another influential work came from Stanford University ecologist Paul Ehrlich, whose *Population Bomb* (1968) warned that the growth of human population would soon threaten the carrying capacity of planet earth. In 1972 a team of researchers at the Massachusetts Institute of Technology (MIT), led by Donella Meadows, published their influential book *The Limits to Growth*, which anticipated a grim outlook for future generations because the present generation was consuming the Earth's resources (Meadows et al, 1972, 2004). Departing from a purely technical or scientific approach to environmental matters, the authors stressed the primacy of ethics and values:

> We affirm finally that any deliberate attempt to reach a rational and enduring state of equilibrium by planned measures, rather than by chance or catastrophe, must ultimately be founded on a basic change of values and goals at individual, national and world levels. (Meadows et al, 1972, p 196)

It was these social protest movements from the 1960s that spurred a revitalisation of political philosophy and applied ethics in the academy, marking a break with the past. During the 1950s philosophical ethics had been dominated by 'meta-ethics' or purely academic concern for linguistic analysis. Ethicists paid little attention to contemporary political and social concerns outside the ivory tower. By the 1960s, the mood had changed. Academics, including philosophers, felt themselves on the front lines of protest and social change.

The landmark event here was the publication of John Rawls' book *A Theory of Justice* (1971), which revived the idea of normative ethics and linked ethics to policy analysis and criticism. It would not be long before philosophers would apply Rawls' thinking to environmental ethics and obligations to future generations. For example, Hans Jonas articulated a 'principle of responsibility' (Jonas, 1979) as part of a broader ethic required by technological civilisation. Eventually, an influential book appeared, *Responsibilities to Future Generations*, a collection of essays published at a time when the philosophical 'problem' of obligations to future generations was just beginning to be widely recognised (Partridge, 1981). Contributors to this volume pointed out that many of the ethical theories that have been taken for granted by moral philosophers for the past two centuries tend to produce strange or counter-intuitive results when extended to include future generations. For example, the ethical system of Utilitarianism would appear to recommend unlimited population increase on the basis of 'the greatest good for the greatest number'. But the result of such a view was that quantity of life took precedence over quality and seemed to put future generations at risk.

Similarly, theories based on the idea of the social contract, dating back to Locke, Rousseau and Kant, seem to present a challenge of understanding reciprocity: after all, where is there any reciprocity if we can affect the lives of future people although unborn generations apparently cannot affect ours? Even a fundamental idea like 'human rights' presents problems when applied to future generations who do not yet exist and may never exist (Govier, 1979; see also Chapter Three). The British philosopher Derek Parfit was one of the most brilliant and creative figures posing these dilemmas (Parfit, 1976, 1982) which seem to involve paradoxes of different kinds (Kavka, 1982): for instance, is there a 'right to be born' (Feinberg, 1980)? How can 'potential' people have a 'right' to be born in the first place? Do 'possible people' have rights at all (Macklin, 1981)?

Responsibilities to Future Generations (Partridge, 1981) created a tremendous intellectual impact. At the time of its original publication, the journal *Ethics* devoted 30 pages to a review of the book, which is still frequently cited and discussed. The basic ethical question has only grown more acute in the years since the book appeared. That question is, simply, 'whether and to what degree it can be morally incumbent on us to make sacrifices to bring happy people into the world or to avoid preventing them being brought into the world'. The ethical issues related to this central question only become more urgent in a world of accelerating economic growth and environmental pollution while populations, in both the developed and developing world, are rapidly ageing.

The call for limits heard so often in the 1970s did not seem at first to apply to programmes for older people. Older people, overall, were presented as 'victims' in need of justified support from the welfare state. Indeed, the 1970s were a decade when books such as Simone de Beauvoir's (1972) *The Coming of Age* and Robert Butler's (1975) *Why Survive?* called attention to older people in need. During the 1970s, ageing began to be understood not as inevitable human fate but as a social problem that could be solved. One example here was dementia, which until the 1970s was largely regarded as 'senility', the inevitable concomitant of age. But, by the mid-1970s, dementia became explained as Alzheimer's disease (Gubrium, 1986) in a process of 'social construction' that gathered force and has continued ever since then. This medicalisation of ageing was decisive. After all, a disease could be treated, prevented, cured. Then, too, we might ask, was old age poverty a problem? It should be rectified. The progressive spirit of the 1960s was increasingly applied to older people, sometimes under the guise of 'compassionate ageism' (Binstock, 1983). This approach to old age advocacy had its merits, but it set the stage for a dramatic challenge in the next decade, when political winds would change.

The 1980s: generational equity and the rise of age-based rationing

The 1980s began with a major political shift: the coming to power of conservative parties in both the UK and the US. The election of Margaret Thatcher (1979) and Ronald Reagan (1980) signalled the ascendance of conservative politics for the rest of the decade and beyond (Ehrman, 2006). In the US, Reagan favoured drastic reform of social security but, whatever his ideological preference, events quickly pushed reform in a different direction. During the late 1970s, US President Jimmy Carter had signed legislation promising to make social security sustainable for a generation. But that promise proved hollow when the economy declined. The economic turbulence of the late 1970s and early 1980s eroded the revenues needed to sustain social security, which was soon threatened with bankruptcy. In Reagan's first term, a bipartisan compromise was required to safeguard the solvency of social security, which was achieved in 1983 (Altman, 2005).

Ironically, the successful resolution of the social security problem set the stage for a dramatic challenge to ageing policy: the rise of generational equity (Longman, 1982). In 1984, just one year after the successful reform of social security, a new organisation in the US came into being, namely Americans for Generational Equity (AGE). Its impact on public policy discussion was profound, even though the organisation itself was negligible in size and actually disappeared after 1990. What AGE did was to change the terms of debate in public policy around population ageing. AGE pushed forward the idea that population ageing was unaffordable and that the old were gaining benefits at the expense of the young.

The framework of justice between generations, familiar in environmental policy, was now applied to ageing, to the dismay of liberal advocates for older people. But the impact of the shift was profound. As Jill Quadagno, no friend of generational equity, put it: "All future policy choices will have to take generational equity into account" (Quadagno, 1989, p 364).

The assault against age-based entitlements in the US reached unprecedented levels during the generational equity debate in the 1980s (see for example, Longman, 1982; Fairlie, 1988). The unprecedented attack on older people was not a spasm of ageism but the result of the history of ageing policy in previous decades. During the 1980s defenders of social security, and other age-based entitlements, had succeeded in reforming the system and doing so on a bipartisan basis. But they had not addressed the festering problem of justice between generations in the environment or in the fiscal domain. Moreover, a further interesting feature of the debate in the 1980s was the role of key political liberals in presenting ideas that could lend support to generational equity. The most prominent of these was Daniel Callahan, whose book *Setting Limits* actually called for rationing healthcare resources on grounds of age and warned that healthcare spending for older people was out of control and unsustainable (Callahan, 1987). Callahan's book and his proposals set off a firestorm of response by gerontologists and ageing advocates and prompted enduring controversy.

Callahan's proposal for age-based rationing sounded outlandish. Yet the practice of age-based rationing, it turns out, has been widespread. For example, it was long the case that people over the age of 55 were excluded from access to kidney dialysis in the British National Health Service (NHS) (Aaron and Schwarz, 2005). Most other advanced industrialised countries excluded the very old from expensive high-tech medicine. But such exclusion was always hidden and indirect, never a matter of public debate, as Callahan called for.

A less inflammatory but parallel approach to allocation of resources was proposed by philosopher Norman Daniels in *Am I my Parents' Keeper?*, which presented itself as a philosophical reflection on justice between the young and old (Daniels, 1988). Daniels had shown himself to be perhaps the foremost interpreter of John Rawls (Daniels, 1985), and he applied his Rawlsian approach to justice to consider competing claims of different age groups. In the 1970s, the Rawlsian framework had been enthusiastically adopted by liberals to call for environmental justice. However, Daniels' work showed that Rawls' ideas could have very different results when applied in a different context: namely, Rawlsian ethics could result in a justification for rationing healthcare resources on grounds of age.

Daniels felt that his formulation could make any problem of 'generational conflict' simply disappear. He proposed framing the issue of "justice between generations" in terms of "justice between age-groups":

> Justice between age groups is a problem best solved if we stop thinking
> of the old and the young as distinct groups. We age. The young
> become the old. As we age, we pass through institutions that affect

> our well being at each stage of life, from infancy to very old age.
> (Daniels, 1988, p 18)

Whatever Callahan and Daniels might say in philosophical terms, the idea of justice between generations – understood as 'generational equity' – was becoming influential among journalists and policy elites concerned about rising government expenditures for the old. Understandably then, gerontologists did not like what generational equity seemed to portend for an ageing society and they responded with strong and repeated attacks on the whole idea. Eric Kingson and colleagues, working under the sponsorship of the Gerontological Society of America, published a rebuttal of generational equity titled *The Common Stake*, emphasising not conflict but the interdependence of generations (Kingson et al, 1987). Kingson, with John Williamson, went on to write what is perhaps the best and most comprehensive book about the whole generational equity debate, a collection including voices from both sides (Kingson and Williamson, 1999). Similar fair-mindedness was evident in a book published by the American Association of Retired Persons (AARP) on the subject of justice between generations (Cohen, 1993).

By the end of the 1980s, concern about generational equity had reached a point where ageing advocates reached out to children's groups to create a new organisation, Generations United, founded jointly by AARP and the Child Welfare League of America. Generations United was designed to be an umbrella organisation uniting all those with an interest in intergenerational programming and intergenerational concerns: for example, the interests of grandparents caring for their grandchildren. Since 1990, Generations United has worked to promote coalitions between young and old, precisely along the lines called for by Kingson and his colleagues (1987) who emphasised interdependence, instead of conflict, between age groups.

The appearance of a movement on behalf of generational equity unsettled ageing advocates because, as a group, they were in large part politically progressive in their thinking. In the US the claim of 'justice between generations' seemed to contradict a fundamental assumption that helping older people would be the vanguard of a movement to help all of society; for example, the hope that Medicare – the key publicly funded programme of health insurance aimed at older and disabled people in the US – would be only the opening victory on behalf of a wider expansion toward national health insurance for all. Elders, then, should be seen simply as 'our future selves', as Daniels (1985, 1988) had argued in the spirit of Rawls. In sum, the deepest values of left-liberal ideology seemed threatened by generational equity.

By the close of the 1980s, the idea of generational equity had spread beyond academic discourse and had begun to shape decisively the way that journalists and others in the policy elite would think about the future of an ageing society. Their pessimism would spread in turn beyond the US. In years to come, generational equity would take on new life through the economic methodology of 'generational accounting', where it proved influential in countries around the world. As it happened, during the 1990s, the US succeeded in reducing the federal government deficit and insuring that social security would long remain solvent. Yet, after 2000, the ethical dilemmas of justice between generations would re-emerge in different forms and in other parts of the globe beyond the US.

The 1990s: generational accounting, sustainability and the environment and the rise of positive ageing

The 1990s marked the end of the Cold War and a growing movement toward globalisation in trade and communications. The concern over generational equity during the 1980s was at its peak in the US, but in the 1990s it spread to other countries. Yet, by the 1990s the terms of the discourse had changed. Instead of philosophical or ethical analysis, the issue of justice between generations became framed in economic terms through the rise of 'generational accounting' developed by Laurence Kotlikoff and colleagues (Kotlikoff, 1993). The appearance of generational accounting as an analytical framework was clearly understood to be a threat to the traditional welfare state and age-based entitlements. In the same year that Kotlikoff published his ground-breaking work, Vern Bengtson devoted his 1990 Presidential Address to the Gerontological Society of America to the question of whether generational accounting would doom the welfare state (Bengtson, 1993). Kotlikoff and his colleagues would go on to apply the generational accounting framework to deficit accounting (Auerbach et al, 1991) and fiscal policy (Auerbach et al, 1994) and the generational accounting methodology would continue to fuel fears about the future of an ageing society (Kotlikoff and Burns, 2004).

The 1990s also witnessed the first widespread application of generational accounting to public policy and governmental expenditures in countries beyond the US. The generational accounting methodology has become influential in analysing benefits and burdens for cohorts in different countries such as Great Britain (Hobman, 1993; Banks et al, 2000), Belgium (Delbecque and Bogaert, 1994), Germany (Hinrichs, 2002) and Japan (Hashimoto, 1996). In Canada there was explicit discussion of intergenerational fairness in reforming policies governing pensions (Good, 1994; Beaujot and Richards, 1996). In Australia there was concern that population ageing would threaten future living standards (Guest, 2001). In sum, by the end of the 1990s, Kotlikoff and other economists had succeeded in introducing an analytical framework that would have influence far beyond the US (Raffelhüschen, 1999).

At the same time, discourse around justice between generations became less polemical and more analytically sophisticated and synthetically comprehensive. Notable here was the landmark collection edited by British historians Peter Laslett and James Fishkin, *Justice between Age Groups and Generations* (Laslett and Fishkin, 1992). Laslett, for example, could ask the question 'is there a generational contract?' in terms less defensive than North American gerontologists who felt themselves to be defending age-based entitlements against a conservative attack.

The 1990s were moreover the decade when the prospect of global warming first became widely understood by the public, spurring a new attention to environmental ethics. In the 1970s, when environmental ethics first came to prominence, the fear was running out of resources and facing the 'limits of growth'. In the 1990s, the fear was too much growth and concomitant climate change. Throughout the decade, the prospect of global warming came increasingly to public attention and environmental thinkers focused attention on justice between generations in that sphere. For example, Auerbach sought to conceptualise the problem in a book provocatively titled *Unto the Thousandth Generation* (Auerbach, 1995), while the philosophical ethicist Brian Barry applied the environmental idea of 'sustainability' to the analysis of justice between generations (Barry, 1999). One of the very few North American analysts who considered environmental issues along with ageing issues was Stanley Ingman who, with colleagues, edited a book significantly titled *An Aging Population, an Aging Planet, and a Sustainable Future* (Ingman et al, 1995).

On the international scene, however, concern about justice between generations continued to grow. One driving force was growing concern about threats to the environment, such as depletion of the ozone layer and global warming. The seeds for action were evident in the influential Brundtland Report specifically defining the key environmental standard of 'sustainability' in terms of justice between generations: "Meeting the needs of the present generation without compromising the ability of future generations to meet their needs" (World Commission on the Environment and Development, 1987, p 43).

By the 1990s, Agenda 21 became a formal programme of the United Nations (UN) favouring the goal of 'sustainable development', which would become a watchword for environmental activists for years to come. Agenda 21 was a comprehensive blueprint of action to be taken globally, nationally and locally by organisations of the UN, governments and major groups in every area in which humans have an impact on the environment. The number *21* refers to the 21st century.

In 1997, the General Assembly of the UN held a special session to appraise five years of progress on the implementation of Agenda 21 (Rio +5). The Assembly recognised progress as 'uneven' and identified key trends including increasing globalisation, widening inequalities in income and a continued deterioration of the global environment. A new General Assembly Resolution (S-19/2) promised further action. The Commission on Sustainable Development was charged with acting as a high-level forum on sustainable development and has served as preparatory committee for later summits and international gatherings to implement Agenda 21.

What was perhaps most notable in the field of ageing during this period was the appearance of a public discourse around 'positive ageing' and the waning of the 'failure model' of earlier years. A key landmark here was the publication of the book *Successful Aging*, supported by the MacArthur Foundation (Rowe and Kahn, 1999). Another example of this line of thinking was the book on *Productive Aging* (Morrow-Howell et al, 2001). Betty Friedan, author of the influential *The Feminine Mystique* (1963), published her long-awaited *The Fountain of Age* (Friedan, 1994). At the end of the decade came Gene Cohen's *The Creative Age* (Cohen, 2000). What all these books had in a common was a resolutely positive vision of ageing, which was a dramatic reversal of the gloomy view so pervasive in the 1970s when age became understood as a 'social problem'. In sum, during the 1990s, not only did public sentiment move toward a positive image of the future, but there was an image of old age, and an ageing society, in more positive terms.

Did this positive image of ageing mean that the old generational equity debate was dead? Not at all. Instead, during the 1990s, the generational equity agenda took on a different form: the concept and methodology of generational accounting. No longer was the problem of fairness put forward in terms of age, but rather in terms of cohort and history. This shift decisively influenced debates about justice between generations in ways that would persist after the turn of the century. The globalisation of the 1990s brought a growing awareness of the global dimension of both environmental problems and population ageing in both advanced industrialised countries as well as the less economically developed. In advanced countries, at least, improvement in the condition of the older population led to a new public discourse about 'positive ageing' that was bound to have consequences for reflection about justice between generations in the future.

The new millennium and the rise of the risk society

Since the turn of the millennium, there has been a growing awareness of the importance of risks facing human society on a global basis, whether the risks were posed by the environment or by population ageing. This theme was first promoted by Ulrich Beck in his formulation of the 'risk society' (Beck, 1992, 1999). In recent years the idea has been given a more precise quantitative formulation by International Monetary Fund economist Peter Heller in his monograph *Who will Pay?* (Heller, 2003). Heller has argued that contemporary society requires greater commitment to long-term planning than ever before. His comprehensive treatment grows out of his earlier economic studies of the impact of population ageing on fiscal trends and social expenditures in different countries around the globe (Heller et al, 1986). The sources of risk are twofold: first, the welfare state entails a commitment to citizens greater than in earlier times, a commitment extending over a longer life span; and, second, because the scale of environmental impact makes the results of technology more uncertain and dangerous than earlier. Both the life span perspective and the environmental perspective had become prominent in the 1990s in the rise of generational accounting and in growing awareness of global warming. What Heller and other analysts have done is to connect these dimensions of our obligations to future generations.

Moreover, as the impact of global warming and planetary resource depletion has gradually been assimilated around the world, leaders in many countries are increasingly thinking about the problem of justice between future generations in terms that would have been unimaginable even in the recent past. For example:

- *Noah's Ark for seeds:* Norway has announced the creation of a 'Doomsday Vault' inside a remote Arctic Island. The vault will hold a seed bank of all known varieties of the world's crops, according to the organiser, the Global Crop Diversity Trust.
- *The Clock of the Long Now:* Stewart Brand, founder of the Whole Earth Catalog, along with a group of scientists and futurists, has led in the planning and development of a '10,000 year clock', the so-called 'Clock of the Long Now', intended to inspire humanity to take account of long-range consequences for future generations inhabiting the earth (Brand, 1999).
- *Guarding nuclear waste:* a repository for nuclear waste deposits planned for a remote location in Nevada has been designed with inscriptions warning future generations about the dangers of radioactivity. The project has entailed far-reaching contemplation of how to communicate with future generations across 'deep time' (Benford, 2000).

In addition, some new themes have been enunciated in the public discussion about ageing and justice between generations. As the reality of population ageing has become more widely understood, some analysts have shifted from worry about population growth to new concern about a 'population implosion' (Eberstadt, 2001). Ben Wattenberg (2004) has long worried about how the new demography will shape our future, while Phillip Longman (2004), a strong voice on generational equity two decades earlier, has became a proponent of 'pronatalism', urging higher birth rates as the solution to problems of equitable distribution across generations.

Concern about justice between generations has not been limited to the US. It has emerged as a significant political issue in Europe. In Germany, for example, there was the creation of a Foundation for Generational Justice, bringing together environmental concerns and ageing policy concerns and associated with the radical Green Party. Also in Germany, a group of 47 members of the federal parliament have proposed a law calling for the right to vote from birth to compensate for the growing power of older voters. A constitutional amendment would permit parents to vote by proxy on behalf of children under 18 years of age. These legislators fear that the ageing of the German population will under-represent the interests of children. Demographic trends suggest why legislators are worried. By 2030 more than a third of the German population will be over the age of 60 and analysts estimate that by next election 60 per cent of voters will be over the age of 50. However, as in the US, generational equity arguments seem to appeal more to political elites than to the electorate.

Increasingly too, analysts have invoked the language of 'sustainability' in thinking about justice between generations: for example, in asking what a sustainable social security system would cost (Lee and Yamagata, 2003; Rurup Commission, 2003). The environmental analyst Clark Wolf applied the framework of sustainability to raise questions about the relationship between poverty and fertility in defining conditions for generational justice and sustainable economic development (Wolf, 2002). As social thought increasingly takes on a global dimension in the new century (Wisensale, 2003), it becomes clear that the ethics of sustainability (Visser 't Hooft, 1999) will be at the centre of debates over justice between generations in the 21st century, both in the environment as well as in social insurance systems.

Conclusion

In short, awareness of the 'risk society' along with what Hans Jonas (1979) called the 'principle of responsibility' has prompted growing recognition of the problem of justice between generations in both the domain of social welfare expenditures as well as environmental ethics. While earlier concerns about generational equity were limited mainly to policy elites, the new concern about risks facing future generations has become far more widespread, even invoking the spectre of societal 'collapse' (Diamond, 2004) or humanity's 'final hour' (Rees, 2003). A forecast of global warming has now joined with gloom about the sustainability of pension plans to put younger people in a position where planning for a hopeful life course seems less and less plausible. But perhaps this gloom is premature. Awareness of genuine risks, whether in the environment or population ageing, could prompt either a call for hope and collective action, or a spreading mood of pessimism and paralysis. Which path we take remains to be seen, but it is safe to say that the challenge of justice between generations will no longer be avoided in the 21st century. As W.H. Auden put it succinctly, "In the end we are all contemporaries".

TEN

Progress in gerontology: where are we going now?

Tony Warnes and Judith Phillips

Introduction

When we first began to address the question in this chapter's title, our first and conventional response was to compile a calendar of the principal institutional and funding developments of recent years. That compilation tells a useful story, but it soon became clear that, to understand the many and sometimes conflicting directions of change in the subject, in research funding and priorities, and in older people's situation in society, analysis was needed. 'Progress' implies goals and destinations and, in the production of knowledge, these are the outcome of a complex interchange of ideas and ambitions between funders and researchers. To understand the roles of gerontological knowledge and gerontologists, it is first necessary to be clear about the interest groups or constituencies that are concerned with the circumstances and welfare of (past and future) older people. When they are specified, we can begin to understand their priority goals and their information needs.

This chapter presents our understanding of the connections in contemporary Britain between, on the one side, the interest groups that are concerned with the well-being of older people and, on the other side, information providers – including gerontologists. It aims to clarify the roles of gerontological knowledge and gerontologists in the debates and decision-making processes. The chapter has three main sections: the first sets out our understanding of the 'stakeholder groups', their interactions with each other and with societal change, and the role of information in both policy debates and administrative and practice change. The second reviews the growth of gerontology and its major branches, and then reports recent institutional developments in Britain as first intended, but with a twist: a case study of the interaction between the members and officials of the Welsh Assembly Government and gerontological advisers. The chapter concludes with an audit of areas of progress.

Stakeholders and objectives

Gerontology encompasses the study of older people and biological ageing. That immediately points to quite disparate topics: on the one hand, the factors and structures that condition the absolute and relative material well-being of older people at different times and places and, on the other, the fundamental genetic and biochemical processes of the ageing of the soma. If the only concern is to maximise the standard of living of today's older people, nothing would be spent on fundamental ageing research, and its funding would be diverted to, say, state benefits for older people. But, biologists argue that by studying the fundamental processes not only will we gain a better understanding of the pathologies and disorders of old age that will lead to new therapies, more effective treatments and a raised quality of old-age lives but also, over a longer time scale, there will be breakthroughs that enable interventions that alter the rate of ageing and longevity. In the long term, they would argue, their research will bring radical improvements in the well-being of older people.

Put in this way, the priority-setting conundrum is over-simplified and falsely suggests that the interests of natural scientists and older people are opposed. In the final sections of the chapter, the issues raised will be examined more subtly, but we first take a more inclusive view of the interest groups or stakeholders in ageing and older people issues. Both the older people and biological ageing enterprises incorporate many and diverse questions and topics, and they engage many different groups. We suggest, however, that they fall into three distinguishable constituencies.

- Older people (and those approaching old age), with contractual and moral claims on younger age groups (see Chapter Nine).
- The government, with massive and expensive responsibilities for funding in whole or part old-age income, healthcare, social care and social housing, and perennially responsible for balancing the competing claims of 'social reproduction' (that is, children, education and parents) and the welfare of the current adult population (see Chapters Three and Four).
- Professional (or producer) interests: the many occupational groups and economic interests that provide services for older people, most especially the health and social care professionals and the organisations that provide medical and long-term care facilities and therapies, including the pharmaceutical industry. Their mission is to raise 'welfare', but their vested interest is to expand their role. The processes that influence their priorities are labyrinthine and require constant appraisal. While this constituency is the main source of expertise and capacity to raise welfare, their contribution is subject to several blights, such as the tendency for inherited or customary practices to outlive their functionality, and the paucity of evidence-based ways of working and, as a result, of sub-optimal resource allocation and outcomes.

The three major constituencies can be conceived as a wheel of interest groups that are constantly interacting and energised by their ceaseless interaction with change, as it were, the slope of social, economic, technological and political developments that imparts energy to the entire system (Figure 10.1). The heat and friction generated at the points of contact with the road, and among the stakeholder groups, can retard forward progress, but each of the constituencies is helped by companion and support organisations that try both to promote their sponsor's interest and to keep things moving. Some specialise in advocacy, like the older people's representative organisations[1]; some in information processing and presentation, like the think-tanks; and some in implementation, especially the civil service and local government. The braking effect is countered by collaboration and good management, appropriate organisations, and by good quality information and better understanding, which is where researchers come in, and indeed their companion organisations, like commercial survey firms, the research councils and charitable foundations. The information generators do not drive the system, but they have an important facilitating or 'lubricating' role. If high-quality information and good understanding is generated and communicated well, then timely and appropriate policy and administrative responses are promoted.

Information is one key lubricant of the system, but another is payment for services rendered. The wheel is also a 'market place' for leverage, persuasion, ideas and information. Occasionally a line of research is driven principally by an intellectual problem, but it is difficult to think of unadulterated examples outside mathematics and the humanities since, say, 1939. In gerontology, the research that is done is guided by the information priorities of government, commerce and, on a much smaller scale, of older people's representative organisations and social research foundations: the key drivers are government research and development and higher education funding. This has been patently obvious in the US for three decades, but only recently has it become clear that the US is not a special case. Indeed, several European governments have decided over the past five years that they need a 'national programme of ageing research' but, what is being funded and why? To begin to understand these changes, we briefly review the growth of gerontology in the English-speaking world and then focus on the UK.

Growth of gerontology

As James Birren concisely introduced his excellent short history, "gerontology is an ancient subject but a recent science" (1996b, p 655). The epithet succinctly describes a paradox: that in all societies, philosophers, theologians and imaginative writers have been fascinated by the processes and stages of human ageing and the experience of old age, but systematic and sustained investigation of these questions began only around 60 years ago. The main phases of gerontology's growth since then are clear. While a few scientists and scholars had taken a

Figure 10.1: The wheel of gerontological interests and the road of change

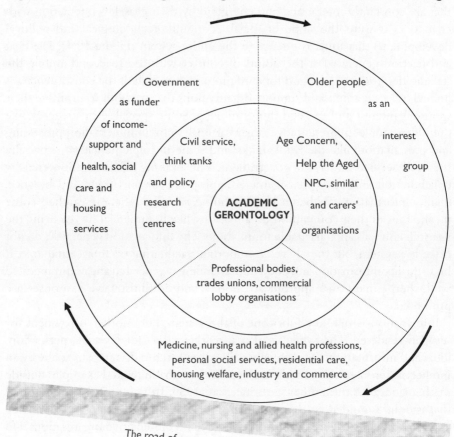

Government
as funder
of income-
support and
health, social
care and
housing
services

Civil service,
think tanks
and policy
research
centres

ACADEMIC GERONTOLOGY

Age Concern,
Help the Aged
NPC, similar
and carers'
organisations

Older people
as an
interest
group

Professional bodies,
trades unions, commercial
lobby organisations

Medicine, nursing and allied health professions,
personal social services, residential care,
housing welfare, industry and commerce

The road of economic, technological, political and social change

Note: NPC = National Pensioners Convention

special interest in ageing and old age for half a century, gerontology as a focus of collective academic effort and with formal structures, took root at the end of the Second World War. The Gerontological Society of America (GSA) and the British Society for Research on Ageing (BSRA) were founded in 1945, and the International Association of Gerontology (IAG) in 1950. In those same years, several disparate events confirmed that in Britain (as elsewhere) a benchmark had been crossed: local authority homes for older people replaced the workhouses; the modern state pension began; geriatric medicine was first recognised as a medical speciality; and, least well known, William Morris (Viscount Nuffield), the car manufacturer, provided the first substantial charitable funding for applied social research in gerontology, for projects in Oxford and Cambridge on age and work performance (see Welford, 1951).

Since that time, gerontological research has grown continuously, until the 1970s very slowly in most countries, but quickly in the US. The differential was further increased by the establishment in 1974 of the National Institute on Aging (NIA) (as one of the National Institutes of Health): "to provide leadership in aging research, training, health information dissemination, and other programs relevant to aging and older people" (see www.nia.nih.gov/). Subsequent amendments to this legislation designated the NIA as the primary federal agency on Alzheimer's disease research. It now has an annual budget of $1,057 million (around £565 million), of which two thirds are expended on research grants, 10 per cent on in-house research and eight per cent on research centres. A substantial majority of the funds support genetic, neurological, biomedical, clinical and epidemiological research. The GSA now has over 5,000 members, most of them academics or social welfare professionals, and the American Geriatrics Society (AGS) has 7,000 members, a substantial minority of whom are researchers.

Developments in the UK

The growth of institutional gerontology and its research capacity was much slower in the UK. The early developments have been documented by Coleman (1975), Warnes (1993) and Bernard and Phillips (2000). The first substantial impetus for the growth of social gerontology was the rapid expansion of the universities from the mid-1960s, and the recognition of a need for teaching and courses in the subject. The British Society of Social and Behavioural Gerontology (now the British Society of Gerontology) was founded in 1971 (for a few years, its meetings attracted no more than 30-50 delegates). The journal *Ageing & Society* was first published in 1981, and then a demand for Masters courses was realised in the late 1980s. At that time, public sector employers were willing to support attendance with job release and fees contributions. Successful postgraduate courses in turn prompted the foundation of several centres and institutes of gerontology, and created a market for teaching texts and collections (Wells and Freer, 1988; Jeffreys, 1989; Warnes, 1989; Bond and Coleman, 1990). The first publicly funded but modest research programme in social gerontology was funded by the Social Science Research Council (SSRC) in the 1980s and directed by Margot Jeffreys. During the 1980s, the growth of social gerontology was appreciable but "from a very low base and without revolutionising the research capacity or public influence of the subject" (Warnes, 1999, p 120).

Until the mid-1990s, the British Geriatrics Society (BGS) prospered, and the British Society for Research on Ageing (BSRA), the society of biological gerontologists, remained small but had considerable intellectual weight[2], while the study of dementia was dominated by epidemiology. The shared research priority of consultant physicians and the public (as represented in the mass media), to concentrate research funding on organ-based diseases and pathologies, swayed the comparatively well-resourced Medical Research Council (MRC) to award relatively little to research on the basic processes of ageing. Through the 1980s it did, however, support a Laboratory of Mathematical Biology at the National Institute for Medical Research in north London, where Tom Kirkwood developed the disposable soma theory (Kirkwood, 1977) and did much else besides. But this was wound up in 1993. It was not only the biologists who looked with envy at their North American colleagues. Social gerontologists' proposals for projects that spanned the concerns of several disciplines (for example, sociology, social work, psychology and healthcare) were finding it hard to win grants from the Economic and Social Research Council (ESRC) (as the SSRC had since become), and had little chance of success with the MRC (although for many years it has funded a centre of excellence in medical sociology in the University of Glasgow).

There was another difficulty: the distrustful relationship between the government and social science researchers during the Thatcher administration (1979-97). In 1997, a booklet was produced to support the bid by the three UK gerontology societies (BSG, BGS and BSRA) to host the 2005 International Association of Gerontology's World Congress. Its preface claimed unashamedly that the collection demonstrated "the pluri-disciplinary character of British scientific and scholarly gerontological societies, and the seamless range of gerontologists' interests from fundamental research through health and social welfare practice to social and 'citizenship' policies". Over the page, however, Margot Jeffreys gave a less bullish view, one that clearly stemmed from her time as an SSRC programme director.

There is a long-standing suspicion and ambivalence with which British politicians, tacitly supported by the general public, regard those academics who believe that their research activities have something to offer society. Added to this deeply embedded scepticism about the ability of the academic social and behavioural sciences to provide guidance on matters of policy was the inward looking, defensive stance of exponents of those newly developing sciences. They were seeking to establish the legitimacy and respectability of their own individual discipline in a conservative academia still dominated by both highly respected 'basic' subjects and long-established professional groups with unquestioned authority. In this concatenation of circumstance, we have explanation for the frankly indifferent collective contribution made by British scholars until relatively recently to gerontological theory and its application (Jeffreys, 1997, p 1).

We shortly continue the story of developments in British gerontology since 1997, but first return to the worldwide expansion of the subject. The IAG now has 70 affiliated societies in 63 countries, with a combined membership of more than 40,000. Its governance continues, however, to be dominated by geriatricians, some of whom bring the attitudes and expectations of a medical society to the organisation: in 2005, it changed its name to the International Association of Gerontology and Geriatrics. One should remember, however, that geriatricians are distinguished among medical consultants for their holistic assessment and diagnostic skills and for their empathy with their patients, and that time and again they have been at the forefront in raising awareness of gerontological issues and in advocating rigorous and well-funded research. In many middle- and low-income countries, they are still the only gerontology researchers.

Multiplication of gerontology journals

Interesting aspects of the pace and stages of the subject's development are indicated by the multiplication of English-language scientific and scholarly journals (Table 10.1). As late as 1959, only two journals with gerontology or ag(e)ing in the title had been founded and, during the 1960s, only three more began. However, 30 new titles were founded during the 1970s and 1980s, and 20 more during the 1990s (Figure 10.2). Altogether 63 substantial titles appeared, of which 61 continued publication in 2005. The early impetus was from biology and geriatric medicine. Among the 22 titles founded up to 1981, 12 were *exclusively* concerned with biomedical topics (that is, both basic science and geriatric practice), and only two were *exclusively* concerned with social science and humanities research. The remainder were either multidisciplinary or related to other professional concerns (one social work, two nursing). Between 1982 and 1991, by contrast, among the 23 journals established, only four were biomedical and nine specialised in social gerontology. There had clearly been a swing, but it was temporary. Among the 18 journals founded between 1993 and 2005, eight were biomedical and five were in social gerontology[3]. Note, however, that around one quarter of all the current serials are professedly multidisciplinary, and that such titles continue to be founded, some as flagship national journals, although in practice the pages of many are dominated by biomedical research.

The titles and presumed readerships reflect a perennial dilemma for both biological and social gerontologists: whether to commit to gerontology or to their base discipline or research field. The dominant influences have been job security and the established disciplines' prestige hierarchies and processes. Many researchers in gerontology decide to stay with their base discipline or, for biomedical researchers, a cadre of organ pathology researchers (for example, in cardiovascular disorders or cancer). Through the 1990s, these responses were both the consequence of and reinforced the UK research councils' no more than mild enthusiasm for, either fundamental biological research or cross-disciplinary and social gerontology projects with a 'welfare-client' rather than 'welfare-producer' orientation. For whatever reasons, a strong constituency of social gerontologists with 'gerontological imagination', who see the issues generally from the point of view of (present and future) older people, did not develop from the foundations laid in the 1980s. Medical, professional, public expenditure and political concerns were the dominant influences, and were reinforced within the universities.

This outcome was reflected by, and interacted with, a similar imbalance among the three constituencies of influence on information requirements and production. In particular, the interests of today's older people, and of those concerned to promote their welfare, have been relatively weak. Alarm about the long-term

Table 10.1: Year of first publication of journals with gerontolog* and ag(e)ing in the titles held by the British Library, 2005

1937 *Growth, Development and Aging*[a]

1946 *Journal of Gerontology* (now four disciplinary-specific journals)

1958 *Gerontology and Geriatrics* (Amsterdam)

1961 *The Gerontologist*

1964 *Experimental Gerontology*

1969 *Indian Journal of Gerontology*

1970 *Aging and Human Development*

1972 Age and Ageing

1972 *Mechanisms of Aging and Development*

1973 *Ageing International*

1974 *Acta Gerontologica* (Milan, Italy)

1975 *Journal of Gerontological Nursing*

1975 *Experimental Aging Research*

1976 *Gerontology* (Basel, Switzerland)

1976 *Biomedical Gerontology* (Tokyo)

1978 *Journal of Gerontological Social Work*

1979 *Journal of Clinical and Experimental Gerontology*

1979 *Current Practice in Gerontological Nursing*

1979 *Research on Aging*

1980 *Neurobiology of Aging*

1981 Ageing & Society

1981 *Australasian Journal on Ageing*

1982 *Archives of Gerontology and Geriatrics*

1982 *Journal of Applied Gerontology*

1982 *Canadian Journal on Aging*

1983 *Journal of Religious Gerontology*[b]

1986 *Journal of Educational Gerontology*[c]

1986 *Journal of Cross-Cultural Gerontology*

1986 *Psychology and Aging*

1986 *International Journal of Geriatric Psychiatry*

1987 *Hong Kong Journal of Gerontology* (until 1995)

1987 *Comprehensive Gerontology*

1987 *Journal of Aging Studies*

1988 *Trends in Biomedical Gerontology*

1989 *Journal of Aging and Health*

1989 *Journal of Women and Aging*

1990 *Abstracts in Social Gerontology*

1990 *Behavior, Health and Aging*

1990 *Ageing: Clinical and Experimental Research*

1991 *European Journal of Gerontology* (1991 and 1992 only)

1991 *Reviews in Clinical Gerontology*

1991 Generations Review (BSG)

1991 *Journal of Geriatric Drug Therapy*[d]

1991 *Southern African Journal of Gerontology*

1993 *Skin and Aging*

1994 *Aging, Neuropsychology and Cognition*

1994 *Contemporary Gerontology*

1995 *Ethics, Law and Aging Review*

1996 *Advances in Cell Aging and Gerontology*

1996 *Journal of Aging and Identity*

1996 *Advances in Anti-Aging Medicine*

1996 *Journal of Aging and Ethnicity*

1996 *Advances in Gerontological Nursing*

1997 *Journal of Nutrition, Health and Aging*

1997 *Aging and Mental Health*

1998 *Chinese Journal of Gerontology*

2000 *Biogerontology*[e]

2001 *Hallym International Journal of Aging*

2001 *Geriatrics and Gerontology International*[e]

2002 *Ageing Research Reviews*

2002 *Aging Cell*

2004 *Ageing Horizons* (Oxford)

2005 *European Journal of Ageing*

Notes: geriatric* was not a search term. [a] Before 1988, *Growth.* [b] Now *Journal of Religion, Spirituality and Aging.* [c] Now *Education and Ageing.* [d] Since 2003, *Journal of Aging and Pharmacotherapy.* [e] Online publication.

Figure 10.2: The foundation of English-language gerontology journals

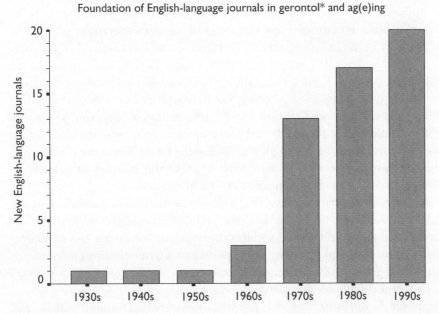

Foundation of English-language journals in gerontol* and ag(e)ing

spending projections of 'elderly care and support' in all its forms has become the key and consensually agreed research problem, while those researchers whose projects imply a need for more spending on the quality of today's support and care of older people are less welcome (but, to be fair, quite often listened to). Over the past decade, there has also been a tendency for public social research funding for gerontology to converge on the technical and operational aspects of service administration.

British gerontology and gerontologists since 1987

For two decades in Britain, there has nonetheless been growth and increasing confidence in academic gerontology, both as a teaching subject and a research field. Educational gerontology has grown with a proliferation of vocationally oriented Masters-level programmes in the universities. More and more gerontology texts are published. Attendance at BSG and BGS annual conferences and related conferences has grown, and responding to 'the ageing population' is on many policy and practice agendas, as notably in the development of new forms of specialist extra-care housing and, most urgently in the eyes of the government, restraining the growth of expenditure on old-age income. Despite such optimism in the field of gerontology, there are cautionary notes in relation to education, policy and practice and research.

Research funding has increased from the European Union, the Department of Health and the UK research councils, as through the Engineering and Physical

Sciences Research Council's (EPSRC) EQUAL Programme, Biotechnology and Biological Sciences Research Council (BBSRC) Experimental Research on Ageing Initiative, the ESRC's 'Growing Older Programme' and, most recently, the multi-Research Council 'New Dynamics of Ageing' Programme (2005-10). In addition, both the Joseph Rowntree Foundation and The Nuffield Foundation have had 'ageing' research programme themes, and the Department of Health established a Funders' Forum as a platform for co-ordinated working and from which to identify the major gaps in support. In March 2004, the National Health Service (NHS) announced that an extra £100 million a year would be made available by 2008 for Research and Development into four major diseases: Alzheimer's, stroke, diabetes and mental ill-health. The success of the 34 National Cancer Research Networks, which have doubled the number of patients in clinical trials, will provide the model to tackle these diseases.

Many of these initiatives have emphasised the merits of multidisciplinary approaches, but different stakeholders interpret this very differently. In one place it means adding strong statistical and health economics competence to a clinical research team; in another pooling the expertise of different health professionals; and in a third getting information scientists to design 'assistive technology' projects in collaboration with designers and care–provider agencies.

Moreover, in *education*, there has not been the growth of undergraduate and postgraduate interest in gerontology, as in the US, for example. The lack of funding for students and excessive workplace-based demands leaving little time to fulfil course requirements is one constraining factor. A further factor is the lack of relevance and vocational skills built into such courses, which has led to the lack of funding support from employers in the social and healthcare fields. Such constraint in the knowledge base of gerontology has meant that the evidence base for policy and practice has not necessarily stemmed from gerontological research. Professional development, particularly in relation to social work and nursing, has been less influential as a driver of gerontology.

Professional development and the impact of gerontology

Research into ageing and later life is becoming increasingly multidisciplinary with a focus on stakeholder involvement. Increasingly there is a need to bridge the research–policy–practice gaps to make research acceptable and applicable to the lives of older people (Nolan and Cooke, 2002; see also Chapter Six). Professional developments in social work and nursing have traditionally not made use of gerontological research and theory, despite a number of gerontology centres establishing their credentials on professional education and training. The context for professional development in this area is increasingly changing in response to:

• demographic trends;
• the visibility of older people on policy and practice agendas, such as the *National*

Service Framework for Older People (DH, 2001) and Better Government for
Older People initiatives, the strategies for older people in Wales and England,
and the Commissioner for Older People in Wales;

- the increasing prominence of frail and vulnerable older people in the case and
patient loads of social work and nursing;
- the specialisation of work with older people;
- retention and recruitment issues among the social care workforce, influencing
the supply of professionals working with older people.

Social work, nursing and gerontology

The two worlds of gerontology and social work have developed separately with
little commonality and crossover between disciplines. The complexity of work
with older people in practice has been simplified under the appearance of the
care management process. Care management procedures increasingly focus on
the measurement of need through defining older people in terms of crisis, risk,
dependency and frailty, and research agendas have mirrored this trend,
concentrating on managerial concerns and methods. Moreover, the research
agendas of the two disciplines of social work and gerontology have developed in
different directions: gerontology accommodating a wider perspective. Gerontology
has become interdisciplinary with skills and techniques of many disciplines –
actuaries, economists, architects and engineers are claiming the territory of driving
gerontology forward. This is reflected in the cross-research council New Dynamics
of Ageing Programme and priorities of the EPSRC through its Strategic
Promotion of Ageing Research Capacity (SPARC) Programme. The programme
objectives of the New Dynamics of Ageing are "to advance our understanding
of the dynamics of ageing from an interdisciplinary perspective" (www.esrc.ac.uk).

Alternatively, social work research has revolved around concerns of dependency
focused on narrow issues of health and social care with the gerontological agenda
having little impact on social work approaches. Consequently, as stated previously,
employers have been reluctant to support educational courses in gerontology,
and the lack of connection between gerontological research and social work
practice has also contributed to a research–practice gap. Similar issues have been
raised in nursing. McCormack (2005) argues that the challenge for nursing is to
break away from a history of service delivery that has been dominated by models
of institutionalisation and routinised care. Similar to social work, education for
nurses working with older people continues to be problematic with a lack of
career structure, and recognition of skills.

Consequently the influence of social work and nursing has declined in influence
on the discipline of gerontology. This can be argued to be a positive development
reflecting a changed construction of older people from 'sick and frail' requiring
treatment to a more affluent, assertive and active group of citizens in society. Yet
the research capacity in social ageing came traditionally from practice routes.

Where are we going in relation to research?

Emerging trends indicate a concentration of funding in large centres of excellence that embrace a multidisciplinary approach, alongside a greater and heightened awareness of ageing as a subject area across society. Mainstreaming age may be a policy initiative that spreads to research. Sarah Harper's 1999 review of research in social gerontology identified 20 major academic centres, groups and networks (Harper, 1999). Since then, there have been changes in the number, focus and development, with some centres moving from teaching gerontology as a major activity to developing a research specialism or specialisms within centres, many around policy-related research; for example, Keele has embraced social exclusion and ageing in urban environments as a major area, providing government with research evidence for its Sure Start to Later Life Initiative (Phillipson and Scharf, 2004; Scharf et al, 2005; ODPM, 2006); Bangor has traditionally concentrated on rural issues and social networks (Wenger, 1984; Wenger and Burholt, 2002, 2004); and the University of Oxford has developed special interests in both actuarial issues of pensions funding and population ageing in developing countries (Aboderin, 2004; Schroeder-Butterfill, 2004). Many disciplines are involved in such centres of expertise highlighting one of the strengths of gerontology. Despite this, funding has been difficult to secure across disciplinary boundaries until recently. The multidisciplinary nature of research into ageing makes it more difficult to attract funding and the Research Assessment Exercise, which places emphasis on competition between centres for research funding, has been particularly disastrous for ageing research because it has discouraged translational research and collaborative approaches.

Traditionally research has focused on health and social aspects of ageing, but there are signs of a broader vision of ageing. There are new areas and opportunities for increasing capacity, for example, through biomedical engineering. There are also signs of other disciplinary agendas impacting on ageing, for example, technology on well-being. This new holistic paradigm of ageing across disciplines and a greater acceptance of interdisciplinary collaboration, mirrors the trend towards more 'joined-up' and systematic thinking in policy and practice and goes beyond just health and social care agendas. The technological, social, economic, physical and environmental aspects impacting on well-being in later life are an example where interdisciplinarity is emerging and new centres are developing as a consequence, for example in Swansea and Southampton.

Innovative ways forward? A research network approach

Developing research capacity is one of the key issues in the progress of gerontology. Within the context of a shrinking social science base in universities (Research Councils UK, 2006), there is an increasing need to enhance and sustain the research community, not only in terms of introducing new researchers to ageing, but also to provide core funding in order to sustain and build future capacity in this area. An example of linking professional practice and policy priorities to gerontological research and education has come through the development of research networks in Wales, one of which focuses on ageing and later life.

The Older People and Ageing Research and Development Network (OPAN Cymru) is one of nine priority areas for research identified and funded by the Welsh Assembly Government[4]. OPAN Cymru was launched in 2006 and is unique, having no parallel in England, Scotland or Northern Ireland. This new development flows from the considerable emphasis on, and raft of policy focusing on, older people in Wales. The network is multidisciplinary and multisectoral, encompassing partners from academia, and from the public, voluntary and independent sectors. The partnership brings together expertise in research, policy development and implementation across the spectrum of health, social and clinical settings. It acts as a bridge between the research community, practitioners and policy makers. The network operates out of Swansea University with regional leads in Bangor and Cardiff universities, each with a particular remit for development and programme of work around certain priority themes (for example, policy/practice/participatory approaches in relation to older people and practitioners; clinical and health issues, particularly stroke and social care).

The network encourages innovative interdisciplinary research groups, strengthens specialisms and fosters interest in older people and ageing in a new generation of researchers. The network aims to enhance the research culture and support the development of the research workforce to address difficulties with the recruitment and retention of suitably qualified researchers. It develops research capacity through regional activities including training sessions, seminars and practice-based research initiatives.

It is anticipated that the network will enhance research capacity and development by:

• enhancing the quality and volume of research;
• improving the integration of policy, practice and research;
• improving the coordination of research both across and within health, social care and clinical specialisms;
• strengthening research collaborations across and within sectors.

Reflections and conclusions

Much has changed in British social welfare and universities over the past 10 years. While it is still difficult to be clear about the main trends, the dominant and critical influences are becoming clear. First was the change of government in 1997, which brought in 'New Labour' and, it was hoped, a 'third way' of balancing policies that promote economic growth with stronger public services and social welfare, but which has turned out to be compliant with 'neoliberal' economic and social policies and marked by increasing inequalities (even in old age). Second was the collapse of the 'dot.com' stock market boom in 2001, which had a devastating effect on private pensions' funding and savings more generally, and brought home to national treasuries, as never before, the huge financial implications of an ageing population. The demographic projections had been much the same for decades, but after 2001, government actuaries were alarmed. Third has been a cocktail of social, lifestyle and policy changes that, for example, have seen increasing numbers of 18-year-olds going to university, and the (partly consequential) concentration of research funding on 'highly performing' individuals and centres. Political influences are increasingly driving the subject with the 'demographic time bomb' raising its head occasionally, not solely driven by the needs of an older society. The drivers are the lack of a younger workforce and the fear of escalating health bills with the consequent need to reduce costs through preventative measures and healthy ageing. As a result a barrage of policy initiatives have been introduced such as National Service Frameworks, Sure Start to Later Life, Strategies and a Commissioner (in Wales). This has increased research capacity, quality and outputs but, at the same time, it has also increased reliance on project and programme grants. In other words, research has been both professionalised and made more policy relevant.

The debate on the 'scientific aspects of ageing research', however, is ongoing. The report from the House of Lords Select Committee on Science and Technology, *Ageing: Scientific aspects*, criticised the poor coordination of research into ageing (House of Lords, 2005) and emphasised at least two issues that have constrained the development of research into ageing. These are, first, a failure to coordinate research in particular between the research councils and, second, a failure to apply existing technologies, for example, assistive technologies and to engage with industry and the private sector to enhance the quality of life of older people.

Where do we go from here?

Gerontology is at a crossroads with a number of choices about its directions. While we cannot deny the need for increased funding of research on the scientific aspects of ageing, it is not fanciful to conclude that research in gerontology that does not aid the drive to support the British biotechnological industries will meet with less enthusiasm. Consider, for example, how the government might respond to applied social researchers who claim that their research can raise the well-being of today's older people. It will be well aware that incomes, housing and healthcare are key to the welfare of older people, but it will also claim that these are massively supported by public expenditure on pensions, other social security, social housing and healthcare programmes. Their estimation might be that social research can make only a tiny contribution: the case is unpersuasive compared to the scientific and potential economic importance of biotechnology.

We argue further that there has been little progress in supporting and raising the quality of life of older people with chronic disorders, and particularly those with depression or dementia and other cognitive disorders. How to fund and deliver care with dignity to very frail and (depressed) older people, without reinforcing stigma, is still highly problematic and the medical/social interface remains an area fraught with difficulty. Holistic care is frequently advocated but rarely delivered. In fact, far from making progress, there has been little or no success in combating the negative images of impaired old age.

One way of addressing this lack of progress is through multidisciplinary approaches. Yet, the difficulties of achieving this should not be underestimated. First, in our view, there needs to be much more dialogue among research funders. For example, the Department of Health's programme of studies on long-term care, care planning, and information technology, needs to establish clear links with the 'New Dynamics of Ageing' research initiative. There is also scope for more commercial and industrial funding of research (and indeed education) as ageing becomes of increasing concern in these sectors, both in terms of ageing consumers and ageing workforces.

Second, disciplines such as nursing and social work need to embrace gerontology wholeheartedly, drawing on its research evidence to reshape practice developments. Sadly, research agendas have for too long been dictated by health and social services agendas. Accepting a broader framework of research that appreciates the diversity of ageing and the need to explore this diversity in relation to professional developments is crucial. Professional education also needs to recognise that working with older people, at both qualifying and post-qualifying level, is a specialist and skilled activity. Gerontology courses need strengthening and placing on a firm financial footing through, for example, local authority and NHS funding.

Third, there are some optimistic signs of progress on which it is worth building. Large investments in longitudinal surveys in England and Europe are beginning to deliver distinctive and original data and analyses (Marmot et al, 2002; Banks et al, 2006) and accomplished researchers have been brought into the ageing field from population epidemiology, medical sociology and even public sector and welfare economics. There are also notable areas of continuing strength in social gerontological research, as on social networks, intergenerational relations and support (Phillipson et al, 2001), with important contributions from cultural studies (the new bastion of the individual teacher-scholar) on the experience of old age and of receiving formal services (see Vincent et al, 2006). The gerontological research community is also moving forward with truly participatory approaches with older people (see Chapters Six and Eight).

In conclusion, gerontology has come a long way over the past 60 years in developing its research, teaching and conceptual bases although it still needs to anchor its status as a discipline if it is not to lose ground to 'medicine, nursing and social work in setting future research, policy and practice agendas. Several questions remain key to gerontology's future development in the UK:

- Should there be a National Institute of Ageing, similar to that in the US and Canada, which coordinates funding for research on ageing?
- Should research be concentrated in designated centres?

- Are research networks, similar to the OPAN development in Wales, the way forward to increasing research capacity and achieving multidisciplinary approaches?
- How can we balance the different interests in gerontology and the disparate agendas of each group?

Notes

[1] The representation of older people and their welfare has shifted solely from voluntary groups such as Age Concern and Help the Aged to the proliferating advocacy and older people's groups that place older people's participation centre stage, the National Pensioners Convention and Better Government for Older People being two such examples tackling specific issues of concern for older people. Older people's champions in every local authority/council have also increased the pressures on councils to take seriously the views and roles of older people. Voluntary agencies such as those above have also broadened their scope as providers of services, and research funders.

[2] Both the Nobel laureate Sir Peter Medawar and the polymath Alex Comfort were active members, and in the 1980s the chair was Tom Kirkwood.

[3] The categorisations are approximate and have not been based on a detailed examination of the contents of the journals. Neurology titles have been allocated to biomedicine, and *Psychology and Aging* to social gerontology. It was thought that *Behavior, Health and Aging* is in both camps.

[4] The other networks parallel some of the funded English networks under the UK clinical research network – diabetes, neurodegenerative diseases, dementia, stroke, cancer, children and medicine, learning disability and mental health.

References

Aaron, H. and Schwarz, W. (2005) *Can we say no? The challenge of rationing health care*, Washington, DC: Brookings Institution Press.

Abel-Smith, B. (1960) *A history of the nursing profession*, London: Heinemann.

Abel-Smith, B. (1964) *The hospitals: 1800-1964*, London: Heinemann.

Aboderin, I. (2004) 'Decline in material family support for older people in urban Ghana, Africa: understanding processes and causes of change', *Journal of Gerontology: Psychological Sciences, Social Sciences*, vol 59, no 3, pp S128-37.

ADSS (Association of Directors of Social Services)/LGA (Local Government Association) (2003) *All our tomorrows: Inverting the triangle of care*, London: ADSS/LGA.

Age Concern (2005) *Age and ... multiple discrimination and older people*, London: Age Concern and Help the Aged.

Allan, K. (2001) *Communication and consultation: Exploring ways for staff to involve people with dementia in developing services*, Bristol/York: The Policy Press/Joseph Rowntree Foundation.

Altman, N.J. (2005) *The battle for social security: From FDR's vision to Bush's gamble*, New York, NY: Wiley.

Andersen, M.L. (1983) *Thinking about women: Sociological perspectives on sex and gender*, New York, NY: Macmillan.

Andrews, M. (1999) 'The seductiveness of agelessness', *Ageing and Society*, vol 19, no 3, pp 301-18.

Arber, S., Davidson, K. and Ginn, J. (eds) (2003) *Gender and ageing: Changing roles and relationships*, Maidenhead: Open University Press.

Archibald, C. (2003) *People with dementia in acute hospitals: A practice guide for registered nurses*, Stirling: Dementia Development Centre.

Audit Commission (2004a) *Older people, building a strategic approach: Independence and well-being*, London: Audit Commission.

Audit Commission (2004b) *Older people, independence and well being: The challenge for public services*, London: Audit Commission.

Auerbach, A., Gokhale, J. and Kotlikoff, L. (1991) 'Generational accounts: a meaningful alternative to deficit accounting', in D. Bradford (ed) *Tax policy and the economy*, vol 5, Cambridge, MA: MIT Press, pp 55-110.

Auerbach, A., Gokhale, J. and Kotlikoff, L. (1994) 'Generational accounts: a meaningful way to evaluate fiscal policy', *Journal of Economic Perspectives*, vol 8, no 1, pp 73-94.

Auerbach, B.E. (1995) *Unto the thousandth generation: Conceptualizing intergenerational justice*, New York, NY: Peter Lang Publishing.

Baars, J. (1991) 'The challenge of critical studies', *Journal of Aging Studies*, vol 5, no 3, pp 219-43.

Baars, J., Dannefer, D., Phillipson, C. and Walker, A. (2006) *Aging, globalization and inequality: The new critical gerontology*, New York, NY: Baywood.

Banks, J., Disney, R. and Smith, Z. (2000) 'What can we learn from generational accounts for the United Kingdom?', *The Economic Journal*, vol 110, no 467, pp F575-97.

Banks, J., Breeze, E., Lessof, C. and Nazroo, J. (2006) *Retirement, health and relationships of the older population in England: The 2004 English Longitudinal Study of Ageing (Wave 2)*, London: Institute for Fiscal Studies.

Barnes, C. (1996) 'Theories of disability and the origins of the oppression of disabled people in western society', in L. Barton (ed) *Disability and society: Emerging issues and insights*, London: Longman, pp 43-60.

Barry, B. (1999) 'Sustainability and intergenerational justice,' in A. Dobson (ed) *Fairness and futurity*, Oxford: Oxford University Press, pp 93-117.

Bauld, L., Chesterman, J., Davies, B., Judge, K. and Mangalore, R. (2000) *Caring for older people: An assessment of community care in the 1990s*, Aldershot: Ashgate.

Beaujot, R. and Richards, J. (1996) 'Intergenerational fairness in reforming the Canada pension plan', *Policy Options*, vol 17, no 9, pp 45-8.

Beck, U. (1992) *Risk society: Towards a new modernity*, Thousand Oaks, CA: Sage Publications.

Beck, U. (1999) *World risk society*, Cambridge: Polity Press.

Becker, H. (2004) 'Photographs as evidence, photographs as exposition', in C. Knowles and P. Sweetman (eds) *Picturing the social landscape: Visual methods and the sociological imagination*, London: Routledge.

Behar, R. (1996) *The vulnerable observer: Anthropology that breaks your heart*, Boston, MA: Beacon Press.

Bell, C. (1977) 'Reflections on the Banbury Restudy', in C. Bell and H. Newby (eds) *Doing sociological research*, London: George, Allen and Unwin, pp 47-62.

Benford, G. (2000) *Deep time: How humanity communicates across millennia*, New York, NY: Harper Perennial.

Bengtson, V.L. (1993) 'Will "generational accounting" doom the welfare state?', *The Gerontologist*, vol 33, no 6, pp 812-16.

Beresford, P. (2003) 'User involvement in research: connecting lives, experience and theory', Making Research Count Conference Paper, Warwick: Warwick University (accessed via www2.warwick.ac.uk on 7 July, 2005).

Beresford, P. and Croft, S. (1993) *Citizen involvement: A practical guide for change*, London: Palgrave Macmillan.

Berman, H.J. (1994) *Interpreting the aging self: Personal journals of later life*, New York, NY: Springer.

Berman, H.J. (2000) 'Self-representation and aging: philosophical, psychological, and literary perspectives', in T.R. Cole, R. Kastenbaum and R.E. Ray (eds) *Handbook of the humanities and aging* (2nd edn), New York, NY: Springer, pp 272-90.

Bernard, M. (2000) *Promoting health in old age*, Buckinghamshire: Open University Press.

Bernard, M. (2001) 'Women ageing: old lives, new challenges', *Education and Ageing*, vol 16, no 3, pp 333-52.

Bernard, M. and Phillips, J. (2000) 'The challenge of ageing in tomorrow's Britain', *Ageing and Society*, vol 20, no 1, pp 33-54.

Bernard, M., Phillips, J., Machin, L. and Harding-Davis, V. (eds) (2000) *Women and aging: Changing identities, challenging myths*, London and New York, NY: Routledge.

Bernstein, R. (1992) *The new constellation: The ethical-political horizons of modernity/postmodernity*, Cambridge, MA: MIT Press.

Berthoud, R., Bryan, M. and Bardasi, E. (2004) *The dynamics of deprivation: The relationship between income and material deprivation over time*, Research Report No 219, London: DWP.

Biggs S. (2001) 'Toward a critical narrativity: stories of aging in contemporary social policy', *Journal of Aging Studies*, vol 15, no 4, pp 303-16.

Binstock, R.H. (1983) 'The aged as scapegoat', *The Gerontologist*, vol 23, no 2, pp 136-43.

Birren, J.E. (1996a) 'Foreword', in J.E. Birren, G.M. Kenyon, J.E. Ruth, J.F. Schroots and T. Svensson (eds) *Aging and biography: Explorations in adult development*, New York, NY: Springer, pp ix-xi.

Birren, J.E. (1996b) 'History of gerontology', in J.E. Birren (ed) *Encyclopedia of gerontology*, San Diego, CA: Academic, pp 655-65.

Birren, J.E. and Cochran, K.N. (2001) *Telling the stories of life through guided autobiography groups*, Baltimore, MD: Johns Hopkins University Press.

Birren, J.E. and Deutchman, D. (1991) *Guiding autobiography groups for older adults: Exploring the fabric of life*, Baltimore, MD: Johns Hopkins University Press.

Blakemore, K. (1997) 'From minorities to majorities: perspectives on culture, ethnicity and ageing in British gerontology', in A. Jamieson, S. Harper and C.R. Victor (eds) *Critical approaches to ageing and later life*, Buckingham: Open University Press, pp 27-38.

Bond, J. and Coleman, P.G. (eds) (1990) *Ageing in society: An introduction to social gerontology*, London: Sage Publications.

Brand, S. (1999) *The clock of the long now: Time and responsibility*, New York, NY: Basic Books.

Braye, S. (2000) 'Participation and involvement in social care: an overview', in H. Kemshall and R. Littlechild (eds) *User involvement and participation in social care*, London: Jessica Kingsley, pp 9-28.

Braye, S. and Preston-Shoot, M. (1995) *Empowering practice in social care*, Buckingham: Open University Press.

Brokaw, T. (1998) *The greatest generation*, New York, NY: Random House.

Browne, C.V. (1998) *Women, feminism and aging*, New York, NY: Springer.

Bruner, J. (1986) *Actual minds, possible worlds*, Cambridge, MA: Harvard University Press.

Bruner, J. (1990) *Acts of meaning*, Cambridge, MA: Harvard University Press.

Bruner, J. (2002) *Making stories: Law, literature, life*, New York, NY: Farrar, Strau and Giroux.

Bulatao, R.A. and Anderson, N.B. (2004) *Understanding racial and ethnic differences in health in late life: A research agenda*, Washington, DC: National Academy Press.

Butler, A., Oldman, C. and Greve, J. (1983) *Sheltered housing for the elderly: Policy, practice and the consumer*, London: George, Allen and Unwin.

Butler, R.N. (1975) *Why survive? Being old in America*, New York, NY: Harper and Row.

Butt, J. and O'Neill, A. (2004) *'Let's move on': Black and minority older people's views on research findings*, York: Joseph Rowntree Foundation.

Bytheway, B. (1986) 'Redundancy and the older worker', in R.M. Lee (ed) *Redundancies, lay-off and plant closures: Causes, character and consequences*, London: Croom Helm, pp 84-115.

Bytheway, B. (1995) *Ageism*, Buckingham: Open University Press.

Bytheway, B. (ed) (2003) *Everyday living in later life*, Representation of Older People in Ageing Research Series, No 4, London: Centre for Policy on Ageing.

Bytheway, B. and Johnson, J. (2002) 'The use of diaries in the study of later life', in A. Jamieson and C.R. Victor (eds) *Researching ageing and later life: The practice of social gerontology*, Buckingham: Open University Press, pp 155-74.

Calasanti, T. (1996) 'Incorporating diversity: meaning, levels or research and implications for social theory', *The Gerontologist*, vol 36, no 2, pp 147-56.

Callahan, D. (1987) *Settings limits: Medical goals in an aging society*, New York, NY: Simon and Schuster.

Campbell, J. and Oliver, M. (1996) *Disability politics: Understanding our past, changing our future*, London: Routledge.

Carson, R. (1962) *Silent Spring*, Boston: Houghton Mifflin

Carter, T. and Beresford, P. (2000) *Age and change: Models of involvement for older people*, York: Joseph Rowntree Foundation.

Catalyst Forum Working Group (2002) *The challenge of longer life: Economic burden or social opportunity?*, Report of the Working Group on the Implications of Demographic Change, Catalyst Paper 7, London: The Catalyst Forum.

Chambers, G. (1998) *Practising human rights: UK lawyers and the European Convention on Human Rights*, The Law Society and Policy Planning Unit Research Study No 28, London: The Law Society.

Chambers, P. (2005) *Older widows and the life course: Multiple narratives of hidden lives*, Aldershot: Ashgate.

Chandler, S. and Ray, R.E. (2002) 'New meanings for old tales: a discourse-based study of reminiscence and development in late life', in J.D. Webster and B.K. Haight (eds) *Critical advances in reminiscence work: From theory to application*, New York, NY: Springer, pp 76-94.

Clark, H., Dyer, S. and Horwood, J. (1998) *'That bit of help': The high value of low level preventative services for older people*, Bristol/York: The Policy Press/Joseph Rowntree Foundation.

Clark, P. (2001) 'Narrative gerontology in clinical practice: current applications and future prospects', in G. Kenyon, P. Clark and B. de Vries (eds) *Narrative gerontology: Theory, research, and practice*, New York, NY: Springer, pp 193-214.

Clough, R., Green, B., Hawkes, B., Raymond, G. and Bright, L. (2006) *Older people as researchers*, York: Joseph Rowntree Foundation.

Cohen, G. (2000) *The creative age: Awakening human potential in the second half of life*, New York, NY: Avon.

Cohen, L. (ed) (1993) *Justice across generations: What does it mean?*, Washington, DC: Public Policy Institute, AARP.

Cohler, B.J. and Cole, T.R. (1996) 'Studying older lives: reciprocal acts of telling and listening', in J.E. Birren, G.M. Kenyon, J.E. Ruth, J.F. Schroots and T. Svensson (eds) *Aging and biography: Explorations in adult development*, New York, NY: Springer, pp 61-76.

Cole, T.R. (1991) *A journey of life: A cultural history of aging in America*, New York, NY: Cambridge University Press.

Cole, T.R. (1995) 'What have we "made" of aging?', *Journals of Gerontology – Series B: Psychological Sciences and Social Sciences*, vol 50, no 6, pp S341-3.

Cole, T.R. and Sierpina, M. (2006) 'Humanistic gerontology and the meaning(s) of aging', in K. Ferraro and J. Wilmouth (eds) *Gerontology: Perspectives and issues* (3rd edn), New York, NY: Springer.

Coleman, P.G. (1975) 'Social gerontology in England, Scotland and Wales: a review', *The Gerontologist*, vol 15, no 3, pp 219-29.

Corti, L. and Thompson, P. (2004) 'Secondary analysis of archived data', in C. Seale, G. Giampietro, J.F. Gubrium and D. Silverman (eds) *Qualitative research practice*, London: Sage Publications, pp 327-43.

Council of Europe (2002) *European Social Charter: Collected texts* (3rd edn), Strasbourg: Council of Europe.

Cribier, F. (1982) 'Aspects of retirement migration from Paris: an essay in social and cultural geography', in A. Warnes (ed) *Geographical perspectives on the elderly*, Chichester, Sussex: Wiley, pp 111-37.

Crowther, M. (1981) *The workhouse system, 1834-1929*, London: Batsford.

Cumming, E. (1963) 'Further thoughts on the theory of disengagement', *International Social Science Journal*, vol 15, no 3, pp 377-93.

Cumming, E. and Henry, W.E. (1961) *Growing old: The process of disengagement*, New York, NY: Basic Books.

Dalley, G., Unsworth, L., Keightley, D., Waller, M., Davies, T. and Morton, R. (2004) *How do we care? The availability of registered care homes and children's homes in England and their performance against national minimum standards 2002-03*, London: The Stationery Office.

Daniels, N. (1985) *Just health care*, Cambridge: Cambridge University Press.

Daniels, N. (1988) *Am I my parents' keeper? An essay on justice between the young and the old*, Oxford: Oxford University Press.

Davies, C.A. (1999) *Reflexive ethnography*, London: Routledge.

Davies, C.A. and Charles, N. (2002) 'The piano in the parlour: methodological issues in the context of a restudy', *Sociological Research Online*, vol 7, no 2 (www.socresonline.org.uk/7/2/davies.html).

Deal, M. (2003) 'Disabled people's attitudes towards impairment groups: a hierarchy of impairments', *Disability and Society*, vol 18, no 7, pp 897-910.

Delbecque, B. and Bogaert, H. (1994) 'L'Incidence de la dette publique et due vieillissement demographique sur la conduite de la politique budgetaire: une étude théorique appliquée au cas de la Belgique', Bureau du Plan, *Planning Papers* No 70, November.

De Beauvoir, S. (1972) *The Coming of Age*, New York: Putnam.

De-Shalit, A. (1995) *Why posterity matters. Environmental policies and future generations*, London and New York, NY: Routledge.

DH (Department of Health) (1989) *Community care in the next decade and beyond*, London: DH.

DH (1994) *Implementing caring for people: Housing and homelessness*, London: DH.

DH (1998) *Modernising social services: Promoting independence, improving protection, raising standards*, London: DH.

DH (2000) *The NHS Plan: A plan for investment, a plan for reform*, London: DH.

DH (2001) *National Service Framework for older people*, London: DH.

DH (2004) *Protection of Vulnerable Adults (POVA) scheme in England and Wales for care homes and domiciliary care agencies: A practical guide*, London: DH (www.dh.gov.uk/PublicationsAndStatistics/Publications/ PublicationsPolicyAndGuidance/PublicationsPolicyAndGuidanceArticle/fs/ en?CONTENT_ID=4085855&chk=p0kQeS).

DH (2005a) *Independence, well-being and choice: Our vision for the future of social care for adults in England*, London: DH.

DH (2005b) *Supporting people with long-term conditions: An NHS and social care model to support local innovation and integration*, London: DH.

DH (2005c) *The National Service Framework for long-term conditions*, London: DH.

DH (2005d) *Research governance framework for health and social care* (2nd edn), London: DH.

DH (2006a) *Our health, our care, our say: A new direction for community services*, London: DH.

DH (2006b) *Feedback: Dignity listening events*, London: DH.

DH and DoE (Department of the Environment) (1997) *Housing and community care: Establishing the strategic framework*, London: DH.

Diamond, J. (2004) *Collapse: How societies choose to fail or succeed*, New York, NY: Viking.

Dimock, G. (1993) 'Children of the mills: re-reading Lewis Hine's child-labour photographs', *Oxford Art Journal*, vol 16, no 2, pp 37-54.

Donahue, W. and Tibbitts, C. (1957) *The new frontiers of aging*, Ann Arbor, MI: University of Michigan Press.

Donkor, K. (2002) 'Structural adjustment and mass poverty in Ghana', in P. Townsend and D. Gordon (eds) *World poverty: New policies to defeat an old enemy*, Bristol: The Policy Press, pp 226-8.

Dowdall, G.W. and Golden, J. (1989) 'Photographs as data: an analysis of images from a mental hospital', *Qualitative Sociology*, vol 12, no 2, pp 183-213.

Dressel, P., Minkler, M. and Yen, I. (1998) 'Gender, race, class and aging: advances and opportunities', in M. Minkler and C.L. Estes (eds) *Critical gerontology: Perspectives from political and moral economy*, Amityville, NY: Baywood Publishing, pp 275-94.

DTI (Department of Trade and Industry) (2004) *Fairness for all: A new Commission for Equality and Human Rights*, London: The Stationery Office.

Dunning, A. (2004) 'Participation and engagement of older people: towards a best practice strategy for Stoke-on-Trent', Unpublished report, Stoke-on-Trent: Health Action Stoke/Beth Johnson Foundation.

DWP (Department for Work and Pensions) (2005a) *Households Below Average Income 2003/4*, London: DWP, Information and Analysis Directorate, London.

DWP (2005b) *Opportunity Age: Meeting the challenges of ageing in the 21st century*, London: DWP.

Dwyer, S. (1998) 'Learning from experience: moral phenomenology and politics', in B. Bar On and A. Ferguson (eds) *Daring to be good: Essays in feminist ethico-politics*, New York, NY: Routledge, pp 28-44.

Eberstadt, N. (2001) 'The population implosion', *Foreign Policy*, vol 123 (November/December), pp 22-45.

Ehrlich, P.R. (1968) *The population bomb*, New York, NY: Ballantine Books.

Ehrman, J. (2006) *The eighties: America in the age of Reagan*, New Haven, CT: Yale University Press.

ESDS (Economic and Social Data Service) (nda) 'Identifiers and anonymisation: dealing with confidentiality', ESDS Access and Preservation (www.esds.ac.uk/aandp/create/identguideline.asp, accessed 03/03/2006).

ESDS (ndb) 'End user licence', ESDS Access and Preservation (www.esds.ac.uk/aandp/access/licence.asp, accessed 03/03/2006).

Estes, C. L. (1979) *Aging Enterprise: A critical examination of social policies and services for the aged*, San Francisco, CA: Jossey-Bass Inc.

Estes, C.L. and Associates (2001) *Social policy and aging: A critical perspective*, Thousand Oaks, CA: Sage Publications.

Estes, C.L., Biggs, S. and Phillipson, C. (2003) *Social theory, social policy and ageing: A critical introduction*, Maidenhead: Open University Press.

Fairlie, H. (1988) 'Greedy geezers: talkin 'bout my generation', *New Republic*, vol 28, March, p 19.

Farber, D. and Bailey, B. (2003) *The Columbia guide to America in the 1960s*, New York, NY: Columbia University Press.

Feinberg, J (1980) *Rights, justice, and the bounds of liberty: Essays in social philosophy*, Princeton, NJ: Princeton University Press.

Feldman, D. (2002) *Civil liberties and human rights in England and Wales* (2nd edn), Oxford: Oxford University Press.

Fernandes, L. (2003) *Transforming feminist practice: Non-violence, social justice and the possibilities of a spiritualized feminism*, San Francisco, CA: Aunt Lute Books.

FIFARS (Federal Interagency Forum on Aging-Related Statistics) (2004) *Older Americans 2004: Key indicators of well-being*, Washington, DC: US Government Printing Office.

Finnegan, R. (1992) *Oral traditions and the verbal arts: A guide to research practice*, London: Routledge.

Flax, J. (1987) 'Postmodernism and gender relations in feminist theory', *Signs*, vol 12, no 4, pp 621-43.

Foord, M. (2005) 'Introduction: supported housing and community care – towards a new landscape of precariousness', in M. Foord and P. Simic (eds) *Housing, community care and supported housing – Resolving contradictions*, Coventry: Chartered Institute of Housing, pp 2-19.

Fraser, N. (1989) *Unruly practices: Power, discourse and gender in contemporary social theory*, Minneapolis, MN: University of Minnesota Press.

Friedan, B. (1963) *The feminine mystique*, New York, NY: W.W. Norton and Co.

Friedan, B. (1994) *The fountain of age*, New York, NY: Simon and Schuster.

Furman, F.K. (1997) *Facing the mirror: Old women and beauty shop culture*, New York, NY: Routledge.

Geertz, C. (1988) *Works and lives: the anthropologist as author*, Cambridge: Polity Press.

Gergen, K. (1991) *The saturated self*, New York, NY: Basic Books.

Gergen, K. (1996) 'Beyond life narratives in the therapeutic encounter', in J.E. Birren, G.M. Kenyon, J.E. Ruth, J.F. Schroots and T. Svensson (eds) *Aging and biography: Explorations in adult development*, New York, NY: Springer, pp 205-23.

Gilbert, N. (1970) *British social policy, 1919-39*, London: Batsford.

Gilleard, C. and Higgs, P. (2002) 'The third age: class, cohort or generation?', *Ageing and Society*, vol 22, no 3, pp 369-82.

Gilliard, J., Means, R., Beattie, A. and Daker-White, G. (2005) 'Dementia care in England and the social model of disability: lessons and issues', *Dementia*, vol 4, no 4, pp 571-86.

Glasby, J. (2006) 'Bringing down the Berlin wall: partnership working and the health and social care divide', *Health and Social Care in the Community*, vol 14, no 3, pp 195-96.

Glendinning, C. and Means, R. (2004) 'Rearranging the deckchairs on the Titanic of long-term care', *Critical Social Policy*, vol 24, no 54, pp 435-57.

Glendinning, C., Hudson, B. and Means, R. (2005) 'Under strain? Exploring the troubled relationship between health and social care', *Public Money and Management*, vol 25, no 4, pp 245-52.

Glover, I. and Branine, M. (eds) (2001) *Ageism in work and employment*, Aldershot: Ashgate.

Gluck, S.B. and Patai, D. (eds) (1991) *Women's words: The feminist practice of oral history*, London: Routledge.

Godfrey, M., Townsend, J. and Denby, T. (2004) *Building a good life for older people in local communities: The experience of ageing in time and place*, York: Joseph Rowntree Foundation.

Good, G.S. (1994) *First call for children and generational equity: Can public policies bridge both principles?*, Ottawa: Canadian Institute of Child Health.

Gordon, D., Nandy, S., Pantazis, C., Pemberton, S. and Townsend, P. (2003) *Child poverty in the developing world*, Bristol: The Policy Press.

Gordon, D., Adelman, L., Ashworth, K., Bradshaw, J., Levitas, R., Middleton, R., Pantazis, C., Patsios, D., Payne, S., Townsend, P. and Williams, J. (2000) *Poverty and social exclusion in Britain*, York: Joseph Rowntree Foundation.

Govier, T. (1979) 'What should we do about future people?', *American Philosophical Quarterly*, vol 16, no 2, pp 105-13.

Green, L.W. and Mercer, S.L. (2001) 'Can public health researchers and agencies reconcile the push from funding bodies and the pull from communities?', *American Journal of Public Health*, vol 91, no 12, pp 1926-9.

Griffiths, R. (1988) *Community care: agenda for action*, London: HMSO.

Grundy, E. (1987) 'Retirement migration and its consequences in England and Wales', *Ageing and Society*, vol 7, no 1, pp 57-82.

Gubrium, J. (1975) *Living and dying at Murray Manor*, New York, NY: St. Martin's Press.

Gubrium, J. (1986) *Old timers and Alzheimer's: The descriptive organization of senility*, Greenwich, CT: JAI Press.

Gubrium, J. (1993) *Speaking of life: Horizons of meaning for nursing home residents*, Hawthorne, NY: Aldine de Gruyter.

Gubrium, J. (2001) 'Narrative, experience, and aging', in G. Kenyon, P. Clark and B. de Vries (eds) *Narrative gerontology: Theory, research, and practice*, New York, NY: Springer, pp 19-30.

Gubrium, J. and Wallace, B. (1990) 'Who theorises age?', *Ageing and Society*, vol 10, no 2, pp 131-50.

Guest, R.S. (2001) 'Ageing, optimal national savings and future living standards in Australia', *Economic Record*, vol 77, no 237, pp 117-34.

Gullette, M.M. (1997) *Declining to decline: Cultural combat and the politics of the midlife*, Charlottesville, VA: University Press of Virginia.

Gullette, M.M. (2000) 'Age studies as cultural studies', in T.R. Cole, R. Kastenbaum and R.E. Ray (eds) *Handbook of the humanities and aging* (2nd edn), New York, NY: Springer, pp 214-34.

Gullette, M.M. (2004) *Aged by culture*, Chicago, IL: University of Chicago Press.

Gunaratnam, Y. (2003) *Researching 'race' and ethnicity: Methods, knowledge and power*, London: Sage Publications.

Habermas, J. (1975) *Legitimation crisis*, Boston, MA: Beacon Press.

Hall, B.L. (1992) 'From margins to center: the development and purpose of participatory action research', *American Sociologist*, vol 23, no 4, pp 15-28.

Handcock, G.A., Woods, B., Challis, D. and Orrell, M. (2006) 'The needs of older people with dementia in residential care', *International Journal of Geriatric Psychiatry*, vol 21, no 1, pp 43-9.

Hanley, B. (2005) *Research as empowerment? Report of a series of seminars organised by the Toronto Group*, York: Joseph Rowntree Foundation.

Harper, S. (1999) *Social gerontology: A review of current research*, London: The Nuffield Foundation.

Harris, C., Charles, N. and Davies, C. (2004) 'Some problems in the comparative use of "class" as a descriptive variable at two different points in time', Department of Sociology and Anthropology Online papers, University of Wales, Swansea (www.swan.ac.uk/sssid/Research/Res%20-%20Sociology.htm).

Hashimoto, A. (1996) *The gift of generations: Japanese and American perspectives on aging and the social contract*, Cambridge: Cambridge University Press.

Hayek, F.A. (1944) *The road to serfdom*, Chicago, IL: University of Chicago Press.

Heaton, J. (2004) *Reworking qualitative data*, London: Sage Publications.

Heller, P.S. (2003) *Who will pay? Coping with aging societies, climate change, and other long term fiscal challenges*, Washington, DC: International Monetary Fund.

Heller, P.S., Hemming, R. and Kohnert, P.W. (1986) *Aging and social expenditure in the major industrial countries, 1980-2025*, IMF Occasional Paper No 47, Washington, DC: International Monetary Fund.

Help the Aged (2002a) *Nothing personal: Rationing social care for older people*, London: Help the Aged.

Help the Aged (2002b) *Age discrimination in public policy*, London: Help the Aged.

Hewitt, P. (2002) *Meeting the challenge of global aging*, Washington, DC: Center for Strategic and International Studies.

Heywood, F., Oldman, C. and Means, R. (2002) *Housing and home in later life*, Buckingham: Open University Press.

Hinrichs, K. (2002) 'Do the old exploit the young? If so is enfranchising children a good idea?', *Archives Européennes de Sociologie*, vol 43, no 1, pp 35-58.

Hobman, D. (ed) (1993) *Uniting generations: Studies in conflict and co-operation*, London: Age Concern England.

Holstein, M. (1994) 'Taking next steps: gerontological education, research and the literary imagination', *The Gerontologist*, vol 34, no 6, pp 822-7.

Holstein, M. (1999) 'Women and productive aging: troubling implications', in M. Minkler and C.L. Estes (eds) *Critical gerontology: Perspectives from political and moral economy*, Amityville, NY: Baywood Publishing, pp 359-73.

Holstein, M. (2006) 'On being an aging woman', in T. Calasanti and K. Slevin (eds) *Age matters*, London: Routledge, pp 313-34.

hooks, b. (1984) *From margin to center*, Boston, MA: South End Press.

House of Lords, Science and Technology Committee (2005) *Ageing: Scientific aspects, Volume 1*, London: The Stationery Office.

Hudson, B. (1999) 'Primary health care and social care working', *Managing Community Care*, vol 7, no 1, pp 15-22.

Hudson, B. (2005) 'Sea change or quick fix? Policy on long-term conditions in England', *Health and Social Care in the Community*, vol 13, no 4, pp 378-85.

Hudson, B. (2006) 'Now it's our say', *Community Care*, 9-15 February, pp 34-5.

Hughes, B. and Wilkin, D. (1980) *Residential care of the elderly: A review of the literature*, Research Report No 2, Manchester: Research Unit, University Hospital of South Manchester Psychogeriatric Unit.

Hughes, M., McNeish, D., Newman, T., Roberts, H. and Sachdev, D. (2000) *Making connections: Linking research and practice*, London: Barnardo's/Joseph Rowntree Foundation.

Ingman, S.R., Pei, X., Ekstrom, C.D., Friedsam, H.J. and Bartlett, K.R. (eds) (1995) *An aging population, an aging planet, and a sustainable future*, Denton, TX: University of North Texas.

Israel, B.A., Schulz, A.J., Parker, E.A. and Becker, A.B. (1998) 'Review of community-based research: assessing partnership approaches to improve public health', *Annual Review of Public Health*, vol 19, no 1, pp 173-202.

Jack, R. (1995) 'Empowerment in community care', in R. Jack (ed) *Empowerment in community care*, London: Chapman and Hall, pp 11-42.

Jackson, B. and Marsden, D. (1962) *Education and the working class*, Harmondworth: Penguin.

Jacob, J. (1999) *Doctors and rules: A sociology of professional values* (expanded 2nd edn), New Brunswick, NJ and London: Transaction.

Jacobs, R.N. (2002) 'The narrative integration of personal and collective identity in social movements', in M.C. Green, J.J. Strange and T.C. Brock (eds) *Narrative impact: Social and cognitive foundations*, Mahwah, NJ: Lawrence Erlbaum, pp 205-28.

JCHR (Joint Committee on Human Rights) (2003) *The case for a Human Rights Commission*, Sixth Report of Session 2002-3, vol I and II, HC 489-I and II, London: The Stationery Office.

JCHR (2005) *The work of the Committee in the 2001-2005 Parliament*, Nineteenth Report of Session 2004-5, HC 552, London: The Stationery Office.

Jeffreys, M. (ed) (1989) *Growing old in the twentieth century*, London: Routledge.

Jeffreys, M. (1997) 'Gerontology and geriatrics in Britain', in J.E. Phillips (ed) *British gerontology and geriatrics: Experience and innovation*, London: BGS/BSRA/BSG, pp 1-4.

Johnson, J. and Bytheway, B. (2001) 'An evaluation of the use of diaries in the study of medication in later life', *International Journal of Social Research Methods*, vol 4, no 3, pp 183-204.

Jonas, H. (1979) *Das prinzip verantwortung. Versuch einer Ethik für die technologische Zivilisation*, Frankfurt am Main: Insel Verlag.

Jones, D. (2002) Business and media supplement, *Observer*, 30 June.

Jordan, D.K. (1981) 'The ethnographic enterprise and the bureacratization of ethics: the problem of human subjects legislation', *Journal of Anthropological Research*, vol 37, no 4, pp 415-19.

Jordanova, L. (2000) *History in practice*, London: Arnold.

JRF (Joseph Rowntree Foundation) (2004) *Older people shaping policy and practice*, York: JRF.

Kaufman, S. (1986) *The ageless self: Sources of meaning in late life*, Madison, WI: University of Wisconsin Press.

Kavka, G. (1982) 'The paradox of future individuals', *Philosophy & Public Affairs*, vol 11, no 2, pp 92-112.

Keady, J., Nolan, M. and Gilliard, J. (1995) 'Listen to the voice of experience', *Journal of Dementia Care*, vol 3, no 3, pp 15-17.

Kellaher, L. and Peace, S. (1993) 'Rest assured', in J. Johnson and R. Slater (eds) *Ageing and later life*, London: Sage Publications, pp 168-77.

Kemshall, H. (2002) *Risk, social policy and welfare*, Buckingham: Open University Press.

Kemshall, H. and Littlechild, R. (2000) 'Research informing practice: some concluding remarks', in H. Kemshall and R. Littlechild (eds) *User involvement and participation in social care: Research informing practice*, London: Jessica Kingsley, pp 233-43.

Kenyon, G.M. (1996) 'The meaning/value of personal storytelling', in J.E. Birren, G.M. Kenyon, J.E. Ruth, J.F. Schroots and T. Svensson (eds) *Aging and biography: Explorations in adult development*, New York, NY: Springer, pp 21-38.

Kenyon, G.M. and Randall, W.L. (1997) *Restorying our lives: Personal growth through autobiographical reflection*, Westport, CN: Praeger.

Kenyon, G.M., Clark, P. and de Vries, B. (eds) (2001) *Narrative gerontology: Theory, research, and practice*, New York, NY: Springer.

Kingson, E.R. and Williamson, J.B. (eds) (1999) *The generational equity debate*, New York, NY: Columbia University Press.

Kingson, E.R., Hirshorn, B. and Harootyan, L.K. (1987) *The common stake: The interdependence of generations*, Washington, DC: Gerontological Society of America.

Kinsella, K. and Velkoff, V. (2001) *An aging world: 2001*, US Census Bureau, Series P95/01-1, Washington, DC (www.census.gov/prod/2001pubs/p95-01-1.pdf).

Kirkwood, T. (1977) 'Evolution of ageing', *Nature*, no 270, pp 301-4.

Koch, T. (2000) *Age speaks for itself: Silent voices of the elderly*, Westport, CT: Praeger.

Kotlikoff, L.J. (1993) *Generational accounting: Knowing who pays, and when, for what we spend*, New York, NY: Free Press.

Kotlikoff, L.J. and Burns, S. (2004) *The coming generational storm: What you need to know about America's economic future*, Cambridge, MA: MIT Press.

Ladd, H.F. and Murray, S.E. (2001) 'Intergenerational conflict reconsidered: county demographic structure and the demand for public education', *Economics of Education Review*, vol 20, no 4, pp 343-57.

Laslett, P. (1989) *A fresh map of life*, London: Wiedenfeld and Nicolson.

Laslett, P. and Fishkin, J.S. (eds) (1992) *Justice between age groups and generations*, New Haven, NJ: Yale University Press.

Le Grand, J. (2003) *Motivation, agency and public policy: Of knights and knaves, pawns and queens*, Oxford: Oxford University Press.

Lee, R. and Yamagata, H. (2003) 'Sustainable social security: what would it cost?', *National Tax Journal*, vol 56, no 1, part 1, pp 267-43.

Lincoln, Y.S. and Guba, E.G. (1985) *Naturalistic inquiry*, Newbury Park, CA: Sage Publications.

Longino, C.F. (1995) *Retirement migration in America: An analysis of the size, trends and economic impact of the country's newest growth industry*, Houston, TX: Vacation.

Longman, P. (1982) 'Taking America to the cleaners', *Washington Monthly*, November, pp 24-30.

Longman, P. (2004) *The empty cradle: How falling birthrates threaten world prosperity and what to do about it*, New York, NY: Basic Books.

Luborsky, M. (1987) 'Analysis of life history narratives', *Ethos*, vol 15, no 4, pp 366-81.

Luborsky, M. (1990) 'Alchemists' visions: cultural norms eliciting and analyzing life history narratives', *Journal of Aging Studies*, vol 4, no 1, pp 17-29.

Luborsky, M. (1993) 'The romance with personal meaning in gerontology: cultural aspects of life themes', *The Gerontologist*, vol 33, no 4, pp 445-52.

Lupton, C., Peckham, S. and Taylor, P. (1998) *Managing public involvement in healthcare purchasing*, Buckingham: Open University Press.

Lyotard, J.-F. (1984) *The postmodern condition: A report on knowledge*, Minneapolis, MN: University of Minnesota Press.

McCormack, B. (2005) 'Gerontological nursing: the state of the art', in M. Johnson (ed) *The Cambridge handbook of age and ageing*, Cambridge: Cambridge University Press, pp 613-21.

McMullin, J.A. (2000) 'Diversity and the state of sociological aging theory', *The Gerontologist*, vol 40, no 5, pp 517-30.

Mac an Ghaill, M. (1999) *Contemporary racisms and ethnicities: social and cultural transformations*, Buckingham: Open University Press.

Macklin, R. (1981) 'Can future generations correctly be said to have rights?', in E. Partridge (ed) *Responsibilities to future generations*, Buffalo, NY: Prometheus Books, pp 151-6.

Macnicol, J. and Blaikie, A. (1989) 'The politics of retirement, 1908-1948', in M. Jefferys (ed) *Growing old in the twentieth century*, London: Routledge, pp 21-42.

Mader, W. (1996) 'Emotionality and continuity in biographical contexts', in J.E. Birren, G.M. Kenyon, J.E. Ruth, J.F. Schroots and T. Svensson (eds) *Aging and biography: Explorations in adult development*, New York, NY: Springer, pp 39-60.

Manheimer, R. (1999) *A map to the end of time: Wayfarings with friends and philosophers*, New York, NY: Norton.

Marmot, M., Banks, J., Blundell, R., Lessof, C. and Nazroo, J. (eds) (2002) *Health, wealth and lifestyles of the older population in England: The 2002 English Longitudinal Study of Ageing*, London: Institute for Fiscal Studies.

Meadows, D.H., Randers, J. and Meadows, D.L. (2004) *Limits to growth: The 30-year update*, London: Earthscan.

Meadows, D.H., Meadows, D.L., Randers, J. and Behrens, W.W. (1972) *The limits to growth*, New York, NY: New American Library.

Means, R. and Smith, R. (1998) *From Poor Law to Community Care: The development of welfare services for elderly people, 1937-1971*, Bristol: The Policy Press.

Means, R., Morbey, H. and Smith, R. (2002) *From community care to market care: The development of welfare services for older people*, Bristol: The Policy Press.

Means, R., Brenton, M., Harrison, L. and Heywood, F. (1997) *Making partnerships in community care: A guide for practitioners in housing, health and social services*, Bristol: The Policy Press.

Mercer, G. (2002) 'Emancipatory disability research', in C. Barnes, M. Oliver and L. Barton (eds) *Disability studies today*, Cambridge: Polity Press, pp 228-49.

Meyers, D. (1997) 'Emotion and heterodox moral perception: an essay in moral social psychology', in D. Meyers (ed) *Feminists rethink the self*, Boulder, CO: Westview Press, pp 197-218.

Miniño, A.M., Heron, M. and Smith, B.L. (2006) *Deaths: Preliminary data for 2004*, National Vital Statistics Report, vol 54, no 19, Hyattsville, MD: National Center for Health Statistics.

Minkler, M. (1996) 'Critical perspectives on ageing: new challenges for gerontology', *Ageing and Society*, vol 16, no 4, pp 467-87.

Minkler, M. and Cole, T.R. (1999) 'Political and moral economy: getting to know one another', in M. Minkler and C.L. Estes (eds) *Critical gerontology: Perspectives from political and moral economy*, New York, NY: Baywood, pp 37-50.

Minkler, M. and Roe, K. (1993) *Forgotten caregivers: Grandmothers raising the children of the crack cocaine epidemic*, Thousand Oaks, CA: Sage Publications.

Minkler, M. and Wallerstein, N. (2003) *Community-based participatory research for health*, San Francisco, CA: Jossey-Bass.

Minnich, E.K. (1990) *Transforming knowledge*, Philadelphia, PA: Temple University Press.

Mitchell, D. (2004) *Cloud atlas*, London: Sceptre.

Moody, H.R. (1993) 'Overview: what is critical gerontology and why is it important?', in T.R. Cole, W.A. Achenbaum, P.L. Jakobi and R. Kastenbaum (eds) *Voices and visions of aging: Toward a critical gerontology*, New York, NY: Springer, pp xv-xli.

Morris, J. (1991) *Pride and prejudice*, London: Women's Press.

Morris, J. (1993) *Independent lives? Community care and disabled people*, Basingstoke: Macmillan.

Morrow-Howell, N., Hinterlong, J. and Sherraden, M. (eds) (2001) *Productive aging: Concepts and challenges*, Baltimore, MD: Johns Hopkins University Press.

Murphy, J., Tester, S., Hubbard, G., Downs, M. and MacDonald, C. (2005) 'Enabling frail older people with a communication difficulty to express their views: the use of Talking Mats TM as an interview tool', *Health and Social Care in the Community*, vol 13, no 2, pp 95-107.

Myerhoff, B. (1980) *Number our days*, New York, NY: Simon & Schuster.

Myerhoff, B. and Ruby, J. (1992) 'A crack in the mirror: reflexive perspectives in anthropology', in B. Myerhoff (ed) *Remembered lives: The work of ritual, storytelling, and growing older*, Ann Arbor, MI: University of Michigan Press, pp 307-40.

Naples, N.A. (2003) *Feminism and method: Ethnography, discourse analysis and activist research*, London: Routledge.

Nisbet, R. (1994) *History of the idea of progress: An inquiry into its origin and growth*, Somerset, NJ: Transaction Books.

Nolan, M. and Cooke, J. (2002) 'The use of gerontological research in policy and practice', in A. Jamieson and C.R. Victor (eds) *Researching ageing and later life*, Buckingham: Open University Press, pp 245-59.

Nuffield Provincial Hospitals Trust (1946) *The hospital surveys: The Doomsday Book of the hospital services*, Oxford: Oxford University Press.

Oakley, K. (2002) 'Emotions and the story worlds of fiction', in M.C. Green, J.J. Strange and T.C. Brock (eds) *Narrative impact: Social and cognitive foundations*, Mahwah, NJ: Lawrence Erlbaum, pp 39-70.

ODPM (Office of the Deputy Prime Minister) (2005) *Creating sustainable communities: Supporting independence – Consultation on a strategy for the Supporting People programme*, London: ODPM.

ODPM (2006) *A Sure Start to later life: Ending inequalities for older people*, London: Social Exclusion Unit, ODPM.

Office for National Statistics (2004) *Focus on older people*, London: Office for National Statistics.

Older People's Steering Group (2004) *Older people shaping policy and practice*, York: Joseph Rowntree Foundation.

Oldman, C. (1988) 'More than bricks and mortar', *Housing*, June/July, pp 13-14.

Oliver, M. (1990) *The politics of disablement*, Basingstoke: Macmillan.

Oliver, M. (1992) 'Changing the social relations of research production', *Disability, Handicap & Society*, vol 7, no 2, pp 101-15.

Opie, A. (1999) 'Being in health: versions of the discursive body', in S.M. Neysmith (ed) *Critical issues for future social work practice with aging persons*, New York, NY: Columbia, pp 187-212.

Pannell, J., Morbey, H. and Means, R. (2002) *Surviving at the margins: Older homeless people and the organisations that support them*, London: Help the Aged.

Parfit, D. (1976) 'On doing the best for our children', in M.D. Bayles (ed) *Ethics and population*, Cambridge, MA: Schenkman, pp 100-15.

Parfit, D. (1982) 'Future generations: further problems', *Philosophy & Public Affairs*, vol 11, no 2, pp 113-72.

Parsons, T. (1942) 'Age and sex in the social structure of the United States', *American Sociological Review*, vol 7, no 5, pp 604-16.

Parsons, T. (1964) *Essays in sociological theory* (paperback edn), New York, NY: The Free Press.

Partridge, E. (1981) *Responsibilities to future generations*, Buffalo, NY: Prometheus Books.

Peace, S. (ed) (1999) *Involving older people in research*, The Representation of Older People in Ageing Research Series, No 2, London: Centre for Policy on Ageing.

Peace, S. (2002) 'The role of older people in social research', in A. Jamieson and C.R. Victor (eds) *Researching ageing and later life: The practice of social gerontology*, Buckingham: Open University Press, pp 226-44.

Peace, S., Kellaher, L. and Willcocks, D. (1997) *Re-evaluating residential care*, Buckingham: Open University Press.

Perrin, T. and May, H. (2000) *Wellbeing in dementia: An occupational approach for therapists and carers*, Edinburgh: Harcourt.

Phillips, J.E. (ed) (1997) *British gerontology and geriatrics: Experience and innovation*, London: British Geriatric Society/British Society of Gerontology. British Society for Research on Ageing.

Phillipson, C. (1993) 'The sociology of retirement', in J. Bond, P. Coleman and S. Peace (eds) *Ageing in society*, London: Sage Publications, pp 180-99.

Phillipson, C. (1998) *Reconstructing old age*, London: Sage Publications.

Phillipson, C. and Scharf, T. (2004) *The impact of government policy on social exclusion of older people: A review of the literature*, London: Social Exclusion Unit, Office of the Deputy Prime Minister.

Phillipson, C. and Walker, A. (1987) 'The case for a critical gerontology', in S. DeGregorio (ed) *Social gerontology: New directions*, London: Croom Helm, pp 1-15.

Phillipson, C., Vincent, J.A. and Downs, M. (eds) (2006) *The futures of old age*, London: Sage Publications.

Phillipson, C., Bernard, M., Phillips, J. and Ogg, J. (2001) *The family and community life of older people*, London: Routledge.

Platman, K. and Taylor, P. (2004) 'Age, employment and policy', *Social Policy & Society*, vol 3, no 2, pp 143-200.

Polivka, L. (2005) 'Aging in a post-traditional society', Unpublished paper, Joint Conference of the National Council on Aging and the American Society on Aging, Philadelphia, PA.

Polkinghorne, D. (1988) *Narrative knowing and the human sciences*, Albany, NY: SUNY Press.

Pollock, A. (2004) *NHS plc – The privatisation of our health care*, London: Verso.

Quadagno, J. (1989) 'Generational equity and the politics of the welfare state', *Politics & Society*, vol 17, no 3, pp 353-76.

Qureshi, H. and Henwood, M. (2000) *Older people's definitions of quality services*, York: Joseph Rowntree Foundation.

Raffelhüschen, B. (1999) 'Generational accounting: method, data, and limitations', *European Economy, Reports and Studies*, no 6, pp 17-28.

Ramazanoglu, C. With Holland, J. (2002) *Feminist methodology: Challenges and choices*, London: Sage Publications.

Randall, W.L. (1995) *The stories we are: An essay on self-creation*, Toronto: University of Toronto Press.

Randall, W.L. (1996) 'Restorying a life: adult education and transformative learning', in J.E. Birren, G.M. Kenyon, J.E. Ruth, J.F. Schroots and T. Svensson (eds) *Aging and biography: Explorations in adult development*, New York, NY: Springer, pp 224-47.

Randall, W.L. (2001) 'Storied worlds: acquiring a narrative perspective on aging, identity, and everyday life', in G. Kenyon, P. Clark and B. de Vries (eds) *Narrative gerontology: Theory, research, and practice*, New York: Springer, pp 31-62.

Randall, W.L. and Kenyon, G.M. (2001) *Ordinary wisdom: Biographical aging and the journey of life*, Westport, CT: Praeger.

Rawls, J. (1971) *A theory of justice*, Oxford: Oxford University Press.

Ray, R.E. (1996) 'A postmodern perspective on feminist gerontology', *The Gerontologist*, vol 36, no 5, pp 674-80.

Ray, R.E. (1999) 'Researching to transgress: the need for critical feminism in gerontology', in J.D. Garner (ed) *Fundamentals of feminist gerontology*, New York, NY: The Haworth Press, pp 171-84.

Ray, R.E. (2000) *Beyond nostalgia: Aging and life-story writing*, Charlottesville, VA: University Press of Virginia.

Ray, R.E. (2003) 'The uninvited guest: mother/daughter conflict in feminist gerontology', *Journal of Aging Studies*, vol 17, no 1, pp 113-28.

Raynes, N., Temple, B., Glenister, C. and Coulthard, L. (2001) *Quality at home for older people*, Bristol: The Policy Press.

Reason, P. and Bradbury, H. (eds) (2001) *Handbook of action research: Participative inquiry and practice*, London: Sage Publications.

Rees, M.J. (2003) *Our final hour: A scientist's warning: How terror, error, and environmental disaster threaten*, New York, NY: Basic Books.

Reinharz, S. (1992) *Feminist methods in social research*, Oxford: Oxford University Press.

Research Councils UK (2006) *Health of disciplines: Annual report 2006 to the UK research base funders' forum*, Swindon: Research Councils UK (www.rcuk.ac.uk/cmsweb/downloads/rcuk/publications/hod06.pdf).

Richardson, L. (1997) *Fields of play: Constructing an academic life*, New Brunswick, NJ: Rutgers University Press.

Robb, B. (1967) *Sans everything: A case to answer*, London: Allen and Unwin.

Roe, K.M., Minkler, M. and Saunders, F.F. (1995) 'Combining research, advocacy and education: the methods of the Grandparent Caregiving Study', *Health Education Quarterly*, vol 22, no 4, pp 458-75.

Rolph, S. (2000) The history of community care for people with learning difficulties in Norfolk, 1930-1980: the role of two hostels', Unpublished PhD thesis, Milton Keynes: The Open University.

Rolph, S. (2005) 'Editorial', *'The last refuge' revisited: Continuity and change in residential care for older people*, Newsletter No 1, October, pp 3-4 (www.lastrefugerevisited.org.uk).

Rosser, C. and Harris, C. (1965) *The family and social change*, London: Routledge and Kegan Paul.

Rowe, J.W. and Kahn, R.L. (1999) *Successful aging*, New York, NY: Dell.

Rowntree Report (1980) *Older people: Report of a survey committee on the problems of ageing and the care of old people*, New York, NY: Arno Press.

Rubinstein, R.L. (2002a) 'The third age', in R.S. Weiss and S.A. Bass (eds) *Challenges of the third age: Meaning and purpose in later life*, New York, NY: Oxford University Press, pp 29-40.

Rubinstein, R.L. (2002b) 'Reminiscence, personal meaning, themes, and the "object relations" of older people', in J.D. Webster and B.K. Haight (eds) *Critical advances in reminiscence work: From theory to application*, New York, NY: Springer, pp 153-64.

Rubinstein, R.L. (2002c) 'The qualitative interview with older informants: some key questions', in G.D. Rowles and N.E. Schoenberg (eds) *Qualitative gerontology: A contemporary perspective*, New York, NY: Springer, pp 137-53.

Rummery, K. (2003) 'Progress towards partnership? The development of relations between primary care organisations and social services concerning older people's services in the UK', *Social Policy and Society*, vol 3, no 1, pp 33-42.

Rurup Commission (2003) *Achieving financial sustainability for the social security systems*, Berlin: Bundesministerium fur Gesundheit und Soziale Sicherung.

Ruth, J.E. and Oberg, P. (1996) 'Ways of life: old age in a life history perspective', in J.E. Birren, G.M. Kenyon, J.E. Ruth, J.F. Schroots and T. Svensson (eds) *Aging and biography: Explorations in adult development*, New York, NY: Springer, pp 167-86.

Samuel, L. (2002) *Fundamental social rights: Case law of the European Social Charter* (2nd edn), Strasbourg: Council of Europe Publishing.

Sarbin, T. (ed) (1986) *Narrative psychology: The storied nature of human conduct*, New York, NY: Praeger.

Schafer, R. (1992) *Retelling a life: Narrative and dialogue in psychoanalysis*, New York, NY: Basic Books.

Schank, R. and Berman, T. (2002) 'The pervasive role of stories in knowledge and action', in M.C. Green, J.J. Strange and T.C. Brock (eds) *Narrative impact: Social and cognitive foundations*, Mahwah, NJ: Lawrence Erlbaum, pp 287-313.

Scharf, T., Phillipson, C. and Smith, A.E. (2005) *Multiple exclusion and quality of life amongst excluded older people in disadvantaged neighbourhoods*, London: Social Exclusion Unit, Office of the Deputy Prime Minister.

Schoenberg, N.E. (2002) '"Let's talk": introduction', in G.D. Rowles and N.E. Schoenberg (eds) *Qualitative gerontology: A contemporary perspective*, New York, NY: Springer, pp 130-6.

Schroeder-Butterfill, E. (2004) 'Inter-generational family support provided by older people in Indonesia', *Ageing and Society*, vol 24, no 4, pp 1-34.

SCIE (Social Care Institute for Excellence) (2006) *Using qualitative research in systematic reviews: Older people's views of hospital discharge*, London: SCIE.

Shaw, C. (2006) '2004-based national population projections for the UK and constituent countries', *Population Trends*, no 123, Spring, pp 9-20.

Shaw, M.E. and Westwood, M.J. (2002) 'Transformation in life stories: the Canadian war veterans life review project', in J.D. Webster and B.K. Haight (eds) *Critical advances in reminiscence work: From theory to application*, New York, NY: Springer, pp 257-74.

Sheets, D., Bradley, D. and Hendricks, J. (eds) (2005) *Enduring questions in gerontology*, New York, NY: Springer.

Sherman, E. (1991) *Reminiscence and the self in old age*, New York, NY: Springer.

Sin, C.H. (2005) 'Experiencing racism: reflections on the practice of research with minority ethnic older people in Britain', *International Journal of Social Research Methodology*, vol 8, no 2, pp 101-15.

Social Research Association (2003) *Ethical guidelines*, London: Social Research Association.

SPA News (2002) 'Peter Townsend – still going strong', *Newsletter* for the Social Policy Association, May/June, pp 1-5.

Spence, D. (1982) *Narrative truth and historical truth*, New York, NY: Norton.

Stacey, M. (1960) *Tradition and change: A study of Banbury*, Oxford: Oxford University Press.

Stacey, M., Batstone, E., Bell, C. and Murcott, A. (1975) *Power, persistence and change: A second study of Banbury*, London: Routledge and Kegan Paul.

Steel, R. (2003) *Brief summary and checklist for researchers, research commissioners and research groups for involving vulnerable and marginalised people*, Hampshire: INVOLVE.

Steinem, G. (1992) *Revolution from within*, New York, NY: Little, Brown.

Stiglitz, J. (2002a) 'Corporate corruption', *The Guardian*, London, 4 July.

Stiglitz, J. (2002b) *Globalisation and its discontents*, London: Allen Lane.

Stout, J.R. (1988) *Ethics after Babel: Languages of morals and their discontents*, Boston, MA: Beacon Press.

Summerfield, P. (1998) *Reconstructing women's wartime lives*, Manchester: Manchester University Press.

Sutherland Report (1999) *With respect to old age: Long term care – rights and responsibilities. A report by the Royal Commission on Long-term Care*, Cm 4192-1, London: The Stationery Office.

Talmon, Y. (1961) 'Ageing in Israel, a planned society', *American Journal of Sociology*, vol 67, no 3, pp 284-95.

Thompson, P. (1998) 'Sharing and reshaping life stories: problems and potential in archiving research narratives', in M. Chamberlain and P. Thompson (eds) *Narrative and genre*, London: Routledge, pp 167-81.

Thompson, S. (2005) *Age discrimination*, Lyme Regis: Russell House.

Townsend, P. (1957) *The family life of old people*, London: Routledge and Kegan Paul.

Townsend, P. (1962) *The last refuge – A survey of residential institutions and homes for the elderly in England and Wales*, London: Routledge and Kegan Paul.

Townsend, P. (1981a) 'The structured dependency of the elderly: a creation of social policy in the twentieth century', *Ageing and Society*, vol 1, no 1, pp 5-28.

Townsend, P. (1981b) 'Elderly people with disabilities', in A. Walker with P. Townsend (eds) *Disability in Britain: A manifesto of rights*, Oxford: Martin Robertson, pp 91–118.

Townsend, P. (1986) 'Ageism and social policy', in C. Phillipson and A. Walker (eds) *Ageing and social policy: A critical assessment*, Aldershot: Gower, pp 15–44.

Townsend, P. (2006) 'Policies for the aged in the 21st century: more "structured dependency" or the realisation of human rights?', *Ageing and Society*, vol 26, no 2, pp 161–80.

Townsend, P. and Gordon, D. (eds) (2002) *World poverty: New policies to defeat an old enemy*, Bristol: The Policy Press.

Townsend, P. and Thompson, P. (2004) 'Reflections on becoming a researcher: Peter Townsend interviewed by Paul Thompson', *International Journal of Social Research Methodology*, vol 7, no 1, pp 87–97.

Tozer, R. and Thornton, P. (1995) *A meeting of minds – Older people as research advisers*, Social Policy Reports, no 3, York: Social Policy Research Unit, University of York.

Tulle-Winton, E. (2000) 'Old bodies', in P. Hancock, B. Hughes, E. Jagger, K. Paterson, R. Russell, E. Tulle-Winton and M. Tyler (eds) *The body, culture and society: An introduction*, Buckingham: Open University Press, pp 64–83.

UN (United Nations) (1995) *Copenhagen Declaration on Social Development and Programme of Action of the World Summit for Social Development*, Report of the World Summit for Social Development, New York, NY: Department of Economic and Social Affairs, UN.

UN (2005) *World population prospects: The 2004 revision. Highlights*, Department of Economic and Social Affairs, Population Division, New York (www.un.org/esa/population/publications/WPP2004/2004Highlights_finalrevised.pdf).

UPIAS (Union of the Physically Impaired Against Segregation) (1976) *Fundamental principles of disability*, London: UPIAS.

Vincent, J., Phillipson, C. and Downs, M. (eds) (2006) *The futures of old age*, London: Sage Publications.

Visser 't Hooft, H.P. (1999) *Justice to future generations and the environment*, Boston, MA: Kluwer Academic Publishers.

Wadsworth, M. (2002) 'Doing longitudinal research', in A. Jamieson and C.R. Victor (eds) *Researching ageing and later life*, Buckingham: Open University Press, pp 99–116.

Walker, A. (ed) (2005) *Understanding quality of life in old age*, Milton Keynes: Open University Press.

Walker, A. and Deacon, B. (2003) 'Economic globalisation and policies on ageing', *Journal of Societal and Social Policy*, vol 2, no 2, pp 1–18.

Walker, A. and Hennessy, C.H. (eds) (2004) *Growing older: Quality of life in old age*, Milton Keynes: Open University Press.

Wallace, J.B. (1992) 'Reconsidering the life review: the social construction of talk about the past', *The Gerontologist*, vol 32, no 1, pp 120–25.

Walmsley, J. (1998) 'Life history interviews with people with learning disabilities', in R. Perks and A. Thomson (eds) *The oral history reader*, London: Routledge, pp 126-39.

Wanless Report (2006) *Securing good social care for older people: Taking a long-term view*, London: King's Fund.

Warburton, R. and McCracken, J. (1999) 'An evidence-based perspective from the Department of Health on the impact of the 1993 reforms on the care of frail, elderly people', in Part One of *Community Care and Informal Care*, Research Volume 3 of the Royal Commission on Long-term Care, London: The Stationery Office, pp 25-36.

Warnes, A.M. (ed) (1989) *Human ageing and later life: Multidisciplinary perspectives*, London: Arnold.

Warnes, A.M. (1993) 'The development of retirement migration in Great Britain', *Espace, Populations, Sociétés*, no 3, pp 451-64.

Warnes, A.M. (1999) 'A decade of gerontology's development in Britain, *Contemporary Gerontology*, vol 5, no 4, pp 120-4.

Watson, J. (2002) *Something for everyone: The impact of the Human Rights Act and the need for a Human Rights Commission*, London: British Institute of Human Rights.

Wattenberg, B. (2004) *Fewer: How the new demography of depopulation will shape our future*, Chicago, Il: Ivan R. Dee.

Weber, M. (1947) *Theory of economic and social organisation* (revised and edited edn), London: Palgrave.

Welford, A.T. (1951) *Skill and age: An experimental approach*, Oxford: Oxford University Press.

Wells, N. and Freer, C. (eds) (1988) *The ageing population: Burden or challenge*, Basingstoke: Macmillan.

Wenger, G.C. (1984) *The supportive network: Coping with old age*, London: Allen and Unwin.

Wenger, G.C. and Burholt, V. (2002) 'Differences over time in older people's relationships with children, grandchildren, nieces and nephews in rural North Wales', *Ageing and Society*, vol 21, no 5, pp 567-90.

Wenger, G.C. and Burholt, V. (2004) 'Changes in levels of social isolation and loneliness among older people in rural Wales – a 20-year longitudinal study', *Canadian Journal on Aging*, vol 23, no 2, pp 477-93.

Westerhof, G.J., Dittmann-Kohli, F. and Bode, C. (2003) 'The aging paradox: toward personal meaning in gerontological theory', in S. Biggs, A. Lowenstein and J. Hendricks (eds) *The need for theory: Critical approaches to social gerontology*, New York, NY: Baywood, pp 127-43.

Whelan, C., Layte, R., Maitre, B., Gannon, B., Nolan, B., Watson, D. and Williams, J. (2003) *Monitoring poverty trends in Ireland: Results from the 2001 Living in Ireland Survey*, Dublin: Economic and Social Research Institute.

White, M. and Epson, D. (1990) *Narrative means to therapeutic ends*, New York, NY: Norton.

Willcocks, D., Peace, S. and Kellaher, L. (1987) *Private lives in public places*, London: Tavistock Publications.

Wisensale, S.K. (2003) 'Global aging and intergenerational equity', *Journal of Intergenerational Relationships*, vol 1, no 1, pp 29-47.

Wolf, C. (2002) 'Poverty, fertility, and opportunity: factors for intergenerationally sustainable development', in Stiftung fur Generationengerechtigkeit (ed) *Generationengerechtigkeit*, Oberursel: Stiftung fur Generationengerechtigkeit.

Wootton, B. (1945) *Freedom under planning*, Chapel Hill, NC: University of North Carolina Press.

World Commission on the Environment and Development (1987) *Our common future*, Oxford: Oxford University Press.

Wyatt-Brown, A. (1992) 'Literary gerontology comes of age', in T.R. Cole, D.D. Van Tassel and R. Kastenbaum (eds) *Handbook of the humanities and aging*, New York, NY: Springer, pp 331-51.

Wyatt-Brown, A. (2000) 'The future of literary gerontology', in T.R. Cole, R. Kastenbaum and R.E. Ray (eds) *Handbook of the humanities and aging* (2nd edn), New York, NY: Springer, pp 41-61.

Young, I.M. (1990) *Justice and the politics of difference*, Princeton, NJ: Princeton University Press.

Yow, V.R. (1994) *Recording oral history: A practical guide for social scientists*, London: Sage Publications.

Index

Page references for notes are followed by *n*

A

Abel-Smith, B. 44*n*, 96
abuse of older people
  violation of human rights 35-7
research indicators 39-41
gerontology
  critical gerontology 18-19, 26
  progress in gerontology 139-54
  see also research
'accelerated prospective' studies 92
'acquiescent functionalism' 30
action research 23, 25
adult development and narrative 61, 62, 67-8
Age Concern 35
age-based rationing of healthcare 131
age-inclusive society 105-21
Ageing and Society (journal) 11-12, 18, 143
ageing societies 4-6, 125, 130-3, 133, 151-2
ageism and age discrimination 7, 11
  attitudes towards 116-18
  definition of age discrimination 106, 118
  and emotional patterns 71-2
  human rights-based approach 6, 9, 27-44
  RoAD project 11, 105-21
  see also generational equity debate
agency of older people vii, 18
  see also participative research
Agenda 21 134
Alzheimer's disease 130
  see also dementia
American Association of Retired Persons
  (AARP) 132
American Geriatrics Society (AGS) 143
Americans for Generational Equity (AGE)
  130-1
Amsterdam Treaty 34, 35
Andersen, M.L. 15
Andrews, M. 118
anonymisation of data 100-1
anti-discriminatory policies 9, 32, 35
archived qualitative data 90
  ethical issues 7, 100-2
Auerbach, A. 134
autobiographical scholarship 68-70
autobiography groups 67-8

B

Baars, J. 13, 77
Bangor University 150, 151
Barker, P. 25
Barry, B. 134
Beck, U. 135
Becker, H. 97
'bed blocking' issues 53
Behar, R. 70
Bell, C. 93
Bengtson, V. 133
Beresford, P. 73, 82, 83
Berman, H.J. 65-6
Berman, T. 62
Bernard, M. 13, 21, 26, 143
Bernstein, R. 13
Better Government for Older People 149, 154*n*
'biographical aging' 62-3
biographical perspectives vii
  see also narrative gerontology
biological ageing 140
Biotechnology and Biological Sciences
  Research Council (BBSRC) Experimental
  Research on Ageing Initiative 148
Birren, J. 63, 66, 67, 141
birth rate *see* fertility rates
Blakemore, K. 15
body: attitudes towards ageing body 16-17
Brand, S. 136
Braye, S. 76
bricolage *see* methodological bricolage
British Association of Social Workers retired
  members' group 91
British Geriatrics Society (BGS) 143
British Institute of Human Rights 34, 36-7
British Society of Gerontology 12, 83, 143
British Society for Research on Ageing (BSRA)
  142, 143
Browne, C.V. 77
Brundtland Report 134
Bruner, J. 61-3
Burke, E. 125
Butler, R. 130
Butt, J. 79
Bytheway, B. 7, 11

C

Calasanti, T. 14
Callahan, D. 125, 131, 132
Cardiff University 151
care homes *see* residential care
care packages
  and funding of social care 27, 51
  and housing 51-2
Care Standards Inspectorate for Wales (CSIW)
  93
Care trusts 52, 53
caregiving and gender 20
Carson, R. 128
Carter, T. 83
Chambers, P. 84
Charles, N. 94-5
children: human rights 33, 39-40
choice: empowerment as policy aim 45, 56, 74
chronic disorders *see* long-term healthcare
  conditions
citizen participation 74-5
'Clock of the Long Now' 136
Clough, R. 81, 83
Cochran, K.N. 66
Cohen, G. 135
Cole, T.R. 15, 19, 59
Coleman, P.G. 143
collective identities and narrative 60-1
Comfort, A. 154*n*
Commission for Equalities and Human Rights
  34, 120
Commission for Social Care Inspection (CSCI)
  93
Commission on Sustainable Development 134
Commissioner for Children and Young People
  34
Commissioner for Older People in Wales 149
Community Care (journal) 55
community care services and re-medicalisation
  of later life 46-56
community matrons 53-4
community-based participatory research 23, 83
consent and confidentiality issues: revisiting *The
  Last Refuge* 99-101
consumerist approaches to participation 75-6
Convention on the Rights of the Child (CRC)
  33, 39, 40
'corporate social responsibility' 42
Corti, L. 90
critical gerontology vii-viii, 6-7
  current assessment of field 13-26
  assessment of progress 139-54
  and social change 60
Cumming, E. 30

D

Daniels, N. 125, 131-2
data
  measuring violation of human rights 32-3
  and revisiting *The Last Refuge* 96-101
Davies, C. 90, 94-5
de Beauvoir, S. 130
death rate *see* mortality rates
dementia
  and participative research 79, 85
  social construction of 130
democratic approaches to participation 74, 75,
  76
Demographic Health Surveys (DHS) 33, 39
demographics *see* population trends
Department of Health 52, 53-4, 153
  Funders' Forum 148
dependency: structured dependency 9, 17, 31-2,
  43
depression and storytelling 64-5
deprivation indicators 38-9, 40
developing countries 4, 43
diaries as research tool
  The Last Refuge 92, 95
  RoAD project 110, 111-17, 118
Dignity on the Ward 35-6
direct payments 49, 55, 74
disabled older people
  and human rights 38
  medical and social models of disability 46
discrimination *see* ageism and age
  discrimination
disengagement theory 77, 105
dissemination activities and participative
  research 81-2
diversity
  of ageing and older people 80, 84, 85, 107,
  153
  'approach diversity' 14, 25
'DNR' ('do not resuscitate') and human rights
  37
domiciliary care
  decrease in 37
  and structured dependency 9, 31
Donahue, W. 30
'Doomsday Vault' 136

E

Economic and Social Data Service (ESDS)
  100-1
Economic and Social Research Council
  (ESRC) 32, 144
  'Growing Older Programme' 148

Economic and Social Research Institute, Dublin
39
economic sociology 31
economic theory and social policy 29, 30
  see also political economy of ageing
Ehrlich, P. 128
elder abuse *see* abuse of older people
Eliot, G. 62
embarrassment and age discrimination 117-18
embodiment of ageing 16-17
emotions
  and experiences of age discrimination 115
  and narrative 62
  and social change 70-2
employment *see* labour market
Employment Equality (Age) Regulations (2006)
  120*n*
empowerment
  and participation 21, 74, 75-6
  as policy aim 45, 56, 74
Engineering and Physical Sciences Research
  Council (EPSRC) EQUAL Programme
  147-8, 149
environmental issues
  and intergenerational justice 127, 128, 134,
  135-6
  see also narrative environments; 'wisdom
  environments'
Equalities and Human Rights Commission 34
equality
  gender and pay inequalities 20, 21
  see also intergenerational justice
Estes, C. vii, 14, 18, 24-5, 77
ethical issues
  archived qualitative data 7, 100-2
  intergenerational justice 129-37
  revisiting *The Last Refuge* 99-101
Ethics (journal) 129
ethnicity *see* racial and ethnic difference
ethnographic research approach 10
  narrativity and storytelling 64-5
European Convention on Human Rights
  (ECHR) 33-4, 35, 38, 39, 40
European Social Charter (ESC) 34-5, 38, 39, 40,
  41
European social model 29, 34
exclusion *see* ageism and age discrimination;
  marginalised groups

F

Fairness for All (White Paper) 105
families: abuse of older people 36-7
Feldman, D. 33
feminism
  and critical gerontology vii, 6, 8-9, 14, 20-1

critique of traditional research 77
first-person approach 21
and narrative gerontology 59-60, 61, 68, 69-70
Fernandes, L. 70
fertility rates
  decline and ageing population 4-5
  pronatalism discourse 136
fieldwork: older people as researchers 109-11
Fifty and Counting Team (FACT) 87*n*
Fishkin, J. 133
focus groups 23, 24
Foord, M. 52
Foundation for Generational Justice (Germany)
  136-7
Friedan, B. 135
Friedman, M. 29
funding
  and participative research 82, 86
  and progress in gerontology 141, 143-4, 147-8
  multidisciplinary research 150, 153
  of social care 27, 51, 52
Furman, F. 16

G

gender
  and autobiography groups 67-8
  and caregiving 20
  emotions and gender relations 71
  gender justice and narrative 61
  life expectancy and gender gap 5
  and moral perspective 20
  pay inequalities 20, 21
general practitioners (GPs) and social care 55
generational accounting 133, 135
generational equity debate 125, 127, 130-3, 135
Generations United 132
Germany
  Ageing Survey 63
  intergenerational justice issues 136-7
Gerontological Society of America 132, 142
Gerontologist, The (journal) 19
gerontology
  progress in 139-54
    historical context 141-47
  see also critical gerontology; social gerontology
Gilbert, N. 47
Gilleard, C. 21
Glendinning, C. 48
global warming 134, 135-6
globalisation
  and human rights of older people 42
  and intergenerational justice 135
Godfrey, M. 83
Grandparent Caregiver Study 23
Gray Panthers vii

'Greatest Generation' 126
Green Paper on Social Care 49-54, 74
Griffiths Report (1988) 48-9, 51, 52-3
Growing Older Programme (ESRC) 32
Grumbach, D. 66
Gubrium, J. 63-4, 65
Gullette, M. 59, 61, 67

H

Habermas, J. 128
Hall, B.L. 23
Hanley, B. 78
Harper, S. 150
Harris, C. 95, 96
Hayek, F. 29, 33
health as measure of success 16
healthcare
    competitive environment 55
    and generational justice debate 131
    professional development and gerontology
        148-50, 153
    re-medicalisation of later life 9, 45-56
    and social care divide 47-9, 52-4, 55
    see also National Health Service
Heller, P. 135-6
Help the Aged 35, 108, 120
hermeneutics and narrative 66-7
Hermoso, M. 15-16
Higgs, P. 21
Holland, C. 11
Holstein, M.B. 4, 6, 7, 8-9, 24, 25, 67
homeless people 51-2
hooks, b. 22
House of Lords Select Committee on Science
    and Technology 152
housing
    and community care 51-2
    and extra-care housing 51
    and findings of *The Last Refuge* 90
Hudson, B. 55
human rights
    as approach to ageism 6, 9, 27-44
        research issues 38-41
    and intergenerational justice 129
Human Rights Act (1998) (UK) 33-4, 35, 37,
    38
humanistic perspectives vii, 6, 59
    humanities as critical gerontology pathway 17,
        18-19, 24-5
    see also narrative gerontology

I

identity formation and narrative 60-1
income maintenance as structural institution 9

Independence, well-being and choice (Green Paper)
    9, 45, 49-54
independent living
    and community care 48, 51-2, 56
    and findings of *The Last Refuge* 90
individual budgets 49, 74
Ingman, S. 134
Institute of Economic Affairs 29
Institute for Social and Economic Research,
    University of Essex 39
institutional ageism 30-1
integrated health and social care support 55
interdisciplinary nature of critical gerontology
    18
interdisciplinary research 82-3, 148, 150-1, 153
intergenerational justice 7, 11, 125-37
International Association of Gerontology (IAG)
    142, 144
International Association of Gerontology and
    Geriatrics 144-5
International Covenant on Economic, Social
    and Cultural Rights 39, 40, 41
interviews as research tool
    The Last Refuge 92, 95
    RoAD project 110, 112

J

Jackson, B. 101
Jacob, J. 44*n*
Jacobs, R.N. 60
Jeffreys, M. 143, 144
Johnson, J. 7, 10-11
Joint Committee on Human Rights (JCHR)
    33, 34, 35-6
Jonas, H. 129, 137
Jones, D. 42
Jordan, D. 100
Joseph Rowntree Foundation (JRF) 38, 46-7,
    49, 148
Journal of Aging Studies 19
journals in gerontology field 145-7
justice *see* intergenerational justice; social justice

K

Kahn, R.L. 135
Keele University, 150
Kenyon, G. 62-3, 64, 66
King's Fund 27, 28
Kingson, E. 132
Kirkwood, T. 144, 154*n*
knowledge
    hierarchies of 76
    narrative knowing 61-3
Kotlikoff, L. 133
Kuhn, M. vii

L

Laboratory of Mathematical Biology 144
labour market
  age discrimination 105, 112–13
  gender inequalities in paid work 20, 21
Laslett, P. 133–4
Last Refuge see Townsend, Peter: revisiting *The Last Refuge*
Law, J. 15–16
'Legitimation Crisis' 128
'liberal-pluralist' tradition 30
life course perspective on ageing vii, 3–4, 7, 26, 135–6
  see also narrative gerontology
life expectancy 5
life history perspectives vii
  see also narrative gerontology
limits: acknowledgment of 128, 130
'lived experience' 111, 126
  and narrative gerontology 63, 67
  and participative research 77, 78, 79, 87
living alone 6
local authorities as lead agencies for community care 49, 50, 52–3, 54
Local Government Act (1929) 47
long-term healthcare conditions and policy 53–4, 55, 56, 152–3
  see also residential care
longitudinal studies 153
  revisiting *The Last Refuge* 90–103
    data collection 96–102
    methodological issues 93–6
Longman, P. 136
Luborsky, M. 64–5
Lupton, C. 75–6, 84

M

MacArthur Foundation 135
McCormack, B. 149
McMullin, J.A. 14, 15
Mader, W. 70–2
Malthus, T. 125
Manheimer, R. 69
marginalised groups 60, 79
  see also ageism and age discrimination; social inclusion
Marsden, D. 101–2
Marx, K. 31
'Master Narrative' of progress 126–7
Meadows, D. 128
meaning *see* personal meanings and narrative
Means, R. 9, 11, 48, 55
Medawar, Sir Peter 154*n*

medical model
  health and social care divide 46, 47–9, 52–4, 55
  research in gerontology 143–4
  social construction of dementia 130
  and 'successful ageing' 15–16
  see also re-medicalisation of later life
Medical Research Council (MRC) 143–4
methodological bricolage 22–4, 25, 26
Meyers, D. 20
migration: changing patterns and ageing population 4, 5
Miles, J. 117–18
Minkler, M. 4, 6, 7, 8–9, 17
  Grandparent Caregiver Study 23
minority ethnic groups: validity of research participation 79
Mitchell, D. 3
Moody, H.R. 6, 7, 11, 20, 60
moral obligation and human rights 32
moral perspective
  and critical gerontology 19–20
  and intergenerational justice 129–37
Morris, W., Viscount Nuffield 142
Morrow-Howell, N. 135
mortality rates: decline and ageing population 4, 5
multidisciplinary research 82–3, 148, 150–1, 153
multiple deprivation 38–9
Multiple Indicator Cluster Surveys (MICS) 33, 39
Myerhoff, B. 69
Myles, J. vii

N

narrative environments 65
narrative gerontology 7, 59–72
narrative knowing 61–3
narrative significance 61–3
'narrative truth' 62
narrativity 61, 63–5
National Assistance Act (1948) 48, 89
National Cancer Research Networks 148
National Care Commission 37
National Health Service (NHS)
  age-based rationing 131
  and health/social care divide 48, 49, 52–4, 55
  marginalisation of older people 48
  prioritised over social services 50
  research funding 148
National Institute on Aging (NIA) 143
National Pensioners Convention 154*n*
National Service Framework for Older People 148–9

National Social Policy and Social Change
    Archive 89, 90, 100
'neoliberal' tradition 30
New Dynamics of Ageing Programme 149, 153
NHS *see* National Health Service
NHS Plan, The 52
normative ethics in 1970s 128-30
nuclear waste repository 136
Nuffield Foundation 142, 148
nursing: professional development and
    gerontology 148-50, 153
nursing homes: violation of human rights 36

O

Oakley, K. 62
Oberg, P. 65, 66
older adults' narratives 61, 65-7
older people
    definition for RoAD project 106-7
    representativeness issues 111-12
    as stakeholders in gerontology 140, 141
Older People and Ageing Research and
    Development Network (OPAN Cymru) 151
Older People Researching Social Issues
    (OPRSI) 91
Older People's Forums (Help the Aged
    network) 108
Older People's Steering Group 78
O'Neill, A. 79
OPAN Cymru 151
Open University 120-1*n*
Opie, A. 80
'oppositional gaze' 22
optimism and intergenerational justice 125, 126
Our health, our care, our say (White Paper) 54-6
Oxford University 150

P

paid work: gender inequalities 20, 21
Parfit, D. 129
Parsons, T. 30
participative research 7-8, 10-11, 153
    critical analysis 73-87
    effectiveness of research 79
    exclusion from participation 79
    historical context 77-8
    involving users with complex needs 84, 85
    older people as researchers 79-82
    traditional user involvement 78-9
    and methodological bricolage approach 22-4,
        25
    older people as researchers in revisiting *The
        Last Refuge* 91-2
    RoAD project 107-21
    stakeholder involvement 148

partnership funding of social care 27
partnership working and health/social care
    divide 52-4, 55
Partridge, E. 129-30
'passionate scholarship' vii-viii, 4, 8, 26
Peace, S. 11
pensions
    gender inequalities 21
    and structured dependency 9, 31
    threat to state pensions 29
personal care: Sutherland recommendations
    27-8, 37-8
personal meanings
    interpretations of age discrimination 116-17
    and narrative 63, 64, 66-7
pessimism and intergenerational justice 125,
    126-7, 137
Phillips, J. 11-12, 21, 26, 143
Phillipson, C. 6, 13, 21, 23
philosophy and intergenerational justice 125,
    129-37
photographs in *The Last Refuge* 97-9
political economy of ageing 17-18, 25
    generational accounting 133-5
    generational justice debate 130-3
politics of rights 33
Polivka, L. 21
Poor Law 47, 102*n*
'population implosion' 136
population trends 4-6
    and intergenerational justice 125, 129, 130-3,
        136
    and role of gerontologists 60
'positive ageing' discourse 134-5
    see also 'successful ageing' ideal
poverty
    and gender 20
    human rights issues 38-9, 40, 41, 43
Poverty and Social Exclusion Survey 38-9
power relations
    in research 10, 76, 77
    and social gerontological approach 14-15
practice-based commissioning 55
Preston-Shoot, M. 76
primary care trusts (PCTs) 53, 55
'productive ageing'
    and gender 20
    see also 'successful ageing' ideal
professional development in gerontology 148-
    50, 153
professional interest stakeholders 140, 141
Programme of Action to Mitigate the Social
    Cost of Adjustment 43
progress
    in contemporary gerontology field 139-54

optimism about future 125, 126-7
pronatalism discourse 136
Public Assistance Institutions (PAIs)
  as replacement for workhouses 47-8
  as residential accommodation for old people
    in 1950s 89, 98

Q

Quadagno, J. 131
qualitative research
  excluded user groups 79
  Last Refuge longitudinal study 90-103
  and understanding ageing experience 22, 24
quality of life perspective
  and chronic disorders 152-3
  marginalisation 53, 56
  and *The Last Refuge* research 95, 96
Quality of Life research studies 32
quality measures for *The Last Refuge* 95, 97
quantitative research 18

R

racial and ethnic difference
  and social gerontology 14
  see also minority ethnic groups
racism: parallels with ageism 119-20
Radcliffe-Brown, A.R. 31
Randall, W. 62-3, 64, 66
Rawls, J. 129, 131, 132
Ray, M. 7, 10
Ray, R.E. 6, 7, 8, 10, 13, 26, 60, 65, 66-7
Reagan, R. 130
reciprocity and intergenerational justice 129
reflective scholarship 7, 8
  self-study of narrating gerontologist 61, 68-70
reflexivity and narrating gerontologist 69
re-medicalisation of later life 9, 45-56
representativeness issues 111
research 7-8, 9-12
  funding
    and participative research 82, 86
    and progress in gerontology 141, 143-4,
      147-8, 150, 153
  on human rights abuses 38-41
  and progress in gerontology 139-54
  researcher as subject 10, 11, 89-103, 107
    self-study of narrating gerontologist 61,
      68-70
  researchers' influence on narrativity 65
  see also academic studies; archived qualitative
    data; participative research; qualitative
    research
Research Assessment Exercise 150
research networks 150-1
residential care

revisiting *The Last Refuge* 10-11, 89-103
and structured dependency 9, 31
Sutherland Report 27-8, 37-8
violation of human rights 35-7
Responsibilities to future generations (Partridge)
  129-30
're-storying the self' 62-3, 67
're-studies' 7
retirement
  deinstitutionalisation 21
  narrativity and life stories 64
  and political economy pathway 18
  retirement migration 5
  'scrap heap' motif 105
  and structured dependency 9, 31
  see also pensions
Richardson, L. 60-1
risk and future generations 126-7, 135-7
'risk society' 135, 137
RoAD (Research on Age Discrimination)
  project 11, 105-21
Roe, K.M. 23
Rolph, S. 10-11
Rosser, C. 95
Rowe, J.W. 135
Royal Commission on Long-Term Care 27-8,
  37-8, 51
Rubinstein, R.L. 78-9
Ruby, Jay 69
Ruth, J.E. 65, 66

S

Sarton, M. 66
Schoenberg, N.E. 81
Scott-Maxwell, F. 66
'scrap heap' motif 105
seed vault 136
self
  history of self in narrative 67
  self-study of narrating gerontologist 61, 68-70
  socially constructed self 62
self-interested choice 24
Shank, R. 62
sheltered housing 51, 90
Sierpina, M. 59
Sin, C.H. 119-20
Smith, R. 10-11
social anthropology 31
social care
  desired outcomes 49, 50
  and health care divide 47-9, 52-4, 55
  human rights-based approach to ageism 32-44
  and re-medicalisation of later life 45-56
  and user participation 74-5

Social Care Institute for Excellence (SCIE)
  85-6
social care plans 55
social change and narrative 60-1, 69-70, 70-2
social construction
  of dementia 130
  socially constructed self 62
social contract theory 129
social development policy: historical perspective
  28-9
social divisions in older population 5-6
Social Exclusion Unit 45, 56
social gerontology 6, 13, 153
  academic history 143-4
  human rights-based approach to ageism 6, 9,
    27-44
  limitations of 14-17
  research review 150
social groups: identity formation and narrative
  60-1
social inclusion: RoAD project 105-21
social justice
  and critical gerontology 60
  gender justice and narrative 61
  and value commitments 21
  see also intergenerational justice
social model of disability 46, 49, 53, 54
social movements
  and intergenerational justice 128-9
  and narrative 60
social protection
  as human right 34-5, 40, 41
  and intergenerational justice 130-1, 137
Social Science Research Council (SSRC) 143,
  144
social services
  as lead agencies for community care 49, 50,
    52-3, 54
  marginalisation 50, 52-5, 55
social work: professional development and
  gerontology 148-50, 153
stakeholders in gerontology 140-1
statistical data and violation of human rights
  32-3
Steinem, G. 69-70
Stiglitz, J. 42
stories
  and narrative knowing 62
  narrativity 63-5
  'storied self' 62
Stout, J. 22
Strategic Promotion of Ageing Research
  Capacity (SPARC) Programme 149
structural adjustment programmes 43
structured dependency 9, 17, 31-2, 43

subjective meanings *see* personal meanings
'successful ageing' ideal 8-9, 15-16, 20, 67
  and older person as researcher 80
  'positive ageing' discourse 134-5
Supporting People funding 51, 52
Supporting people with long term conditions 53-4
sustainability and intergenerational justice 134,
  137
Sutherland Report 27-8, 37-8, 51
Swansea University 151

T

Talmon, Y. 31-2
therapy: narrative therapies 62
Thompson, P. 89, 90
Thornton, P. 23
Tibbitts, C. 30
Toronto Group review 78
Townsend, P. vii, 6, 8, 9, 17, 30
  The Family Life of Old People 89
  revisiting *The Last Refuge* 10-11, 44*n*, 89-103
  data issues 96-101
  methodological challenges 93-6
Tozer, R. 23

U

United Nations
  Agenda 21 134
  Convention on the Rights of the Child
    (CRC) 33
Universal Declaration of Human Rights 33, 40
universality of human rights 32, 42-3
University of Essex: Townsend archive 89, 90,
  100, 101
University of the Third Age (U3A) 91
urbanisation and population trends 5
user participation *see* participative research

V

value commitments 7, 15, 17, 19-21, 77-8
very sheltered housing 51
victim mentality and age discrimination 116-17
Vietnam War 128
visual material in *The Last Refuge* 97-9
voluntary sector 154*n*
volunteer researchers 91-2
voting and intergenerational justice 136-7

W

Wadsworth, M. 92
Walker, A. vii, 6, 13, 23
Wallace, J.B. 64
Wanless Report 27
Ward, R. 11

Warnes, A.M. 11-12, 143
Watson, J. 34, 36-7
Wattenburg, B. 136
Webb, S. and B. 31
Weber, M. 31
welfare
  critiques of concept 29, 31-2
  and human rights 32-3
  and intergenerational justice 130-1, 133, 137
  and stakeholders in gerontology 140
  see also healthcare; social protection
well-being paradigm 150
Welsh Assembly 11-12, 151
Westerhof, G.J. 63
White, P. 25
White Paper on Community Care 51
Williamson, J. 132
'wisdom environments' 64, 65, 67
Wolf, C. 136
Wootton, B. 29
workhouses 47
World Summit Action programme (1995) 41, 42
Wyatt-Brown, A. 65

Y

young people
  older people's perceptions of 113, 114, 115, 119
  youth culture of 1960s 127-8
  see also intergenerational justice